Magnolias

Magnolia 'Ann Rosse'. Photo by Jim Gardiner.

Magnolias
A Gardener's Guide

JIM GARDINER

An expanded and revised edition
of Jim Gardiner's *Magnolias*, 1989

TIMBER PRESS
Portland, Oregon

An expanded and revised edition of Jim Gardiner's *Magnolias,*
published in Britain by Cassell, 1989;
and in North America by The Globe Pequot Press, 1989.

Published in 2000 by
TIMBER PRESS, Inc.
The Haseltine Building
133 S.W. Second Avenue, Suite 450
Portland, Oregon 97204, U.S.A.

Printed in Hong Kong
Designed by Susan Applegate

Library of Congress Cataloging-in-Publication Data

Gardiner, James M. (James Milton), 1946–
Magnolias: a gardener's guide/Jim Gardiner.—expanded and rev. ed.
p.   cm.
Includes bibliographical references (p.   ).
ISBN 0-88192-446-6
1. Magnolias. I. Title.
SB413.M34 G37 2000
635.9'77322–dc21
99-057402

For Allison, Jillian, and Andrew

Contents

Foreword

The planting of a magnolia is an important event in any garden and in the life of any gardener. It will be there, increasing in splendour every year, long after the planter is no longer able to admire it. The choice of a magnolia to plant is therefore an important decision. Until quite recently, it was a simple matter. There were the species and their varieties, and there were the hybrids raised by the Chevalier Soulange in France after the Napoleonic wars when the cavalry officer turned to plant breeder. His was a daunting undertaking. There is a wait of several years to see a flower on a new magnolia seedling, and in the search for excellence it is necessary to bring a considerable number of plants to flowering size. The Chevalier performed a great service to horticulture, and his work went unchallenged until relatively recent times. In later years a few hybrids were raised in England, most of them chance seedlings. This was the situation when, in 1970, I retired and decided to conduct a trial of the magnolias in the favourable climate of my garden on the Italian Lakes.

All nurseries were offering the *Magnolia ×soulangeana* hybrids, as they still do, but I suspected that the then-new Gresham hybrids raised in the United States would surpass them. These incorporated the genes of the magnificent Himalayan *Magnolia campbellii*, which the Chevalier did not have available as a parent. My lucky guess proved to be correct. The Greshams were superior on all points. New hybrids were also just beginning to arrive from other American breeders and from New Zealand. After a prolonged search, I planted approximately 150 different species and named hybrids, about one-third of which I discarded after trial.

Since 1970 a steady stream of new magnolias from both countries and new species has been introduced into the blood lines. In *Magnolia* breeding the torch has passed from Britain across the Atlantic and to the Antipodes. There is much American expertise to be found in these pages. At the latest roundup presented here, there is a bewildering—and exciting—choice of planting material. But not all magnolias are happy in every temperature climate and on every soil, and the success of selection depends upon a careful examination of the peculiarities of individual species and of their progeny. Many new hybrids are still untested as to hardiness, however much may be deduced from the characteristics of the species parents.

This book is, so far as I know, the most comprehensive treatment of every aspect of magnolias ever made available to cultivators. It includes much material that will be new to most readers. Importantly, it is backed up by the professionalism of the author, who has served in five botanic gardens and who is now curator of the Royal Horticultural Society's great garden at Wisley. He is also president of the Magnolia Society, and he has travelled worldwide to study plants, both in their native habitats and in cultivation.

Gardening is an absorbing and refreshing part of the lives of many of us who hesitate to call ourselves horticulturists. Adam was not a horticulturist, but a gardener, and a beginner at that. It is often thought that gardening is indeed the province of amateurs, and we are certainly in the majority. But there is little that we could have achieved without the professional foundations of systematic, scientific research and the study of species in their native habitat. This book is readable and enjoyable, as any work should be that is aimed at the general gardening public. But its value lies in the vast amount of underlying professional knowledge, experience, and judgement that is artfully concealed from our view within its pages.

SIR PETER SMITHERS
Vico Morcote, Switzerland

Acknowledgements

Magnolias grow worldwide under differing conditions, so in the preparation of this book friends in many countries have helped me by contributing their knowledge and expertise. My many friends in the Magnolia Society have helped with information on climate data, propagation, cultivation, and individual snippets on species and cultivars and how they performed in gardens.

Sir Peter Smithers, an especial thanks for writing the Foreword.

In the United Kingdom, John Bond for reading through the text and offering expert advice, Graham Adcock, Barry Ambrose, Peter Borlase, Philip McMillan Browse, Peter Catt, David Clark, Ambrose Congreve, Allen Coombes, Duncan Donald, Peter Dummer, Maurice Foster, John Gallagher, John Hillier, Nigel Holman, The Lord Howick, David Hunt, Chris Lane, John Ravenscroft, Mike Robinson, Chris Sanders, Tony and Vicky Schilling, Michael Siddons, and Barry Unwin.

In the United States, Dick Figlar, Roger and Marj Gossler, Roberta Hagen, Harry Heineman, August Kehr, Lola Koerting, Larry Langford, Phil Savage, the late Dr. John Allen Smith, Stephen Spongberg, John Tobe, Peter Del Tredici, Charles Tubesing, and Judy Zuk.

In Europe and Scandinavia, Otto Eisenhut, Kenneth Lorentzon, H. P. Nooteboom, Dr. Helmut Orth, Vicomte Philippe de Spoelberch, and Dick van Gelderen.

In temperate East Asia and New Zealand, Peter Cave, Mark and Abbie Jury, Ferris Miller, Mikinori Ogisu, Sun Weibang, and Seiju Yamaguchi.

The superb line drawings and photographs speak for themselves. Special thanks to Pauline Dean (drawings) and the following for loaning their photographs: Abbie Jury, Peter Cave, John Gallagher, John Hillier, Dr. Helmut Orth,

Roger Phillips, Ken Robertson, Sir Peter Smithers, Vicomte Philippe de Spoelberch, Donal Synnott, John Tobe, and Sun Weibang.

To Neal Maillet, executive editor of Timber Press, and Rosemary Foster, formerly consulting editor of Timber Press, for suggesting the idea and being patient.

To Joyce Stewart for her support and all staff at Wisley, primarily Anne Eve, for helping with this project. Last but by no means least, to Allison, Jillian, and Andrew for their patience and understanding while I burnt the midnight oil.

Introduction

Among the most influential of all plant collectors, E. H. "Chinese" Wilson, wrote of magnolias:

> Aristocrats of ancient lineage, possessed of many superlative qualities are the magnolias. They have the largest flowers and largest individual leaves of any hardy group of trees. No other genus of hardy or half-hardy trees and shrubs can boast so many excellences. . . . Their free-flowering character and great beauty of blossom and foliage are equalled by the ease with which they may be cultivated.

Wilson was right. Magnolias are very variable in habit, from a small shrub to a large tree. Their flowers differ in size, in scent, and in colour, from a pure white to a rich royal purple. Plants can be seen in flower over a nine-month period beginning in February. The leaves are either deciduous or evergreen, sometimes with a rich russet-brown indumentum on the underside.

My first real encounter with the richness and diversity of magnolias was as a student gardener in the gardens of the Great Park at Windsor. *Magnolia stellata* 'Waterlily' and *Magnolia campbellii* (Raffillii Group) 'Charles Raffill', that sensational tree magnolia, were my favourites at that time. At Windsor 'Waterlily' snuggles among drifts of dwarf rhododendrons, which created just the right contrast in colour and habit, while the Valley Gardens, where the land falls away towards Virginia Water, made the perfect setting for 'Charles Raffill'.

The intimate part of the Hillier Gardens and Arboretum known as Ten Acres is studded with a multitude of magnolias. Walking through this area on a still summer evening yields a variety of scented flowers, each attracting its own pollinators and visitors of the human type. Often out of reach are the big, creamy white, richly scented flowers of *Magnolia obovata*, a forest tree from the island of Hokkaido, Japan. The fragrance of this species is surpassed only by *M. ×wieseneri*, which combines the intense fragrance of *M. obovata* with the more subtle scents of *M. sieboldii.*

Arriving at the Royal Horticultural Society's Garden at Wisley soon after the great storm of 1987, I was able to help develop many areas, including Battleston Hill and the Wild Garden where magnolias would flourish. Once the major work of reshaping and providing the infrastructure had been done, the exciting task of bringing together species and new hybrids for planting took place.

Time has moved on since my first book on magnolias was published. Since then many new and exciting hybrids have been produced, either by magnolia breeders around the world or by Mother Nature lending a helping hand. I have also had the good fortune to see many magnolias in Europe, Korea, New Zealand, North America, and the British Isles in the company of like-minded enthusiasts. *Magnolia* is indeed an international genus, attracting attention from a wide audience; irrespective of their knowledge, they are linked by their common interest and love of magnolias.

The main body of the text covers the range of species and hybrids that can be grown in the British Isles and other areas of the world where average minimum winter temperatures exceed −18°C (0°F). Considerably more species grow in the warm temperate and subtropical regions of the world that cannot be grown outdoors. Dorothy J. Callaway, in her excellent book *The World of Magnolias* (1994), covers these.

Comparatively few places in the British Isles cannot grow magnolias. With the introduction of a greater range of hybrids that flower later and that are tolerant of wider climatic conditions, more magnolias are available today for the gardener than there were even 10 years ago. Many of these can be found in gardens or from suppliers listed at the back of the book.

Magnolias can be grown in many countries around the world where they are not native. Climatic differences obviously weigh heavily on the choice; however, friends who grow magnolias have kindly contributed information that will help those who wish to grow them in those countries.

Information on the origins, classification, medicinal and economic uses of magnolias, as well as how to grow and use them in the garden, is included at the beginning of the book. A small section on pests and diseases, for there are comparatively few that affect magnolias, and a note on propagation are also provided.

I hope the book will stimulate those who have yet to discover the charms of magnolias, as well as encourage those who have already been hooked, to seek out more, and delight in the magic of the magnolia.

CHAPTER ONE
The Story of the Magnolia

H ENRY Compton (1632–1713) was among the great gardeners of his day. He was also Bishop of London from 1675 until his death and head of the church for the American colonies, then known as "The Plantations." In this capacity he sent to North America missionaries charged with sending back plants as well as spreading the gospel. One of these was John Bannister (1654–1692), who had shown a great interest in botany while an undergraduate at Oxford. In 1678 he arrived at Charles Court County, Virginia, to take up his appointment as chaplain. Whilst he was there "he industriously sought for plants, described them and drew the figures of the rarer species." On 16 April 1687 Compton received from Bannister the sweet bay magnolia, *Magnolia virginiana*, thus introducing the first magnolia to the British Isles.

Magnolia grandiflora, perhaps the most cultivated of all evergreen ornamental trees, was introduced into Britain before 1730. Phillip Miller, in the first edition of *The Gardeners' Dictionary* (1731), wrote:

> There is also another species (apart from *Magnolia virginiana*) which has lately been brought to England. This is esteemed one of the most beautiful trees in America, where they usually grow in moist swampy woods and do often rise to a height of 18 m (60 ft.) or more. . . . Since they are hardy enough to endure the cold of our climate in the open ground, I doubt not but in a few years we shall have the pleasure of seeing its beautiful flowers.

Among the first to grow this plant were the Duchess of Beaufort at Chelsea, Peter Collinson at Peckham, and Sir Charles Wager at Parsons Green (who was the first to flower the species). It is thought, however, that Sir John Colliton of Exeter was the first to grow the species, not only in the British Isles but also Europe. J. C. Loudon in *Arboretum et Fruticetum Britannicum* (1844) reported:

Previous pages: *Magnolia campbellii*. This magnificent tree in the National Trust Garden at Overbecks, in South Devon, attracts considerable attention as it can be seen up to 5 km (3 mi.) away across the Salcombe Estuary. For those who live further away and want a daily update of the condition of the flowers, the Overbecks telephone number is published in the gardening press. In 1999 this tree celebrated its 100th year.

[This tree had been] much disfigured from the great number of layers that had been taken from it . . . it had been surrounded by scaffolding for many years on which tubs were placed to receive the branches laid down for propagation. The tree seems to have

been rented by different gardeners, who at first sold the layers
at five guineas each, but the price gradually fell to half a guinea.

Interest quickly shifted to the Asiatic species, which started coming in about 50 years later. *Magnolia denudata*, the Chinese yulan or lily tree, was the first temperate Asiatic species to be introduced, by Sir Joseph Banks (1743–1820), in 1789. The yulan is thought to have been cultivated in China since the seventh century, where it was found in the gardens of the emperor. Not only was it grown in the open, but it was also grown in pots and forced throughout the winter months, so as to keep a perpetual supply of bloom in the apartments of the imperial palace; however, it was not commonly grown in European gardens until well into the nineteenth century.

The third Duke of Portland (1738–1809), in between his prime ministerial duties, introduced *Magnolia liliiflora*, the purple magnolia or woody orchid, in 1790. He found it as a cultivated plant in Japan, but, like *M. denudata*, it had been grown in China for centuries.

The combined resources of *Magnolia denudata* and *M. liliiflora* resulted in the ubiquitous *M. ×soulangeana* arriving on the scene, producing its characteristic waxy flowers in a variety of colours. We have Chevalier Etienne Soulange-Bodin, formerly a French cavalry officer, to thank for this splendid hybrid. Sickened by the Napoleonic wars in Europe, he wrote in the *Gardeners' Magazine* of 1819:

> It had doubtless been better for both parties to have stayed at home and planted their cabbages. We are returned there and the rising taste for gardening becomes one of the most agreeable guarantees of the repose of the world.

Soulange-Bodin founded the Royal Institute of Horticulture at Fromont, near Paris, and became its first director. His most celebrated horticultural deed was to cross *M. denudata* with *M. liliiflora* and to raise this famous group of hybrids. In the *Transactions of the Linnaean Society* of Paris of 1827 we read:

> By the crossing of a Magnolia Yulan [*Magnolia denudata*] grown from seed with the pollen of the *Magnolia discolor* [*Magnolia liliiflora*], the Fromont gardens have witnessed the birth, growth, and establishment, amongst the varied specimens to be admired there of a new hybrid

which is remarkable for its treelike habit, its handsome foliage, and above all for its widespread brilliant flowers, in which the purest white is tinged with a purplish hue. My worthy colleagues have named this beautiful species *Magnolia ×soulangeana.*

It was probably around this time that *M. ×soulangeana* was first introduced to the British Isles, as a description and an illustration drawn from a plant growing at Young's Nursery at Epsom appeared in the *Botanical Register* of 1828.

It was not until 1852, when Commodore Perry's American squadron opened up Japan to foreign trade, that Japanese plants became available to the Western world. *Magnolia stellata*, the star magnolia, reached Britain only in 1877; it flowered a year later at Veitch's Coombe Wood Nursery. Several attempts had been made to introduce this species prior to this time. In the end the successful route was via New York, through George Roger Hall who had had been growing the species in Bristol, Connecticut, since the winter of 1861.

The Himalayan species, by and large, were not introduced until the early part of the twentieth century, when they were sent back by famous plant collectors such as Ernest Wilson, George Forrest, and Frank Kingdon Ward. *Magnolia campbellii*, the queen of magnolias, was introduced, however, midway through the nineteenth century, probably in 1868. When it was featured in *Curtis's Botanical Magazine* of 1885, Sir Joseph Hooker recorded that a flower of this species "was sent from Mr. Crawford's well-known garden at Lakeville near Cork in 1878," thus making the original introductory date somewhat earlier than indicated.

Magnolia introductions into the British Isles have continued throughout the twentieth century. During the 1970s, Roy Lancaster, Tony Schilling, and Geoffrey Herklots reintroduced *Magnolia campbellii* var. *alba* from Nepal, and Sir Harold Hillier and James Russell introduced *M. macrophylla* subsp. *dealbata* from Mexico. *Magnolia amoena* and *M. zenii* were both introduced to the Arnold Arboretum from China during the 1980s and made the short trip to the British Isles not long after.

THE NAME

Pierre Magnol, after whom the magnolia is named, was a physician and botanist of Montpellier in southern France and an inspired teacher. He had been nominated for the chair of botany and the directorship of the botanic garden in 1667, but was not appointed until 1694.

ORIGINS

Magnolias are believed to be some of the most primitive flowering plants. Evidence of fossil remains are found in rock belonging to the Tertiary period (2–65 million years ago). At that time much of the present Arctic zone was probably free of ice and enjoying a European climate typical of the present day. Vast forests encircled the Arctic regions, with species of *Magnolia, Liriodendron, Liquidambar, Ginkgo*, and many others enjoying widespread distribution.

In the journal of the Magnolia Society (1994) Dick Figlar of Pomona, New York, related how in 1971 Francis Krenbaum had been grading a section of his

Magnolia campbellii. Intrepid travellers seeing these blooms in the wild for the first time would have been overwhelmed. Frank Kingdon Ward, who first saw them in Sikkim, India, marvelled at their appearance, likening them to "a fleet of pink water lilies riding at anchor in a green surf." Photo by John Gallagher.

land near Clarkia, Idaho, in the valley of the St. Maries River, when he uncovered the best-preserved Miocene (5–25 million years ago) plant fossil site in the world. What he had exposed were black leaves being turned in the soft shale; some were even blowing in the wind. Charles Smiley of the University of Idaho at Moscow over the ensuing years discovered more than 130 plant species in the 9 m (30 ft.) thick fossil sediments, including two or three species of *Magnolia* thought to be 17–20 million years old. As well as those trees associated with the modern-day North American flora, including species of *Liriodendron, Liquidambar, Taxodium, Diospyros, Nyssa*, and so on, they also found several genera confined to eastern Asia, including *Metasequoia, Cunninghamia, Zelkova*, and *Paulownia*. Figlar related how in 1991 he and his wife, Anita, were allowed to visit the main site and to dig for fossil leaves including those of *Magnolia latahensis* and a second species that resembled *M. acuminata*. Also discovered by Smiley was an immature fruit aggregate resembling *M. grandiflora*. Close examination indicated nine tepals, about 250 stamens, and 120 carpels, all well within the ranges of today's *M. grandiflora*.

Margarita A. Maranova of the V. L. Komarov Institute of the Russian Academy of Sciences and Dick Figlar of Pomona, New York, presented a paper titled "Leaf Cuticular Features of (Fossil) Miocene *Magnolia latahensis*" at the International Symposium of the Family Magnoliaceae in Guangzhou, China, during May 1998. In this study they scrutinised fossil leaves of *M. latahensis* using cuticular analysis, which showed the most similar living species to be *M. grandiflora*. Other Miocene fossil records exist throughout western North America at San Pablo (west central California), Spokane (Washington), and Puente (Los Angeles), showing *Magnolia* leaves resembling those of the Clarkia site.

Figlar went on to speculate about how the world's climate changed. During the early Miocene, magnolias would have been present over a wide area in North America, from western Canada to Mexico and Central America and then through south central United States to New England. With the increased aridity during the middle Miocene, *Magnolia* populations would have shrunk, with western populations disappearing by the end of the Miocene. It would have been at that time (late Miocene and early Pliocene) that global climatic change took place with the formation and expansion of the polar ice cap. The ice destroyed vast forests in Europe, including many of the so-called primitive plants. Only China, Japan, Korea, and regions of eastern North America would have been saved. The link that probably existed during the early Miocene or late Oligocene (30–25 million years ago) is between *M. acuminata*, which would have been found as far north as Alaska, and its close relative *M. liliiflora* found in China, Korea, and Japan.

CLASSIFICATION AND DISTRIBUTION

The genus *Magnolia* is the largest of the six genera belonging to the family Magnoliaceae. The family itself is divided into two subfamilies, Magnolioideae and Liriodendroideae, the latter containing *Liriodendron* (tulip tree), a genus of two species from eastern North America and China. Within the Magnolioideae are several genera which, depending on current taxonomic thinking, have from 6 to 10 species. These species grow in two distinct temperate and tropical regions of the world—eastern America and eastern Asia. The majority are found in eastern Asia from Manchuria, Korea, and Japan, south through Taiwan, China, and the eastern Himalaya to Java, New Guinea, and Malacca in the Malay archipelago. The American magnolias are found from southern Canada south through the eastern United States, the West Indies, Mexico, Central America, Venezuela, and southeastern Brazil.

The late J. E. Dandy, keeper of botany of the British Museum (Natural History), was the greatest authority on the family Magnoliaceae, having started this study in 1925 when under John Hutchinson at Kew until his (Dandy's) death in 1976. Being a perfectionist, he was continually revising his findings. Consequently, the monograph on which he worked for nearly 50 years went unpublished. Acknowledging this as a basis for further work, H. P. Nooteboom of the Rijksherbarium, Leiden (1985 and 1987) and Law Yuh-wu of the Academia Sinica (1984) have assessed the generic limits. Nooteboom considers that *Talauma, Alcimandra, Manglietiastrum*, and *Aromadendron* should be sunk within *Magnolia* and that *Manglietia, Kmeria, Pachylarnax, Michelia*, and *Elmerrillia* be maintained as genera. Nooteboom indicates that *Talauma, Aromadendron*, and *Alcimandra* differ from *Magnolia* because of the concrescence (growing together) of the carpels. This character, however, is now evident in *Magnolia*, so he sees no grounds for maintaining them as separate genera.

Between 120 and 128 species are formed within the genus *Magnolia*. Nooteboom has modified Dandy's original key to provide the most recent treatment.

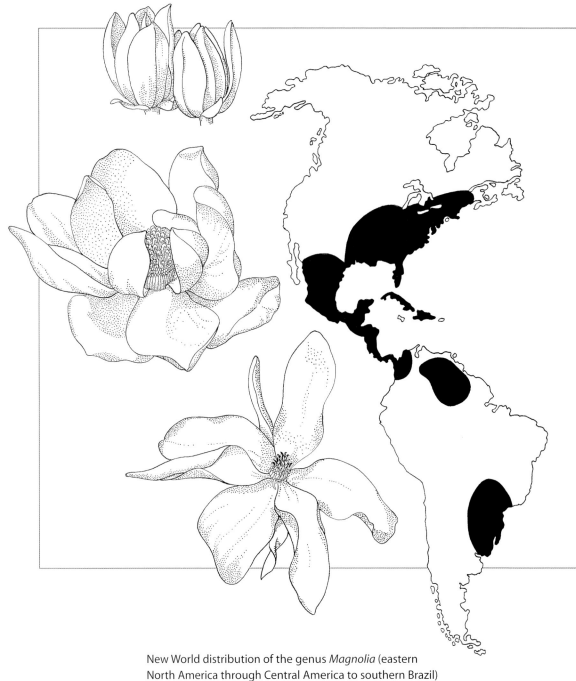

New World distribution of the genus *Magnolia* (eastern
North America through Central America to southern Brazil)
with selected flower shapes of New World magnolias: (from
top to bottom) *Magnolia acuminata*, *M. grandiflora*, and *M.
macrophylla* subsp. *dealbata*. Map and drawings by Pauline
Dean.

Old World distribution of the genus *Magnolia* (temperate and tropical Southeast Asia from the Himalaya to China, Japan, Korea, Taiwan, and Malaysia) with selected flower shapes of Old World magnolias: (clockwise from top) *Magnolia wilsonii*, *M. liliiflora*, *M. denudata*, *M. stellata*, and *M. campbellii*. Map and drawings by Pauline Dean.

Subgenus: *Magnolia*
   Section: *Magnolia* (1 species)
       Atlantic coastal plain of the United States
       Type species: *M. virginiana*
   Section: *Gwillimia* (c. 15 species)
       Southeast Asia from southern China to the Malay archipelago
       Type species: *M. coco*
   Section: *Lirianthe* (1 species)
       Central Himalaya through Assam, Bangladesh to Myanmar
         (Burma)
       Type species: *M. pterocarpa*
   Section: *Rytidospermum* (9 species)
       Asia and America
       Type species: *M. tripetala*
   Section: *Oyama* (c. 3 species)
       Temperate East Asia
       Type species: *M. sieboldii*
   Section: *Theorhodon* (c. 18 species)
       All tropical New World, except *M. grandiflora*
       Type species: *M. grandiflora*
   Section: *Gynopodium* (c. 4 species)
       Southeast Asia from southeastern Tibet (Xizang Zizhiqu),
       northeastern Myanmar (Burma), through southern China to
         Taiwan
       Type species: *M. nitida*
   Section: *Maingola* (c. 14 species)
       Assam southwards into the Malay Peninsula, Java
       Type species: *M. maingayi*
   Section: *Alcimandra* (1 species)
       Sikkim to Assam and northern Myanmar (Burma) and Tonkin
       Type species: *M. cathcartii*

Subgenus: *Yulania*
   Section: *Yulania* (c. 7 species)

Temperate East Asia from the central Himalaya to eastern
China

Type species: *M. denudata*

Section: *Buergeria* (5 species)

Temperate East Asia (China, Korea, and Japan)

Type species: *M. stellata*

Section: *Tulipastrum* (2 species)

Southern and eastern North America and eastern China

Type species: *M. acuminata*

Subgenus: *Talauma*

Section: *Talauma* (c. 12 species)

Tropical America from southern Mexico, Cuba, through lesser
Antilles and central America to eastern Brazil

Type species: *M. plumieria*

Section: *Blumiana* (c. 40 species)

Tropical and sub-tropical Southeast Asia, from Central Himalaya

through Malay Peninsula, into New Guinea

Type species: *Talauma candollei*

Section: *Aromadendron* (c. 4 species)

Sumatra, Malay Peninsula, Java and Borneo

Type species: *Aromadendron elegans*

Section: *Manglietiastrum* (1 species)

Yunnan

Type species: *M. sinica*

Following on from Nooteboom's work on generic limits, Dick Figlar has examined the generic delimitation of *Michelia* and *Magnolia*. In a paper deliv-
ered to the International Symposium of the Family Magnoliaceae in Guangzhou, China, during May 1998, he examined the contrasting types of branch
initiation in *Michelia* and two subgenera of *Magnolia*. He suggested that this
feature uniquely links *Michelia* with subgenus *Yulania*. He supported his theory with the apparent ease of hybridisation between the two groups and other

common characters such as lateral and/or sublateral dehiscence of the anthers and precocious flowering. He proposed that *Michelia* should be treated as a subgenus of *Magnolia* and the related *Elmerrillia* similarly reduced to *Magnolia* as a section of subgenus *Michelia*.

Nooteboom's and Figlar's revisions will, I am sure, be discussed long and hard by botanists and horticulturists alike. It is not within the scope of this book, however, to challenge their theories. Figlar's assessment will be debated far more fiercely than Nooteboom's revision, which will be accepted by the majority.

POLLINATION

Magnolias evolved many millions of years before bees and wasps and butterflies, so rely on beetles as their pollinator. No one family of beetle is more important than another; however, those belonging primarily to the family Nitidulidae, containing small scavenging beetles mostly under 5 mm (ca. ¼ in.) long, are seen. Larger Scarabaeidae have also been seen visiting magnolias.

Beetle-pollinated flowers are characterised by their large size, white or pink or red colour, abundance of pollen, lack of nectar, and fragrance. Several *Magnolia* species secrete a nectarlike substance at the base of the tepals and between the beaklike stigmas that curve outwards from the carpels. These carpels are arranged in spiral formation on the stigmatic column that becomes the basis of the fruit cone if fertilised. As beetles have strong mandibles, magnolia embryos need to be protected inside tough carpels that beetles cannot penetrate. This sugary substance is only produced when the flower is in bud and will only be receptive at this time, prior to opening. Once the flower opens, the stamens release pollen. The beetles are fond of this pollen, which is a rich food source. Their bodies become covered with it when they are feeding. On

Magnolia 'Manchu Fan'. One of the original Gresham hybrids, this clone has smaller white flowers that are borne in considerable profusion. It is regarded by many as their favourite white-flowered Gresham. Photo by Jim Gardiner.

visiting unopened flowers, the pollen smeared on their bodies becomes attached to the sugary substance, thus effecting pollination.

FLOWERS AND FRUITS

The late G. H. Johnstone, whose garden at Trewithen near Truro in Cornwall was the inspirational reference for his *Asiatic Magnolias in Cultivation* (1955), was the first to coin the term "tepal" as the majority of magnolias show no differentiation between sepal and petal. Tepals are arranged in two or more whorls; each whorl has from three to six tepals. In some magnolias the outer whorl, composed of tepals that are reduced in size and substance, resembles a false calyx. Before the tepals appear, the flowers are protected by perules, which in the case of precocious-flowering species (those that flower before the leaves appear) are intensely furry. These are shed as the tepals expand with the flower opening fully within a few days of the perules being shed.

The male part of the flower (the androecium) is composed of numerous free stamens arranged as a boss around the female part (the gynoecium). The boss protrudes above the stamens as a stigmatic column of cone consisting of numerous carpels that also are arranged spirally.

Provided that pollination has taken place, seed is produced in varying amounts depending on the species. In the British Isles, those species flowering very early (*Magnolia campbellii*) or late (*M. grandiflora*) generally fail to set seed. In species where fertilisation has occurred, however, the fruiting cones turn pink or red as they ripen and vary in size from 2.5 to 20.0 cm (1–8 in.) long. They are often distorted in shape due to the irregular fertilisation. When ripe the carpels split longitudinally, so that the ripe seed becomes partially exposed. The seeds vary in colour from pink, orange, scarlet, or crimson depending on the species. The seeds

Magnolia campbellii var. *alba* 'Strybing White'. Unlike the outer tepals of most flowers of *M. campbellii*, which are flat and saucer-shaped, the outer tepals of 'Strybing White' are lax and drooping. Seed of this distinctive clone was received from G. Ghose and Company of Darjeeling and flowered for the first time at Strybing Arboretum, San Francisco. Photo by John Gallagher.

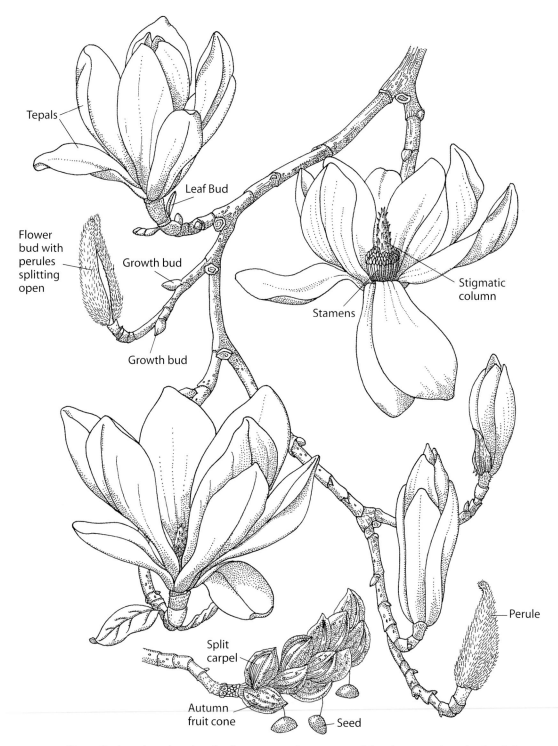

Tepals

Leaf Bud

Flower bud with perules splitting open

Growth bud

Growth bud

Stamens

Stigmatic column

Perule

Split carpel

Autumn fruit cone

Seed

Magnolia denudata, showing the flowers at various stages of development, from bud to full flower and its fruiting cone with seeds. Drawing by Pauline Dean.

are suspended on a fine silk thread, making them more likely to be blown clear of the parent tree's canopy, ensuring adequate light for growth once germination has occurred the following spring.

Leaves of most magnolias are arranged alternately along the stems, however on *Magnolia tripetala* they tend to be grouped together in false whorls at the end of branches.

MEDICINAL USES

The medicinal qualities of magnolias have been known for centuries in China, the first reference being in the *Cheng Lei Pen Tshao* (Chinese Pharmaceutical Natural History) published originally in 1083. *Magnolia officinalis* (hou-phu or hou-po) was so-called by Rehder and Wilson for the epithet "officinalis" meaning "of the shops." It is a species most commonly cultivated for medicinal use, especially in Sichuan and Hubei, where the thick bark and flower buds are used. An infusion of the bark (known to contain the alkaloid magnocurarine) yields a cure for coughs and colds and is used as a tonic during convalescence. The flower buds (known as yu-po) are used for feminine ailments and intestinal problems. During May, 20-year-old trees of *M. officinalis* are cut back and stripped of the bark from the roots, trunk, and branches. After the bark is dried in the shade, then the sun, the harvesters steam it, roll it into tubes, and sort ac-

cording to the part of the tree from which it comes (for example, tube hou-po from the trunk, root hou-po, and branch hou-po). Since it is toxic in large doses, it is never given to pregnant women and always presented with other herbs.

Magnolia liliiflora (mu-lan) is also recorded in the Pharmaceutical Natural History as a drug plant for headaches and nasal disorders. *Magnolia denudata* (hsin Iyu-lan or yulan) has been used for centuries as a food plant and supplier of medicinal preparations. The tepals are pickled and used as a flavouring in rice, while the bark has medicinal uses for treating colds. A

Magnolia officinalis. Within the plant collections at Villa Taranto on the shores of Lake Maggiore in northern Italy can be found many fine specimen trees including *M. officinalis.* Known to the Chinese as the hou-po tree, this species is much prized for its medicinal qualities. Photo by Dr. Helmut Orth.

similar preparation made from the bark of *M. kobus* is considered effective by the Ainu in Japan. Leaves are also used as a flavouring when powdered and sprinkled on food. The flower buds of *M. biondii* and *M. denudata* account for 70 percent of xinyi (used in Chinese traditional medicine) produced in China each year with 200,000 kg (196 tons) being collected from the Funiu Shan in Henan Province.

The young leaves and flower buds of *Magnolia obovata* are boiled and eaten as a vegetable while whole dried leaves are placed on a charcoal brazier or barbecue, filled with miso, leeks, daikon, and shiitake, and grilled. The aroma of the leaves permeates the mixture, called hoba miso, which is then served with rice.

Alkaloids and neolignans have been extracted from dried buds of *Magnolia salicifolia*. It was found that these compounds acted as anti-inflammatory agents, neuromuscular blocking agents, anti-allergy agents, and central nervous system inhibitors. The species is also thought to have potential as an anticancer drug.

American species, too, are used in local medicines, with the bark of *Magnolia grandiflora* providing a stimulant, tonic, and drug. The bark of *M. virginiana* is credited with powerful medicinal qualities—as an astringent, diaphoretic, febrifuge, general astringent, and tonic. It is claimed to be beneficial in cases of dyspepsia, dysentery, and erysipelas and other skin diseases. Tea made from its bark is said to help break the tobacco habit, and an infusion used as a gargle or mouthwash cures various mouth and gum ills.

The genus *Talauma*, recently sunk into *Magnolia*, is restricted to the tropics of Asia and America, and has medicinal value. *Talauma mexicana* was known to the Aztecs as yolloxochitl, meaning "heart flower," referring to the shape of the flower buds. It was cultivated in the fifteenth and sixteenth centuries for its bark, which was used for various medicines considered effective against fevers, heart diseases, paralysis, and epilepsy.

ECONOMIC USES

The timber from several species is used for various purposes. *Magnolia obovata* and *M. kobus*, both Japanese species, have a close-grained, light yellow, soft wood, which is easily worked. *Magnolia obovata* is used for furniture making, utensils, cabinet work, and engraving. North American species are also used. *Magnolia acuminata* and *M. macrophylla* both have soft, durable, close-grained yellow-brown wood that is widely used for flooring and cabinet work. The wood of *M. virginiana* is sometimes used to manufacture broom handles.

Michelia is closely allied to *Magnolia* and is restricted to warm, temperate, and tropical Asia. Many species are used locally for their light yet durable timber in houses, furniture, and coffin construction. All the parts of *Michelia champaca* plants seem to have a practical use. In Thailand the flowers are used as a cosmetic, and a volatile oil extracted from them is used in perfumes. The bark is used in a drink with febrifugal properties, while the timber is used extensively for furniture making, door panels, and tea chests. Even the leaves are used—they are a source of food for the silk worm.

Liriodendron, another *Magnolia* ally from eastern North America, has similar wood properties to those already mentioned, but is also the source of tulipiferine, an alkaloid that acts violently on the heart and nervous system.

ART AND FOLKLORE

The flowers of *Magnolia denudata* are often pictured on Chinese porcelain, paintings, and tapestries of the T'ang dynasty (A.D. 618–907), because they were regarded as symbols of candour and purity.

Among the first illustrations of a magnolia to appear in Britain was a drawing by Georg D. Ehret of *Magnolia grandiflora* that was published in *The Natural History of Carolina* in 1737. To make the drawing Ehret walked the 5 km (3 mi.) from Chelsea to Parsons Green to watch the tree, which was in the garden of Sir Charles Wager, open its first blooms. Ehret was regarded as among the finest botanical artists of his time. He was the son of a Heidelberg market gardener and after brief training as a gardener took up botanical draughtsmanship. After spells in Switzerland and France, he moved to England in 1735. At that time, plants were being introduced mainly from North America, and many patrons wanted paintings of the new plants.

The New World is not without its intriguing tales. In the Carolinas, *Magnolia grandiflora* emits a powerful fragrance, which, from a distance, is delicious but up close is over-powering. Native American tribes are said to avoid sleeping under this magnolia when it is in blossom, and a single bloom placed in a bedroom is said to cause the death of any person who sleeps there.

CHAPTER TWO
Cultivation

T HE CHAPTER on *Magnolia* species discusses the type of habitat in which these plants are found growing in their native environments. The understanding of these conditions can be of great benefit to the gardener when choosing a site and deciding which magnolia to plant—after all, much of the art of successful gardening lies in reproducing for our plants the conditions in which they will be most comfortable, deceiving them into believing that they are in their natural habitat.

It is worthwhile recalling some remarks made by people who have seen magnolias growing in the wild in North America and Asia and learning from their observations. Ernest Wilson (1906), who introduced more *Magnolia* species into cultivation than any other plant collector, wrote:

> In China, and for that matter in Japan and Korea also, magnolias are found in moist woods growing in association with broad-leaved, deciduous trees among which coniferous trees are scattered. They love a cool soil rich in woodland humus.

Euan Cox, plant collector, grower, and author, who accompanied Reginald Farrer to northern Myanmar (Burma), commented:

> Even in that climate [Hpimaw in northern Myanmar] where summer sun is at a premium, all magnolias seem to prefer company and grow either in medium woodland or on the outskirts of the thick jungle. An odd thing about those magnolias is we never saw a poor specimen . . . every tree was shapely and every tree was healthy; this was all the more striking in comparison with the general decrepitude around them.

Maurice Foster from Sevenoaks, Kent, saw *Magnolia campbellii* var. *alba* in Bhutan.

> The damp forest between 2500 m (8000 ft.) and 3000 m (10,000 ft.) that clothes the eastern flanks of the Himalayan outliers falling south from Tibet into India is its "locus classicus". . . . The mixed forest is unimaginably rich in species ranging from the warm temperate zone of *Michelia doltsopa* and *Rhododendron griffithianum* set about with evergreen

oaks and laurels with *R. lindleyi* perched epiphytically in the dark tops; up through cool temperate mixed *Tsuga* and deciduous forest with *R. arboreum, R. falconeri, R. kesangiae* up to 18 m (60 ft.) high; *Acer, Betula, Quercus, Sorbus, Hydrangea*, an understory of *Osmanthus, Viburnum, Daphne, Berberis, Lindera, Litsea*, and groundlings like *Gaultheria, Vaccinium, Begonia, Primula*, and *Arisaema*. Lord of this realm is *Magnolia campbellii* var. *alba*.

J. Ohwi in the *Flora of Japan* (1965) pointed out that "magnolias are constituents of the temperate and boreal regions and are found predominantly in mixed deciduous coniferous woodland but can (*Magnolia stellata*) be found on open boggy sites." T. D. Elias in *Trees of North America* (1980) noted that all native magnolias grow in moist soils along the margins of streams and ponds and lower mountain slopes. They are seen at their best in deep rich woodlands of the Southeast.

CLIMATIC CONDITIONS

Climatic data applicable to our own garden should now be assessed to see whether the site is too hot or cold, too wet or dry, too sunny or cloudy for our proposed magnolia planting plan to take shape. But this is where the difficulties begin, since a whole book on climatic data could be written on the British Isles alone, let alone North America, continental Europe, and the other countries where magnolias are grown.

Cultivating Magnolias in the British Isles

The British Isles is an archipelago of islands and seas that has a greater diversity of scenery than perhaps any other part of the globe of similar size. It consists of only 314,000 sq. km (121,000 sq. mi.), which on the global scale is small, equating in size to the State of Pennsylvania. In evolutionary terms its landscape has been carved out during the comparatively recent past. Eighteen thousand years ago, ice covered most of the islands; however, it took some 12,000 years for the ice sheet to recede leaving the shape that everyone is familiar with today.

The British Isles sit on the edge of continental Europe on the eastern edge of the North Atlantic Ocean lying between the latitudes of 50° and 60° north. It is only 1040 km (650 mi.) from Cornwall to Sutherland in northern Scotland. Be-

cause of the influence of the North Atlantic drift, the British Isles enjoy a remarkably uniform climate. We know this because weather records have been
kept by dedicated observers since the seventeenth century, so we have a fairly
accurate idea of how temperature and rainfall have varied over the past
200–300 years. Data that are available indicate no change to the annual rainfall
figures. While winters have become wetter, increasing by 75 mm (3 in.) of rain
annually, summers have become drier. Temperatures show no change overall,
but the winter half of the year is warmer by 1°C (c. 2°F) and only slightly warmer
in July and August. These long-term records hide substantial fluctuations that
occur from year to year. The three months from January to March 1990 were
the three warmest months at the start of any year since 1659, and November
1994 was the warmest on record. The summer of 1995 was the hottest on record,
while the winter of 1995–96 was the coldest, certainly in Scotland for some considerable time, with Glasgow recording –25°C (–13°F).

The British Isles lie in the path of the Gulf Stream. Starting in the Gulf of Mexico, this ocean current is deflected by the cold waters off Labrador. Because the
sea is slow to warm up, its maximum temperature cannot be attained until August, but it is also slow to cool, so temperatures are maintained well into autumn. Temperatures vary around the coast from 14° to 17°C (57°–63°F) in August, but are cooler around northeastern Scotland. Coastal influences are
particularly apparent along the west coast of England and southwest Scotland
as well as the east coast of Ireland. They are most marked around the southwest of England, but provide surprises elsewhere.

Despite its reputation, Britain's climate and day-to-day weather can be predicted to a limited extent. The storms of 1987 and 1990, however, were not predicted, so violent storm force winds wrought havoc initially in the southeast of
England and over most of the south in 1990. Similar storms have affected the
northwest of England and southwest of Scotland, but not to the same extent.

If the climate has some predictability then the contents of British gardens
cannot. Despite having a poor native flora, the British zest for collecting and
the country's imperial past have enabled a plethora of introductions from the
four corners of the globe to be gathered together. We can arguably describe the
British Isles as the world's clearing house of plants with more than 70,000 plant
names being commercially available.

So where are magnolias grown in the British Isles? All magnolias discussed in this book can be found growing in the British Isles—somewhere! Inevitably tender species such as *Magnolia rostrata* and *M. nitida* can only be found in mild locations such as southwest England and southern Ireland with the southern and southeastern counties of England containing the best collections after the southwest of England.

The southwest of England, particularly the southern coastal regions of Cornwall and Devon, provides climatic conditions ideally suited to the cultivation of magnolias. In fact, probably the finest Asiatic tree magnolias including *Magnolia campbellii*, *M. sprengeri*, and *M. sargentiana* var. *robusta* are found here. The numerous gardens often occupying sheltered valleys with unique microclimates differ slightly from one another, which makes them so distinct. Throughout the entire southwest, rainfall varies dramatically between 775 mm (31 in.) and 2050 mm (82 in.), depending on the situation. June is the sunniest month, averaging nearly eight hours a day. Average temperatures range from 27°C (80°F) in August to –6°C (21°F) in January and February. It is rare, however, to find minus temperatures from March to October inclusive. Many gardens have relied on extensive shelter belts to protect themselves from the gales that sweep through from late autumn to early spring.

Gardens in Ireland enjoy similar environmental conditions to those found in south Cornwall and Devon. Temperatures range from 26°C to –4°C (79°– 25°F) in November to January. Frosts are seen during February and March, but generally are not debilitating. Rainfall inevitably varies. The great magnolia collection at Mount Congreve in County Waterford has less than 400 mm (40 in.) per year.

The southern counties of England are some of the sunniest in the country with 2000 hours of sunshine being recorded during a year. Rainfall tends to be lower than that of the southwest with 700–850 mm (28–34 in.) per year being seen.

The southeast of England has lower rain-

Magnolia 'Caerhays Surprise'. This superb hybrid was raised by Philip Tregunna, head gardener at Caerhays Castle in Cornwall. It combines the ease and frequency of flowering from an early age that *M. liliiflora* 'Nigra' provides with the poise of *M. campbellii* subsp. *mollicomata*. Photo by Dr. Helmut Orth.

fall still, which varies between 625 mm (25 in.) and 750 mm (30 in.) per year. The long-term average rainfall at Wisley is 625 mm (25 in.) with this evenly spread. In the short term, January, March, and April are the driest months and November the wettest.

Temperatures show marked variations from 36°C (97°F) in August to −15°C (5°F) in January. The real danger lies in temperature fluctuations that are seen from November through April. If temperatures were to fall and stay low, there would not be any problems; however, temperatures vary between −15°C (5°F) on the one extreme and +15°C (59°F) on the other. Spells of mild weather followed by periods of subzero temperatures have a dramatic effect on magnolias

Magnolia sprengeri. The gardens at Mount Congreve outside Waterford in southern Ireland contain one of the most comprehensive collections of magnolias in the Western world. Here seedlings are planted on sloping ground leading to the river Suir. Photo by Jim Gardiner.

CHAPTER TWO: CULTIVATION   41

especially around flowering time and beyond. It is not uncommon to find air frosts into April that will either blacken the flowers or the foliage or both.

The influences of the city on climate are noticeable. In central London, close to the river Thames, air frosts with temperatures falling to 1°–3°C (35°– 37°F) rarely occur during December to February, and maximum temperatures are similar to those at Wisley. Rainfall too is lower with approximately 500 mm (20 in.) per year.

Southern Scotland provides probably some of the greatest climatic diversity found in Britain. The coastal influence and shelter created by the Pentland Hills provide Edinburgh with an excellent micro-climate. Rainfall readings here are similar to those of southeast England. The Edinburgh Botanic Garden, for example, has the same rainfall as Wisley, though the extremes of temperature are not as great. Its satellite gardens provide an interesting diversity. Logan in the extreme southwest enjoys a subtropical climate. The temperature rarely drops below 0°C (32°F), although in some years, with 1996 being an example, temperatures fell as low as –10°C (14°F). Rainfall varies between 825 mm (33 in.) and 1125 mm (45 in.) annually. Some 128 km (80 mi.) due north of Logan is Younger Botanic Garden in Argyll where rainfall can reach 2800 mm (112 in.) per year. Low temperatures in Argyll are similar to those in Logan but are more frequent. Although few magnolias are represented at the third garden at Dawyck, the climatic conditions there illustrate the complexities of the British climate. Only 32 km (20 mi.) south of Edinburgh, Dawyck has an annual rainfall up to 1100 mm (44 in.) with minimum temperatures around –25°C (–13°F).

Cultivating Magnolias in North America

North American weather patterns are enormously complex, with tremendous variations occurring. Before looking at specific areas in North America where magnolias are cultivated, mention should be made of the chart giving North American Cold Hardiness Zones. This chart, prepared by the United States Department of Agriculture and the Arnold Arboretum, divides the northern part of the continent into ten hardiness zones. Each zone equates to a minimum winter temperature banding. Zone 1, for example, equates to temperatures below –45°C (–50°F), such as found in areas of northern Canada. Zone 8 has temperatures ranging between –7°C (20°F) and –12°C (10°F), such as found in parts of Oregon, California, Georgia, and North Carolina. Zone 8 is similar, in fact, to most of the British Isles. Zone 10 equates with −1° to 5°C (31°–41°F), such as found in Los Angeles and San Francisco in California, and southern Florida.

This assessment of a woody plant's ability to withstand cold temperatures is valid only when the plant has acclimatised for winter. There are cases where freezing damages plants that normally can withstand these temperatures. The zoning does not take account of premature freezing, late frosts, and wide fluctuations during the winter months.

Possibly of equal benefit to the gardener is the American Horticultural Society Plant Heat-Zone Map. The effects of heat damage are more subtle with lingering effects affecting many parts of the plant. This map is used in a similar way to the Hardiness Zone map. It divides the continent into 12 zones based on the average number of days that a given region experiences "heat days." A heat day is any day where temperatures over 30°C (86°F) are found. It is at this temperature that plants suffer physiological damage from heat. Zone 1 has no heat days and Zone 12 has 210.

In addition to these nationwide maps is the one used in western North America and developed by Sunset Books. The 24 Sunset Zones are defined by many variables including high and low temperatures, dry desert winds, rainfall and other moisture sources (for example, fog). This system is useful to pinpoint microclimates especially important as great variations in climate occur over short distances in this region.

It is particularly helpful to use local knowledge when it comes to selecting magnolias to grow across the North American continent. Who better to ask than Charles Tubesing, former president of the Magnolia Society and horticulturist at the Holden Arboretum in Kirtland, Ohio (U.S. hardiness zone 5), where testing conditions in the extreme are found?

> The rainfall in our area averages 112 cm (44 in.) per year, and is fairly evenly distributed through the seasons. The normal snowfall totals over 2 m (6½ ft.) through the winter, and a 30–40 cm (12–16 in.) blanket of snow is usually present when we experience our lowest temperatures.
>
> Although acidic, soils in our area are mostly clay-based and often poorly drained except for the occasional occurrence of sandy soils where old lake shores used to be. Incorporating organic matter into the backfill soil when planting and providing an organic mulch are helpful in improving the soil texture near the plant.

Summer (June–August) average daily temperatures run from a low of 12°C (54°F) to a high of 28°C (82°F). Our record low is 0°C (32°F), with a high of 40°C (104°F). Winter (December–February) average daily temperatures run from a low of −8°C (18°F) to a high of 6°C (43°F), with records of −29°C (−20°F) and 25°C (77°F). It is normal to reach temperatures in excess of 21°C (70°F) for a few days in late March or April, only to plunge below 0°C (32°F) again.

Overcast days are few during the growing season.

Exotic magnolias that are grown alongside *Magnolia acuminata*, *M. fraseri*, and *M. macrophylla* are *M. kobus*, *M. obovata*, *M. sieboldii*, and *M. stellata*, with *M. salicifolia* flowers being frosted most years. Hybrids and cultivars grown in this region include the de Vos and Kosar hybrids, *M. ×brooklynensis*, *M. ×kewensis*, *M. ×loebneri*, *M. ×soulangeana* (flowers frosted most years), *M. ×wieseneri*, *M.* 'Butterflies', *M.* 'Elizabeth', *M.* 'Gold Star', *M.* 'Marillyn', *M.* 'Yellow Bird', and *M.* 'Yellow Lantern'. *Magnolia* 'Spectrum' and *M.* 'Iolanthe' have been killed while *M.* 'Royal Crown' sustains considerable damage and *M. denudata* has been killed to the ground.

Dick Figlar, former president of the Magnolia Society, lives in Pomona, New York (U.S. hardiness zone 6), about 48 km (30 mi.) northwest of New York City. The average annual precipitation is 102 cm (40 in.) distributed evenly throughout the 12 months of the year (7 cm [2½ in.] in October to 12 cm [5 in.] in August).

The soil type is known locally as Henkly soil. It is excessively drained, extremely acid (pH 4.5 to 5.5), and thin soil: surface 0–10 cm (0–4 in.) gravelly loam, 10–25 cm (4–10 in.) brown gravelly soil, and 25–43 cm (10–17 in.) dark yellow soil.

The coldest month is January with an average daily maximum temperature of 1°C (35°F) and an average daily minimum tem-

Magnolia 'Yellow Bird'. Flowering in May, this hybrid has particularly dark yellow flowers, which are seen as the first flush of leaves has unfurled. This fine specimen plant was photographed on the Borromean island of Isola Madre in Lake Maggiore, Italy. Photo by Dr. Helmut Orth.

perature of –8°C (18°F). T he average coldest temperature per season is –21°C (–5°F) and the extreme coldest –26°C (–14°F). The warmest month is July with an average daily maximum temperature of 29°C (84°F) and an average daily minimum temperature of 16°C (61°F). The average warmest temperature per season is 37°C (98°F) and the extreme warmest 40°C (104°F).

Magnolia 'Elizabeth'. This hybrid is probably the most famous yellow magnolia. It was raised by the Brooklyn Botanic Garden, where the original plant can still be found growing luxuriantly. Photo by Donal Synnott.

Exotic magnolias that are grown alongside *Magnolia acuminata, M. virginiana, M. fraseri, M. fraseri* var. *pyramidata, M. tripetala*, and *M. grandiflora* 'Bracken's Brown Beauty' include *M. obovata, M. officinalis* var. *biloba, M. sieboldii, M. sieboldii* subsp. *sinensis, M. denudata, M. sprengeri* var. *sprengeri* 'Diva', *M. kobus, M. stellata, M. cylindrica, M. biondii, M.* 'Elizabeth', *M.* 'Spectrum', *M.* 'Galaxy' (not as good as 'Spectrum'), *M.* ×*soulangeana*, and *M.* 'Big Dude'. Those that have failed to thrive include *M. sargentiana* var. *robusta, M. campbellii* subsp. *mollicomata*, and *M.* 'Caerhays Belle'.

Dick Figlar also grows magnolias at the Magnolian Grove Arboretum in Pickens, South Carolina (U.S. hardiness zone 7), 37 km (23 mi.) west of Greenville.

The average annual precipitation is 122 cm (48 in.) evenly distributed through the 12 months (7.5–12.5 cm [3–5 in.] per month).

The soil type is known as Laterite soil. Locally it is referred to as Saprolite soil or red soil. The surface layer is deep to moderately deep sandy loam. Subsoils range from sandy clay-loam to clay. These are very acidic soils estimated at pH of 4.5 to 5.5. *Magnolia acuminata* and *M. fraseri* are native to the existing forest and frequently self-seed in the arboretum area—which itself is a cut-away woodland.

The coldest month is January with an average daily maximum temperature of 11°C (51°F) and an average daily minimum temperature of −1°C (31°F). The average coldest temperature per season is −12°C (10°F) and the extreme coldest −18°C (0°F). The warmest month is July with an average daily maximum temperature of 31°C (87°F) and an average daily minimum temperature of 21°C (70°F). The average warmest temperature per season is 37°C (98°F) and the extreme warmest 39°C (102°F).

An extremely wide range of species and hybrids has been planted over the past few years since 1992 so no clear picture on hardiness has developed.

Roger Gossler with Marj and brother Eric runs Gossler Farms Nursery and Garden in Springfield close to Eugene in Oregon's fertile Willamette Valley (U.S. hardiness zone 8). Lying about 100 km (60 mi.) due east of the Pacific Ocean, the Coast Range tempers the winds and reduces the rainfall. The climate is essentially maritime for most of the year.

Rainfall is generally in excess of 100 cm (40 in.), which falls between October and April. Minimum temperatures range from −2° to −17°C (28°–1°F) in the extreme with summer temperatures up to 41°C (106°F).

The Willamette Valley is among the most favoured magnolia-growing regions in the United States. The Gossler Farms Nursery has up to 500 species and cultivars. *Magnolia sargentiana* var. *robusta* can get cut back, though 'Blood Moon' grows strongly and is now 9 m (30 ft.). *Magnolia sprengeri* var. *sprengeri* 'Diva' flowers and seeds well, so that many of Roger's grafting understocks are 'Diva' seedlings.

Cultivating Magnolias in Continental Europe

Some of the finest collections of magnolias can be found in southern Switzerland and northwestern Italy, an area that has been described as having a Mediterranean climate in an alpine setting. The collections of Sir Peter Smithers at Vico Morcote, Switzerland; Piet van Veen at Vira Gambarogno, Switzerland; Villa Taranto at Pallanza and Isola Madre, both on Lake Maggiore in Italy; and the nursery and garden of Mr. and Mrs. Otto Eisenhut at San Nazzaro in Ticino, Switzerland, can boast some of the finest magnolias in the Western world. The setting in which they are found is quite captivating. Sir Peter in his book *Adventures of a Gardener* (1995) described them as replacing native forest trees as the main structure of the ecosystem: "Now at 25 years or so from planting, some of them are forest trees 12 m (40 ft.) high and I have a woodland of exotics!"

Not only do magnolias flourish with such profusion in the hands of knowledgeable and dedicated gardeners, they are also found extensively in public parks and private gardens in this area with *Magnolia grandiflora* and *M. liliiflora* being the dominant plantings. Sir Peter Smithers has provided the following data on climate at Vico Morcote.

Rainfall is 190–250 cm (75–100 in.) which in a normal year would be heaviest in summer and early autumn with little rain in midwinter. However, the climate has become unstable in recent years. Snowfall occurs at relatively warm temperatures, therefore of short duration but may be up to 60 cm (24 in.) in depth.

Soil type is a degraded micaceous schist overlying that rock. pH varies somewhat throughout the garden, but is always on the acid side of neutral but not by more than a point. The soil is quick draining.

Temperature—this is a mountain climate at an altitude of about 365 m (1200 ft.) with mountains above us. There is therefore a very sharp differential between night and day. That is to say temperature rises rapidly at sunrise and falls rapidly at sundown. Winter minimum in 27 years is –17°C (1°F) in 1985 with the "normal" winter minimum being –8° to –12°C (10°–18°F) but only once (1996–97) have we had frost of duration longer than a couple of days.

Daily summer maximum is normally around 35°C (95°F) from June to September, but with a rapid dip at sundown as cool air comes down from the mountains above.

It is among the sunniest areas in Switzerland with more than 2000 hours annually.

Northern Europe has probably been better known as one of the main suppliers of magnolias. Firma C. Esveld (Dick van Gelderen) and Bulkhard Nurseries, both of Boskoop, and Wim. Rutten of Leende, all of the Netherlands, carry extensive lists. Magnolias are found at the Trompenburg Arboretum in Rotterdam and the Gimborn Arboretum at Doorn, both in the Netherlands.

In recent years, however, through the enthusiasm of Vicomte Philippe de Spoelberch at Herkenrode in Belgium, collections of magnolias have been successfully established here. The collection at Herkenrode was started in 1970. After 25 years more than 6000 trees and shrubs have been planted, of which 500 are magnolias. Of the climate in Belgium, Vicomte de Spoelberch has supplied the following:

Cultivation of *Magnolia* in Belgium is determined by the existence of three main areas: western maritime low lands, central intermediate, and eastern mountainous and more continental.

In low (western) Belgium, near the North Sea, rainfall is approximately 750 mm (30 in.) per year; this is half the rainfall of the eastern part of the country (city of Spa). The soil is generally lighter. Spring may be very early, and late frosts will be most damaging. Good collections in this area are to be found at Kalmthout, Hemelrijk, and Arboretum Het Leen (Eeklo). Average minimum January temperatures range from –9°C to –11°C (12°–16°F).

In mid-Belgium, one finds the best soils, intermediate climate, and probably the best possibilities for growing *Magnolia*. Spring frost is very damaging, especially in open sites (early start and lack of protec-

At Vico Morcote in Switzerland, Sir Peter Smithers has filled the painter's palette with a breath-taking array of shades of pinks, white, and purples as the land falls sharply to Lake Lugano. Photo by Sir Peter Smithers.

tion). Rainfall around Brussels will be approximately 1000 mm (40 in.) per year. Average minimum temperatures in January are −11° to −13°C (9°–12°F). Magnolia collections are to be found at Herkenrode (Wespelaar), Mariemont, and Scrawelle (Seneffe). *Magnolia obovata*, *M. officinalis* var. *biloba*, *M.* 'Charles Coates', *M.* 'Leda', *M.* 'Hot Lips', *M. sieboldii*, *M.* ×*kewensis* 'Wada's Memory', *M. kobus*, and *M.* ×*loebneri* do particularly well at Herkenrode, while *M. campbellii*, *M. dawsoniana*, and *M. sargentiana* are always frosted and not worth growing. *Magnolia* 'Iolanthe' and *M.* 'Star Wars' are damaged by winter or spring frosts. Bokrijk Arboretum (near Hasselt) has a good magnolia collection in this clay pocket of the more generally sandy (and cold) Kempen area of northern Belgium. Parc Tenbosch in Brussels grows *Magnolia sprengeri* var. *sprengeri* 'Diva', thanks to the microclimate of the city.

In eastern Belgium the more continental climate (distance from the sea) and altitude will further reduce the January minimum tempera-

Magnolia 'Hot Lips'. This tree was named by Vicomte Philippe de Spoelberch of Herkenrode, Belgium, for the "rich voluptuous base of the tepals"! Spoelberch received the plant from Dick van Gelderen of Boskoop, who grew it as seed-raised *M. campbellii* subsp. *mollicomata*. When, however, it flowered towards the end of April, it evidently was a hybrid because of its shape, flower colour, and hardiness. It is possibly a hybrid with *M. sprengeri* var. *sprengeri* 'Diva'. Photo by Vicomte Philippe de Spoelberch.

tures to −13° to −17°C (1°–9°F). Magnolias will only grow in valley bottoms (heavy, acid, loam and clay). In protected sites (shade) they will be later in vegetation and escape spring frosts! There may be up to two weeks delay in coming into growth. Average January minimum temperatures will drop to −17°C (1°F) with peak years at −25°C (−13°F). Rainfall will reach 1500 mm (60 in.) per year on the Ardennes plateau (Spa). Arboretum Lenoir (Rendeux) in the bottom of the Ourthe valley has a good collection of magnolias with *Magnolia fraseri* and *M. acuminata* growing well for many years.

Cultivating Magnolias in Sweden

It may sound surprising to find so many collections of *Magnolia* growing successfully in Sweden. Karl Flinck and Kenneth Lorentzon have been actively growing and promoting these plants for many years. The latter supplied the following information:

To grow magnolias 6° north, more than their most northern natural stands, is of course troublesome. The surprising thing is that magnolias can be grown at all, and as many as 400 cultivars, species, and selections are grown at Arboretum Flinck in southern Sweden, our most extensive collection. In the best zone in Sweden the minimum temperature could reach as low as −25°C (−13°F) and in a normal winter could drop down to −18° to −20°C (0° to −4°F). The growing season is rather short with about 220 days having a mean temperature above the freezing point. This many cold days means that the duration of frost could be severe, and a day maximum of −10°C (14°F) for a fortnight is not rare. Combined with a lack of snow in the southern parts of the country, the cold temperatures could be lethal after a dry summer. Solid frozen ground is a normal part of our winter and the depth that could be expected in bad winters over a 20-year period is 100 cm (40 in.)!

In the summer the temperature is not high enough to compensate for the low ones in winter. Average mean July temperature is 16°C (61°F).

Watering is recommended as growth starts in May through June, as well as mulching in late August or early September to keep the warmth as long as possible throughout the autumn. Spring is the best season for planting, and a container-grown plant is superior to a ground-dug plant.

The rainfall in the *"Magnolia* belt" is 500–750 mm (20–30 in.) per year. Ideally this should be 1000 mm (40 in.). The difference has to be compensated with irrigation and this is very important.

Since the first magnolias were introduced to Sweden, many forms have been tried, with some remarkable results. Regularly seed-crops could be expected on *Magnolia kobus, M. sieboldii, M. ×loebneri,* and *M. obovata,* with occasional crops on *M. ×kewensis, M. ×proctoriana, M. wilsonii,* and *M. sieboldii* subsp. *sinensis.*

The following are grown and could be found in amateur collections: *Magnolia officinalis* var. *biloba, M. fraseri, M. obovata, M. tripetala, M. sieboldii, M. wilsonii, M. sieboldii* subsp. *sinensis, M. kobus, M. stellata, M. salicifolia, M. biondii,* and *M. cylindrica.* Among hybrids are *M. ×kewensis* 'Wada's Memory'; *M. stellata* 'Centennial', 'Royal Star', and

Magnolia kobus 'Norman Gould'. This colchicine-induced clone was named for the botanist of the Royal Horticultural Society at Wisley between 1931 and 1960. Photo by Jim Gardiner.

Magnolia ×*brooklynensis* 'Woodsman'. This cross by Professor Joe McDaniel between *M. acuminata* 'Klassen' and *M. liliiflora* 'O'Neill' is similar to 'Eva Maria', the original cross, except different clones of the species were used. Photo by Jim Gardiner.

'Waterlily'; *M.* ×*loebneri* 'Leonard Messel' and 'Merrill'; *M.* 'George Henry Kern'; *M.* 'Ann'; *M.* 'Pinkie'; *M.* 'Susan'; and *M. kobus* 'Norman Gould'. *Magnolia acuminata*, its subsp. *subcordata* and cultivars such as 'Skylands Best' are grown, as are *M.* ×*soulangeana* and its cultivars 'Alexandrina', 'Lennei', Picture', 'Rustica Rubra', and 'Verbanica', and *M.* 'Sundew'. *Magnolia* 'Galaxy' performs splendidly.

The preceding conditions include most of Scandinavia except for the western coast of Norway, which has a mild rainy climate with moderate low winter temperatures and low in summer too. *Magnolia sieboldii* and its companions in section *Oyama* grow to perfection, but the summer temperature is too low for growing several of the others.

Cultivating Magnolias in South Korea

In April 1997 I was fortunate to visit South Korea with the Magnolia Society. The highlight of the trip was to visit Chollipo Arboretum on the T'aean Peninsula in northwestern South Korea. Chollipo, meaning "the beach 1000 ri long" (1000 ri equal 40 kilometres or 25 miles), was founded by Carl Ferris Miller who became a Korean citizen in 1979 and in doing so is known as Min Pyong-gal. He first purchased land at Chollipo in 1962, but it was not until 1970 that three traditional buildings were constructed, marking the start of development. In 1973 it was decided to develop the garden beyond a seaside garden, thus making it the first private arboretum in Korea. By 1978 the arboretum covered some 60 hectares (148 acres) with 450 species, hybrids, and cultivars of *Magnolia* planted within it.

The arboretum rises from sea level to 129 m (420 ft.) and faces the Yellow Sea. The soil varies from pure sand through decomposed granite and hard clay to good loam, the last in fairly limited supply, while poor drainage presents a problem in several areas.

Since the Chollipo climate is moderated by its location beside the sea—areas only a few kilometres inland from the arboretum have considerably harsher climates—most plants listed as hardy in U.S. hardiness zone 8 survive the cold. In favourable pockets some plants hardy to U.S. hardiness zone 9 thrive, even surviving the winter of 1976–77, which was the worst in memory of any of the villagers. Conversely, the winters are of sufficient duration and severity for colder-climate trees and shrubs also to do well. Rainfall comes very unevenly as it does throughout South Korea where about half of the annual precipitation comes between late June and early August. The annual average will probably prove to be in the neighbourhood of 100 cm (40 in.). During the storms that ravaged South Korea in August 1998, 30 cm (12 in.) of rain fell during one night!

Normally the temperature in winter does not fall below −10°C (14°F), although during the very cold 1976–77 winter a low of −14.5°C (6°F) was recorded on 26 December 1976. The first frost of autumn usually comes sometime after mid-November, with the last one around the middle of March. Because the rainy season comes at the hottest time of year, the cloud cover and sea proximity keep temperatures well below what might be expected. Temperatures in excess of 30°C (86°F), however, normally occur on at least a few days in July and August. The long, sunny, comparatively dry autumn ensures that sufficient hardening of plants occurs before winter sets in. Although Chollipo's climate is generally salubrious, it suffers from strong winter winds and considerable salt

Magnolia ×*loebneri* 'Raspberry Fun'. Ferris Miller (Min Pyong-gal) selected this hybrid in 1987 from open-pollinated seed of 'Leonard Messel' growing at the Chollipo Arboretum in South Korea. The arboretum contains one of the most comprehensive magnolia collections in the world. Photo by Jim Gardiner.

spray, which means that protective shelter belts have had to be planted in some areas.

Cultivating Magnolias in China

Kunming is the capital of Yunnan Province in southwest China and is situated in the middle of the Yunnan Plateau at an altitude of 1894 m (6214 ft.). The Chinese Academy of Sciences runs the botanical gardens at Kunming where the deputy director is Sun Weibang. Sun has provided the following information about magnolias and related genera growing in Yunnan.

Yunnan is a mountainous province with altitude varying from 76.4 m (250 ft.) to 6740 m (22,110 ft.). This makes it special for geographical features and various climatic conditions—four seasons can be witnessed within an area of 10 sq. km (4 sq. mi.) but naturally, Magnoliaceae plants are mainly distributed in the area at an altitude of 1200–2600 m (3940–8530 ft.). *Magnolia henryi*, big leaf magnolia, can be found at an altitude of 540–1500 m (1770–4920 ft.). Southeast Yunnan is the most concentrated distribution centre for Magnoliaceae plants in Yunnan.

For growing Magnoliaceae in Yunnan, the most important factor to limit their cultivation is the altitude. Generally places with altitude under 3000 m (9840 ft.) can grow Magnoliaceae plants, but in the areas with an altitude over 2000 m (6560 ft.) only genus *Magnolia* and a few michelias can be grown.

At present, few family gardens grow Magnoliaceae, but public parks, botanic gardens, streets in cities, towns, and villages, as well as the temple or monastery yards are the most popular places to grow them.

For high-altitude areas the most popular species to be grown are from the genera *Magnolia* and *Michelia*. Other genera are cultivated in low areas (subtropic and tropic regions). *Liriodendron chinense* and *L. tulipifera* are big trees grown for timber. *Magnolia grandiflora, M. delavayi, M. liliiflora, M. denudata, M. coco, M. ×soulangeana, M. officinalis* (the red one called *M. officinalis* var. *punicea*), *M. kobus*, and *M. campbellii* can be found. *Magnolia delavayi* of Cao-Xi Temple in central Yunnan was planted 300 years ago. The *M. delavayi* of Yufeng Temple of Lijiang (see accompanying photo), at an altitude of about

2800 m (9180 ft.), is 230 years old; the plant is about 10 m (33 ft.) high, and the base diameter of its trunk is 137 cm (55 in.). The village of East Kunming, 100 km (60 mi.) away, has a 300-year-old *M. denudata* 16 m (52 ft.) high.

Michelia yunnanensis, *M. figo*, *M. alba*, *M. champaca*, *M. floribunda*, *M. megalimba*, *M. fallax*, *M. sphaerantha*, *M. xanthantha* (a very nice flowering shrub with yellow flowers), *M. wilsonii*, *M. maudiae*, and *M. macclurei* are also grown. *Michelia yunnanensis* in Yufeng Temple of Lijiang is 10 m (33 ft.) tall and was planted about 230 years ago. Xiangbopin Village in Nanjian County has a 150-year-old *Michelia sphaerantha* that is about 32 m (105 ft.) tall.

Magnolia delavayi. Planted around 1750, this tree grows at the Yufeng Temple in Lijiang, China. Photo by Sun Weibang.

Manglietia duclouxii and *M. insignis* are the most popular species grown for the streets and in the parks. *Parakmeria yunnanensis* and *P. nitida* are grown for their deep green shiny leaves and very straight trunk, and their attractive flowers. *Paramichelia baillonii* is an excellent timber tree grown commonly in the tropical regions of southern Yunnan. *Tsoongiodendron odorum*, a monotypic species, is endemic to Yunnan. It is cultivated for conservation purposes in gardens or parks.

For about half the year most parts of Yunnan have a dry season. Rainfall in the regions where the Magnoliaceae grow is between 800 mm (31 in.) and 2200 mm (87 in.) with Kunming averaging 1060 mm (42 in.).

Yunnan has natural acid red soil (pH 4.0 to 6.8) which occupies about 50 percent of the total. Another major soil type is acid yellow soil.

The average maximum temperature in the Kunming district varies from 15°C (59°F) in December and January to 21°–24°C (70°–75°F) between April and September, with the extreme maximum of 30°C (86°F) in April–June. The average minimum temperature is 1°–2°C (35°–36°F) in December and January and 12°C (54°F) in June–August, with the extreme minimum of −5°C (23°F) in December and January.

Cultivating Magnolias in New Zealand

New Zealand is home to some of the finest hybrids currently being bred with Oz Blumhardt, Mark and Abbie Jury, and Peter Cave leading the way. Without detracting from the ability and foresight of the breeders, the climate of New Zealand provides some of the finest conditions in which magnolias can grow.

Mark and Abbie Jury at their nursery in Waitara have contributed the following information:

New Zealand consists of two main islands, both relatively long and narrow, lying on a north–south axis. Consequently most of the country enjoys a mild maritime climate. Some coastal and northern areas are frost-free and only a few inland areas experience snow settling for more than a day (at low altitudes).

A band of mountains down the centre of the islands means that west coast areas are damper and milder, with east coast areas being correspondingly drier and experiencing greater extremes of temperature. Daytime highs rarely exceed 30°C (86°F) in summer, and winter daytime averages rarely drop below 5°C (41°F), even in the coldest areas. Most of the country has a winter daytime average of 8°–12°C (46°– 54°F). The prevailing pattern of weather is westerly.

On the eastern side of the North Island, rainfall varies between 760 mm (30 in.) and 1050 mm (41 in.), while on the northwestern side it is 1440 mm (56 in.). On the eastern side of the South Island rainfall is 660–850 mm (26–34 in.), while on the western side it varies from 610 to 1073 mm (24–42 in.). This hides the wider variations that exist, in particular in the extreme southwest corner of the South Island where 7600 mm (300 in.) of rain fall in the Milford Sound area.

In growing deciduous magnolias, the only real limitation is in frost-prone areas where early flowering varieties can have buds burnt by frost. No areas are cold enough to split bark, except a few inland areas of the South Island, and hardiness is generally measured by flowering time only.

New Zealand as a whole tends to be windy and some care needs to be taken to select more sheltered sites. Soils vary from volcanic to clay but as a whole are acidic or neutral. No areas are particularly alkaline.

Magnolias flower over an extended period of time. *Magnolia campbellii* is the first to flower, opening in late June to early July in the warmer north (months that are midwinter) but waiting until late August for cooler areas. Flowering of different spring cultivars is then staggered throughout the season, finishing in November.

In this mild climate, growth rates of plants are much stronger and faster than is expected overseas. In the milder areas younger plants of the evergreen species seldom have a dormant period until they are well established. Most of the country can grow a wide range of *Michelia* and evergreen magnolias, the only limitations being in a few inland areas or those with inland altitude.

Magnolia 'Iolanthe'. Among the most popular New Zealand hybrids, this cultivar produces abundant, large soft pink flowers continuously during March and early April, even on plants under five years of age. Photo by Jim Gardiner.

Magnolia 'Sweetheart'. The value of *M.* 'Caerhays Belle' as a parent was appreciated in New Zealand when Peter Cave of Hamilton selected a seedling with a columnar growth habit and with flowers that were held more upright than those of its parent. Photo by Peter Cave.

HARDINESS, SHELTER, AND SHADE

The question is often asked, is the plant hardy? More often than not a straight yes or no is given without further qualification. But what is meant by hardiness, and why do plants from the same genus or even the same species react in different ways?

When magnolias are introduced into areas of the world that are outside their natural distribution, they have to adjust to new climatic conditions. This is often a severe test. How successfully a plant meets the challenge depends on the degree of natural hardiness that it has developed through the evolutionary process and the level of temperature drop to which it is accustomed in its home habitat. For instance, *Magnolia grandiflora* in its natural geographic range can experience minimum temperatures between 6°C (43°F) and −12°C (10°F), depending on the location. When introduced into an alien environment, however, it is often expected to grow in conditions where temperatures can drop to −18°C (0°F).

A plant's ability to withstand low temperatures can also often depend on its geographic origin, its age, and its health. What then are the environmental factors that affect a plant's performance?

Cold Damage

Cold damage may be best considered under two main headings: winter injury when the plants are relatively dormant, and autumn or spring injury when there is some active growth.

The climate in which a magnolia grows in the wild is usually a good guide as to its relative hardiness. There are always one or two surprises, however. *Magnolia delavayi*, for example, is proving more resilient than was first expected. Plants from northerly latitudes, such as *M. acuminata* and *M. tripetala* from the New World and *M. kobus*, *M. obovata*, and *M. sieboldii* subsp. *sieboldii* from the Old, are proving to be the most hardy. Magnolias from southern locations, especially evergreens, such as *M. grandiflora* and *M. nitida*, are vulnerable to winter injury, along with the deciduous *M. globosa* (the Chinese form). Differences between clones and species will show clearly here, with some plants coping while others suffer from dieback, defoliation, or death. Age and the physiological condition of the plant can also affect its chances of survival. Young plants (under approximately seven years) and plants whose growth rate is generally poor are more susceptible to freezing conditions. It is worth mentioning here that containerised magnolias are particularly susceptible to frost damage. (It is root systems that are killed during periods of severe winter weather, so it is the roots that should be given protection.) Although evergreens can take up water when temperatures are as low −2°C (28°F), a combination of biting winds and frozen ground is particularly damaging, as the foliage becomes dehydrated also.

Autumn injury is noticed with some North American deciduous species. *Magnolia macrophylla* in particular continues growing late into the season and consequently suffers from dieback when frost affects the soft shoots.

Spring injury is probably the most damaging, primarily to the flowers but also to the survival of the plant itself. In maritime climates, wintry conditions often return after cold spells during December or January, when buds have already started to swell. The consequences can be disastrous. The entire flower crop may be frosted, with the tepals "browned" completely or just at the margins, or bleached of their colour. Early flowering varieties, such as *Magnolia campbellii* and its close relatives and *M. kobus*, are particularly susceptible. Some of the most debilitating frosts are those late spring air frosts of around −3°C (37°F) when a plant's first shoots are in active growth. Waking up to a bright sunny morning in early April with a white frost covering the ground is a recipe for disaster. The strong early morning sun not only causes all new growth to brown but causes bark to split on the sunny side even on mature specimens. Provided there is sufficient ground moisture, plants will recover strongly.

Plant breeders give considerable thought to improving the hardiness ratings of plants by selecting specific clones or by taking a species known to be very hardy and hybridising it with another species not known for this quality. In the de Vos and Kosar hybrids, for example, *Magnolia stellata* improves the hardiness of *M. liliiflora* 'Nigra' flowers. The inclusion of *M. acuminata* as a seed parent as well as adding interest through flower colour improves considerably the hardiness ratings of its progeny. Not only has this species improved the hardiness ratings and diversified flower colour, but it has also delayed flowering times to later in the year, which may be the difference between successful flowering and frosted buds.

Heat

Heat does not appear to trouble magnolias in the British Isles, unless it is a dry heat coupled with dry soil conditions. Several species and hybrids such as *Magnolia grandiflora* have been planted widely in the tropics without adverse effect; however, some growers believe that deciduous plants need low temperatures at certain times of the year, otherwise their flower development will be adversely affected. On the other hand, magnolias need adequate summer temperatures to ensure shoot growth and ripening. If this shoot ripening does not take place, plants that are normally tolerant of low winter temperatures suffer from shoot dieback or even death. This effect is particularly evident in northern regions of the British Isles and Scandinavia.

Heat also has an effect on flower colour especially in the red-purple end of

Magnolia ×soulangeana 'Coates'. At its peak during late April at the Chollipo Arboretum in South Korea, this specimen illustrates how temperatures (primarily) can affect the flower colour. The warmer spring temperatures of Chollipo (compared to England's temperatures) intensify the flower colour. Photo by John Gallagher.

the spectrum. Many Gresham hybrids appear to be different cultivars when seen in different temperature regimes. In the warmth of a North American spring in Washington, D.C., or New York, the colours are distinctly red-purple, while in the British Isles, where the temperature is several degrees cooler, the colours are pink. *Magnolia ×loebneri* 'Leonard Messel' is distinctly pinker when flowering in warmer conditions.

Shelter

In the wild most magnolias are woodland plants and like companionship. In other words, they are found growing in close association with other plants. They need a gradual build up of leaf litter and humus around them to provide their roots with a soil rich in nutrients. They also require a soil that is shaded by a leaf canopy so that it does not heat up and dry out too quickly.

In cultivation these conditions can be reproduced artificially by feeding and mulching around the base of the plant so that it can be "isolated," for example, when planted as a lawn specimen. The need to mulch and keep the roots shaded decreases as rainfall and atmospheric humidity increase.

October 1987 saw hurricane-force winds batter the southeast corner of England. Many magnolias were lost because other trees fell on them; other magnolias had branches ripped off, but most came through unscathed —a telling demonstration of how the magnolia's pliancy gives it the ability to withstand such winds. A specimen of *Magnolia sargentiana* var. *robusta* at High Beeches Garden in Sussex blew down, however, and the main trunk is more or less parallel to the ground. I saw the tree with the Magnolia Society in 1996 when epicormic growth had sprouted from all the way along the trunk—such is the power of regeneration.

Magnolia ×soulangeana 'Coates'. The flower colour of this specimen in Dorset, England, is not as intense as that of the plant growing in the warmer climate of South Korea (facing page). Photo by John Gallagher.

Some species demand some degree of wind filtration. Despite being surprisingly hardy, the American species *Magnolia macrophylla* indicates by the size of its foliage a need for some shelter, although it adapts to more exposed positions by producing smaller foliage.

Magnolias are also tolerant of urban areas, which tend to have warmer temperatures and "shelter" provided by buildings. They grow surprisingly well when planted in small beds or adjacent to houses with only paving slabs or setts surrounding them. It can be assumed that their root systems find their

Magnolia ×*soulangeana* 'Pickard's Hybrids'. Amos Pickard of Pickard's Magnolia Gardens in Kent produced an array of hybrids by selecting out the best seedlings from selfed *M.* ×*soulangeana* 'Picture'. These hybrids have very full flowers, often bicoloured, and are seen over several weeks. Sir Peter Smithers at Vico Morcote flowers many of them to perfection with fantastic displays in evidence. Photo by Sir Peter Smithers.

way underneath the paving slabs and have an uninterrupted root run without disturbance. The latter is the key to their success. Magnolias do not have deep penetrating root systems, and so can be planted close to buildings that have the appropriate foundations.

When planting a new garden, consider traditional wind breaks such as species of *Betula* (birch), *Larix* (larch), *Alnus* (alder), *Ilex* (holly), or *Pinus* (pine), or even the ubiquitous ×*Cupressocyparis leylandii* (Leyland cypress), to give instant shelter to magnolias. If there is no room for these traditional shelter plants, try some of the smaller magnolias, which are more tolerant of exposure.

Shade

Certain *Magnolia* species under certain climatic conditions are grateful for some shade. As a rule, the hotter and drier it is, the greater the need for shade. In most places in the British Isles it is unnecessary to provide shade—most magnolias simply enjoy any sun. Of the exceptions, *M. wilsonii*, *M. sieboldii* subsp. *sinensis*, *M. sieboldii* (and its hybrids), *M. macrophylla*, and *M. globosa* need shade where the summers are hot and dry, but are quite happy in full sun where moisture and humidity levels are high. In certain instances the light levels are not good enough for successful cultivation. The Pickard hybrids, raised by Amos Pickard of Canterbury, are very successful in the high light areas of Kent and central and southern Europe, but in more northerly latitudes their flowering is not nearly so spectacular.

CHAPTER THREE

Magnolias in the Garden

T HE MAGNOLIA is undoubtedly among the most glamorous and effective woody plants for gardens of all sizes. It is quite magnificent on the grand scale, but can be equally effective in a small suburban garden. *Magnolia stellata*, one of the de Vos and Kosar hybrids known as the "Eight Little Girls," or *M. sieboldii* subsp. *japonica* is quite suitable for the smallest gardens. Even *M. grandiflora* 'Little Gem' or 'Bracken's Brown Beauty' can be used here.

Magnolia ×*soulangeana*, which can be seen in many suburban gardens, or the Gresham hybrids have potential in larger suburban or country gardens. Tree magnolias are particularly effective in the larger garden when set against a dark background of evergreen plants, where they visually dominate the landscape with their glowing white or rich pink blooms. Evergreen magnolias themselves can be used for background planting.

If your garden is undulating, take care not to plant in the bottom of a hollow, which may be a frost pocket. Most of the time, planting in the bottom of a hollow means that you are forever looking skyward to witness the tree's riot of colour, but that is far better than finding the blooms bleached of their colour because of frosting. If your garden is in a frost pocket, select plants whose blooms have a degree of frost hardiness such as *Magnolia* ×*loebneri* 'Leonard Messel'. You could also select plants that flower continuously over a long period, such as *M. stellata*, *M.* 'Star Wars', or *M.* 'Galaxy', so that if the early blooms are frosted, there is a good chance that the later ones will not. A third solution is to select plants that flower after the damaging effects of frosts are over such as *M. wilsonii* 'Highdownensis', *M. grandiflora*, or one of the *M. liliiflora* hybrids.

It can be a positive advantage to view from below *Magnolia wilsonii* 'Highdow-

Magnolia wilsonii 'Highdownensis'. Described by J. E. Dandy in 1950 from a plant growing in the garden of Sir Frederick Stern at Highdown in Sussex, this clone is more vigorous than the species. Its flowers are larger and not so cup-shaped as those *of M. wilsonii* and bloom for six weeks from late May to early July in southern Britain. Photo by Jim Gardiner.

Previous pages: One of the most famous collections of magnolias in the world can be found at Vico Morcote in Switzerland. Photo by Sir Peter Smithers.

nensis', *M. sieboldii* subsp. *sinensis*, and *M. sieboldii*, with their pendent or nodding flowers. Otherwise, if your garden is large and steeply sloping, you may be able to plant below a terrace so that you can "stand in the crown" and soak up the overwhelming display of flower power.

LAWNS

Lawn specimens can be particularly effective. The archetypal *Magnolia* ×*soulangeana* or one of the Gresham hybrids is very useful in medium-sized to large gardens, but there is a magnolia to suit most garden sizes. Magnolias with an upright habit, such as *M.* ×*kewensis* 'Wada's Memory', *M.* 'Daybreak', or one of the *M. acuminata* hybrids, provide a useful focal point and do not take up too

much space. Lawn specimens normally do well, because a covering of grass means no root disturbance, so essential in the cultivation of this genus. It is important, however, to feed the ground around the plant with a proprietary turf fertiliser (lime-free) each spring (using one with supplementary nitrogen) and early autumn (using a high potash feed). The nutrients will reach through to supply the magnolia with a balanced feed. Lawn-planted magnolias almost certainly have to be pruned at some time.

CONTAINERS

The Japanese are particularly fond of planting *Magnolia stellata* and its cultivars in containers, so they can bring the plants into their homes to appreciate the delicate fragrance when in flower. The de Vos and Kosar hybrids can be treated in a similar fashion. From my experience, considerable expertise is needed to retain magnolias in a container for any length of time. The roots are

Magnolia 'Daybreak'. The outcome of crossing *M.* ×*brooklynensis* 'Woodsman' with *M.* 'Tina Durio' was something of a pleasant surprise for August Kehr, who rates this hybrid among his most promising because of its upright-growing habit, rate of growth, flower colour, and floriferousness. It is seen illuminating a dull, rainy April day at Otto Eisenhut's nursery in Ticino, Switzerland. Photo by Jim Gardiner.

Magnolia ×*kewensis* 'Wada's Memory'. One of the most elegant specimens of this hybrid, stunning in flower and habit, can be seen at the Henry Francis du Pont Museum in Winterthur, Delaware. Photo by Jim Gardiner.

particularly sensitive to being hot and dry during the summer months and frosted during the winter months. If these difficulties can be resolved, then the experience of seeing a well-grown specimen of the "magnolia of the houses" in a conservatory during flowering time can be particularly satisfying.

Evergreen magnolias and clones of *Magnolia grandiflora*, in particular *M. grandiflora* 'Gallissonniere', can be grown in very large containers for indoor use in atria. As well as being attractive in flower and scent, and having foliage throughout the year, the plants' upright pyramidal form is very useful when seen in this context.

MIXED BORDERS

Many magnolias are planted in mixed borders with shrubs, herbaceous plants, and bulbs for company. Why not try magnolias with shrub roses, thereby extending the period of interest? The autumn crocus, *Colchicum*, is also useful; although its heavy spring leaves are quite difficult to hide, the plant is complementary when in flower. Care must be taken that the plants chosen to surround magnolias do not need constant soil cultivation at their bases. Magnolias dislike soil being disturbed around their roots.

WALLS

Many a country-house wall would look naked had a *Magnolia grandiflora* not been planted against it. *Magnolia grandiflora* 'Exmouth' was the clone generally used. Sites of similar size and scale are not too readily available today. Slow-growing clones of *M. grandiflora* such as 'Little Gem' or less-vigorous hybrids such as *M.* 'Maryland' are now available for more limited spaces. Early flowering deciduous species such as *M. campbellii* and the beautiful *M. campbellii* subsp. *mollicomata* 'Lanarth' have also been planted against walls. North walls are preferred as they heat up more slowly and do not force the plant into bloom too early so that the flowers run the risk of damage from severe frosts.

PLANT SELECTION

From the outset you should consider what you want of your magnolias. Are you simply growing for aesthetic appeal, or are you planting a collection of species and cultivars that are true to name? Either way, you still want to know how your plant is going to grow and whether it is going to perform the function for which it was selected.

Most reputable suppliers of magnolias raise plants vegetatively by cuttings, grafting, or budding, although some still raise species by seed. With seed-raised plants from cultivated collections, however, there is doubt about their authenticity. There are arguments for and against this technique. Undoubtedly, very interesting and desirable hybrids have been introduced in this way (for example, *Magnolia* 'Charles Coates', *M.* 'Princess Margaret', and *M.* 'Eric Savill'), and importantly hybrids will flower more quickly. Against this, however, there are several poor forms of species in circulation today, and only particular clones should be sought. For example, the Korean form of *M. sieboldii* is the most horticulturally desirable form of this species and should be raised from a known source.

Magnolia grandiflora. This wall-trained specimen at Orchards, near Godalming in Surrey, was planted around 1900. The house was designed by Edwin Lutyens for Lord and Lady Chance and the garden was designed and planted by Gertrude Jekyll. Photo by Jim Gardiner.

Magnolia 'Eric Savill'. This seedling of *M. sprengeri* var. *sprengeri* 'Diva' grows into a broad-spreading small to medium-sized tree that flowers freely each year. It is seen here in the Savill Gardens with a carpet of *Narcissus bulbocodium* in front. Photo by John Gallagher.

Purchasing and Planting Magnolias

Most magnolias purchased today are containerised plants. Pay particular attention to the root systems by examining whether the plant is well established in the container, but not over established with the root system growing out of the bottom of the pot. Many deciduous tree species are either budded or grafted. Better plants (a better union between the stock and the scion) are produced by budding. This advantage does not, however, preclude the purchase of a grafted plant, provided the scion is vigorous and held sturdily in the pot.

Autumn planting is recommended. The soil is warm and the roots will continue to grow for a short time after planting. The plant should have been hardened off by the nursery beforehand—if it has just come out of a greenhouse or a polythene tunnel, growth may be too soft and dieback may take place if early autumn frosts occur.

Equally good results are obtained by spring planting from March to the end of April, depending on the site and situation, provided that container plants are protected from frost during the winter months. When magnolias have been standing out at plant centres during severe winters, they start to break out into growth in the spring and then collapse, indicating that their root system was killed by severe chilling while in the containers. Temperatures that fluctuate widely just as plants are coming into growth are particularly damaging. Sap will be rising, which can become frozen if the temperature drops below 0°C (32°F). As well as killing the new growth, the sap will "explode," causing the bark to split. Split bark can be potentially fatal, even to mature plants. If a plant is purchased in the autumn and for one reason or another it cannot be planted until the spring, heel in the plant still in its pot in a protected site until you are ready to plant.

Summer planting from a container is possible provided you are not in the middle of a drought. Always water freely if there is no significant rain after a week.

Bare-root plants are seldom seen from suppliers and generally arrive at the beginning of the winter. At no time allow the root system to dry out. Care should be taken when containerising and with the subsequent after care, as damaged roots are likely to rot during the dormant period. The smallest possible container should be chosen and the compost must be moist but not wet. Once the plant is established in the spring, it can either be potted up for planting the following autumn or directly planted out in early summer, provided that it is large and vigorous enough and that irrigation is available.

SOIL PREPARATION

It is axiomatic that magnolias benefit from thorough ground preparation prior to planting, but how much preparation is needed depends upon the existing state of the soil. The object of the exercise is to produce a rich, fertile loam that is moisture retentive and on the acid side of neutral. If you are fortunate enough to have this "perfect" soil already, then nothing needs to be done. If, as is more likely, you have not, then you should incorporate liberal amounts of well-rotted bulky organic matter into the soil. This adds "body" to sandy or thin soils and opens up heavy soils and is imperative if success is to be achieved. With clay soils, it is important to incorporate grit along with the organic matter.

What is the best type of organic matter to use? This depends upon where you live and what is available to you. Well-rotted animal manure (horse manure being the best), leaf mould (which is rich in nitrates), conifer needles, shredded bark, coarse sawdust, and chopped bracken are all suitable. Care should be taken before items such as bark or sawdust are used. These should be stacked long enough for their natural toxins to be neutralised and for the damaging nitrites contained in them to be converted by bacterial action into useful nitrates.

Whether planting in sandy or heavy soil, a large planting pit is always to be recommended. For a lawn specimen, the ground should be cultivated to two spits deep (or twice the depth of a spade blade) and a planting pit 1.2 m (4 ft.) in diameter at the very minimum should be dug. If this preparation is being carried out immediately prior to planting, the soil should be broken up into a fine tilth. If a planting pit is being prepared in the autumn for spring planting, it should be left as open as possible (especially with heavy clay soils) to allow weathering to take place.

There is a clear distinction between a moisture-retentive soil and water-logged soil. Magnolias are generally not swamp plants and therefore, if your heavy soil is rather too moisture retentive, it will be worthwhile draining the site prior to planting. When preparing a planting pit where the clay content of the soil is high, always "rough up" the vertical sides by penetrating them with a garden fork or a similar piece of equipment. If smooth sides are left, the roots will often have great difficulty penetrating them and this will drastically reduce the rate of growth of the plant in the future. If planting on a heavy or poorly drained soil, mound up the soil so that the planting pit is artificially raised above the normal ground level.

pH

The term used to define the acidity or alkalinity of the soil is pH; pH 7 is neutral, numbers below 7 indicate acidity, numbers above 7 indicate alkalinity.

Soil pH is a contentious issue amongst magnolia growers. All agree that an acidic soil is suitable for cultivation, with 5.5 to 6.5 being considered the most desirable range. But some accept that many magnolias can be grown successfully in an alkaline soil. Certainly plants growing on thin soils over chalk or limestone do not flourish, but this may be because these soils heat up quickly in the spring and dry out precisely when water is called for. Most successful magnolia collections are growing where the annual rainfall exceeds 81 cm (32 in.) and where a more-or-less even precipitation occurs throughout the growing season. Some magnolias (*Magnolia grandiflora* and other evergreen species) are more tolerant of drought than others; these are able to tolerate life on the chalk, although they may not perform spectacularly.

There are, however, many alkaline soils which are deep and moisture retentive, not only in the British Isles but also in North America and Europe. On moisture-retentive soils with an alkaline pH to 7.5–7.7, an extensive range of magnolias can be cultivated, although they would not succeed on thin dry soils of a similar pH value. No information is available on magnolia tolerance to higher levels of alkalinity. It seems apparent that moisture levels play a significant role in magnolia cultivation on alkaline sites. The risk of chlorosis on alkaline soils remains, but there are additives such as sulphur that will reduce the soil pH.

Sulphur powder or sulphur chips are used and can be applied when plants are in growth. Not only do they acidify the soil, but these supplements also have a nutritional effect. This process is slow and, being a biological process, the warmer the temperature (within reason) the better. As a guide you will need to apply 135–270 gm/sq. m (4–8 oz./sq. yd.) into the top 15 cm (6 in.) of soil if you want to reduce the pH from 7.0 or 7.5 to 6.0 or 6.5.

PLANTING

Referring back to soil preparation, the planting pit will have been prepared, with copious quantities of well-rotted organic matter added. This site should be chosen with care, as it should also be the final position of the plant. I will not go into the detailed nitty-gritty of planting and staking requirements as these aspects are more than adequately covered in most gardening books available today. A few points to consider are summarised here.

When planting in the spring, incorporate 135–270 gm/sq. m (4–8 oz./sq. yd.) of a balanced organic or inorganic fertiliser. Never plant magnolias too deep. The top layer of soil should be just proud of (above) the top of the existing compost level. Great care should be taken to avoid breaking any of the roots. Magnolias have a fleshy root system which, if not in active growth, will not heal over sufficiently quickly. If, however, the plant is root bound, then tease out the root system when planting. A plant should be firmed in according to the prevailing soil conditions.

Where possible, magnolias should be planted when they are small, between 46 cm (18 in.) and 1.2 m (4 ft.), depending on the variety. This way the magnolia will quickly adjust to the surrounding soil conditions. Magnolias planted in late spring or summer need to be watered in well during the first growing season. Watering can be extended into the second season, depending on the situation.

March to the end of April is the optimum planting period, provided that a containerised plant has been given frost protection during the winter months. If there is a likelihood of sharp frost soon after planting, cover the plant with fleece or something similar. Mid-September to early November is the second-best planting period. Avoid the height of summer unless you can irrigate, and avoid January and February (in northern Europe and the British Isles) because of the likelihood of severe weather.

TRANSPLANTING

A fair amount of information has been written about the varying degrees of success achieved when transplanting magnolias from one site to another. Both J. G. Millais and Neil Treseder report considerable success in moving large specimens.

The following summary of points to consider when moving a large plant refers to the moving of an 2.4 m (8 ft.) tall and wide specimen of *Magnolia stellata*. Transplanting was carried out during open weather in March. The crown was tied in and a trench opened up around the tree to reveal a root ball 1.8 m (6 ft.) in diameter. The root ball was gradually reduced in size with a fork, exposing the root network. After damaged roots were pruned, a 1.4 m (4½ ft.) root ball remained. It was undercut and was not deeper than 38 cm (15 in.). The root ball was wrapped in hessian to ensure that the root system neither dried out nor disintegrated. The plant was moved into the prepared pit, the hessian was removed, and friable soil backfilled around the plant and firmed. The crown was then untied and reduced in size by about a quarter or a third so that the plant would lose less water by transpiration and recover more quickly.

If a tree magnolia is moved, the tree should be guyed to ensure that the root system remains firmly anchored, which is essential for quick recovery. Water applied at regular intervals during the summer months certainly aids recovery.

If smaller plants are being transplanted, similar procedures should be adopted. Successful transplanting of young deciduous plants has also been carried out during early September.

MULCHING

A wide range of suitable organic mulches can be used effectively around magnolias. Well-rotted farmyard manure, processed conifer bark, leaf mould, and pine needles are probably the most satisfactory. Wood chippings or sawdust can be used, but have a tendency to cap and deplete soil nitrogen levels. A 5–10 cm (2–4 in.) layer of mulch spread over the top of the soil holds additional moisture that may well prove crucial in times of drought. Provided it is weed-free, the mulch also virtually eliminates the need to cultivate the soil around the base of the magnolia. It is important to not cultivate near the base of young and old plants because their fleshy roots resent disturbance. Depending on the site and situation, it is probably appropriate to give an annual topdressing during the early spring. Never mulch right up to the stem.

PRUNING

Generally speaking, magnolias do not need pruning as a regular cultivation requirement. It is only necessary if the plant has to be trained against a wall, becomes too large for its location in the garden, is misshapen, has been damaged, or has been transplanted.

When a light prune or formative pruning is required, a good rule is to prune plants that flower in spring and early summer between late July and early September. Late-summer flowerers, such as *Magnolia grandiflora*, should be pruned in the spring, when growth begins. Severe pruning of either deciduous or evergreen magnolias should be done immediately before active growth commences in the spring.

Magnolias often show considerable regenerative powers by throwing strong shoots from old wood. This ability can be advantageous if branches are torn off by strong winds or for reshaping misshapen plants. If new shoots are selected to regrow in the affected areas, little damage will be evident several years later.

A wall subject, such as *Magnolia grandiflora*, should be trained up for approximately two-thirds of its ultimate height on a central leader, with only the main laterals being held in.

FERTILIZERS

Coming, as many of them do, from wooded or forested areas, magnolias perform well given high nutrient levels. When buying fertilisers, it is generally appropriate to buy a compound or complete fertiliser, that is, one that contains the three primary nutrients of nitrogen, phosphorus, and potassium. Nitrogen promotes strong shoot growth and gives the plants a greater tolerance to drought and low temperatures. Phosphorus is beneficial for flower-bud production. Potassium ripens the current season's growth shoots and, with magnesium, is particularly useful in reducing chlorosis.

A range of proprietary quick-release and slow-release organic or inorganic fertilisers is available. These should be applied during March or April and in September or October as a supplementary feed in the British Isles. The spring feeding should be high in nitrogen, while the autumn feeding should be high in potash. Quick-release organic fertilisers are beneficial when applied in early spring, and dried blood is a useful additive.

WEED KILLERS

The information here applies to the British Isles. Always check out regulations in your country before using weed killers. It is inevitable that different regulations apply and different products may be available for use. The range of weed killers available enables us to control all weeds around the base of a magnolia without having to carry out surface cultivations such as hoeing, which should be avoided at all costs. Once you have purchased the chemical, keep it in its labelled container or packet in a waterproof, sealed container out of the reach of children, if possible in a locked cupboard. It is crucial to follow the manufacturer's instructions to the letter as well as conform to suggested protective clothing requirements for the operator. A record of chemical applications and where the chemical was applied is useful. Always use up all the spray you have mixed. Once the task is completed, wash out the sprayer and spray out on the same plot of land. Never use the sprayer for operations other than spraying.

Four tried and tested herbicides (active ingredient names only) are mentioned here. The first is dichlobenil, a broad-spectrum granular herbicide that is absorbed by plant roots. It kills annual and perennial weeds as well as grasses. Granules are spread by a hand-held applicator around plants that have been established for at least two years. Weed control can be expected for up to six months from application time, which is during February or March.

Glyphosate, an extremely effective and widely used chemical, is a translocated herbicide for the control of annual and perennial weeds during the growing season. A wetting agent can be used with this chemical. The visual effects can take up to 20 days to show, depending on the time of year and the health, vigour, and condition of the weeds being sprayed.

Paraquat or diquat is a widely used contact herbicide that kills off all annual weeds and burns the tops off perennial weeds in active growth.

Triclopyr, 2,4-D, dicamba, or mecoprop is a translocated herbicide used to control woody weeds such as brambles. For the most effective control, this chemical should be sprayed on during the dull days of summer; it should never be applied during hot sunny days.

CHAPTER FOUR
Propagation

M

AGNOLIAS can be successfully propagated in several different ways—from seed, by cuttings, by layering, by chip-budding, by grafting, and more recently by micropropagation.

SEED

The advantages of raising magnolias from seed are several. It is a means of introducing new cultivars through either controlled or uncontrolled hybridisation. It widens the gene pool. It is cheaper than raising plants by vegetative growth. It generally gives fast establishment and good growth. It produces vigorous root systems, which is particularly beneficial when seedlings are used as understocks. Seed can easily be moved from one country to another, although most countries today endorse the Convention on Biological Diversity (Rio de Janeiro 1992), which requires gardens and institutions to comply with Article 15 (access to genetic resources) concerning the exchange of plant material. Finally, considerable genetic variation is found in seed collected from a cultivated source where open pollination has taken place.

A disadvantage is that seed-raised plants generally take longer to flower than vegetatively raised plants, though many deliberate hybrids raised from seed are flowering in under 10 years.

Availability of seed from species grown in the British Isles varies widely. The very early flowering species, like *Magnolia campbellii*, do not set seed primarily because of low temperatures and lack of pollinators at the time of flowering. Late flowerers, like *M. grandiflora*, do not fruit because temperatures are generally too low at the other end of the season, during the autumn. Several species, such as *M. wilsonii*, *M. obovata*, and *M. campbellii* subsp. *mollicomata* do, however, seed prolifically.

Ripening of the mature fruiting cones can take three or four weeks in the British Isles, by which time seeds can be seen when the fruiting-cone carpels split open, normally in October. It is important that the fruiting cones are left on the plant until this time as it is difficult to extract the seed any earlier. Once this stage is reached, the fruiting cones can be collected, dried, and the seed shaken free.

The seed should not be overdried to the point where the coat becomes shrivelled, as the seed's viability will then be impaired.

Previous pages: *Magnolia stellata*. The star magnolia is native to Japan, where it is often found growing in damp areas close to streams, as seen here in Honshu (Atsumi Gun). In Japan it has a cult following with its own society—the Japan Association for Shidekobushi Conservation—formed in 1991. Photo by Jim Gardiner.

The coat's bright colouring attracts mammals and birds, which assist with the seed's dispersal. Being oily and sticky, the coat also waterproofs the seed and forms a protective covering that prevents germination as long as it remains intact.

The seed should be cleaned by soaking in warm or hot water to which a detergent has been added to remove any remaining traces of the oily film. Seed can be sown either in the autumn or in the spring. The timing ultimately depends on the scale of operation and the facilities available.

The following method can be employed for small-scale production with limited facilities. Sow the seeds thinly in a seed tray or similar container filled with a soil-less seed compost during autumn. Lightly cover the seed with compost followed by approximately 6 mm (¼ in.) depth of grit that is 3 mm (⅛ in.) in diameter. The addition of grit has the advantage of reducing the amount of moss or liverwort that will grow on the surface of the compost. After watering the seed, place the labelled and dated seed tray in a cold frame where the seed will be exposed to winter temperatures. This exposure to cold will remove any germination inhibitors prior to the seeds germinating in the warmth of spring. As this system is not "controlled," germination of some seed may be delayed for a season, so retain the seed tray for an additional 12 months.

The second system is far more controlled. In fact a timetable could be prepared to determine when you store, when you sow, and when to expect germination. Cleaned seed is mixed with moist peat or peat and sand or vermiculite and stored in labelled polythene bags in a refrigerator at a temperature held between 1°C (35°F) and 3°C (37°F) for two months. (Forty-two days has, in fact, been shown to be sufficient.) The addition of a 5-percent fungicidal solution to the stratification medium helps to reduce the incidence of damping off diseases at the germination

Magnolia kobus. Among the first magnolias to bloom in the British Isles from late February to early March, this species is disadvantaged in one way by flowering in one flush, but has the advantage of flowering very profusely. Periodically it seeds freely. The seeds are sown and grown on as understocks for grafting because of their tolerance to a wide range of soil types. Photo by Jim Gardiner.

stage. At this stage the seed can be sown in a similar way to that mentioned above (however, cover with vermiculite instead of grit) and kept at a temperature of 21°C (70°F). Germination can be expected within 30 to 40 days of placing the seed in the higher temperature.

Seedlings are then pricked out into individual 9 cm (3½ in.) pots into a well-drained soil-less compost incorporating a slow-release fertiliser.

CUTTINGS

The main advantages of raising magnolias from cuttings are that an exact copy of the parent plant is produced and that plants flower from an earlier age (as compared with seed-raised plants). The main disadvantages are that cuttings are more costly to produce, and they are less easily transported from country to country because of import-export restrictions. Most magnolias can be propagated by cuttings, so a knowledge of the techniques is useful. There are essentially two types of cuttings, based on the stage of stem development, namely, softwood cuttings (deciduous species and cultivars) and semi-ripe cuttings (evergreen species and cultivars).

Softwood Cuttings

The cuttings are removed at the junction of the current season's growth with the previous year's hardwood. The material is taken when the base of the cutting has become firm. The time at which this occurs depends on several factors that mainly revolve around whether the parent plants have been forced into growth under glass or polythene or are growing in the garden. Growth responses vary from species to species or cultivar to cultivar. This also affects the time at which cuttings are taken, as does the geographical location of the source of the cutting material.

Where container plants are kept under glass or polythene, sun heat alone induces early shoot growth, which can firm sufficiently in early May for cuttings of 7.5–13.0 cm (3–5 in.) long, depending on species or cultivar, to be taken. The growing tip is generally removed, which often induces quicker rooting, due to the redistribution of auxins within the cutting. Wounding is also beneficial and can be either light or heavy, depending on the plant being rooted. *Magnolia stellata*, for example, would have a light wound, whereas the thicker stemmed *M. ×soulangeana* would have a heavy wound. Wounding increases the quantity and quality of the roots, and it increases water uptake by the cutting prior to rooting. With larged-leaved subjects such as *M. ×soulangeana*, approximately half the leaf blade is removed, which reduces water loss and increases the number of cuttings inserted into a given area. In this situation, fungicidal treatment is very important as disease is more likely to occur because of the increased number of cut surfaces on the cutting.

The application of hormone rooting powder is very effective, with up to a 90-percent take being expected. For thin-stemmed subjects such as *Magnolia stellata* a 0.5-percent IBA (Indole butyric acid) in talc is recommended, and for thicker stemmed subjects such as *M. ×soulangeana* an 0.8-percent IBA in talc is recommended. The right time to take cuttings of garden plants in southern England is late June or July.

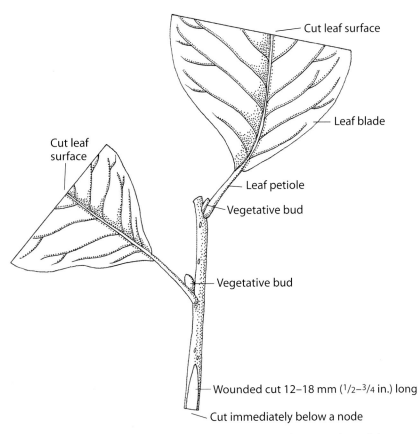

A softwood cutting of *Magnolia ×soulangeana*, showing the wounding of the stem and the reduction of each leaf blade by 50 percent. The cutting is about 12.5 cm (5 in.) long. Drawing by Pauline Dean.

The key to success in rooting softwood cuttings is to take cuttings from healthy plants. Plants that are in a poor state of health, either through age or growing conditions, generally take far longer to root (if they root at all) than do strong, vigorous plants. Cuttings should be kept turgid from the time of collection until they are rooted by observing the conventional methods described in propagation manuals. They can be rooted in various protected structures: cold frames, mist propagation units, closed cases, or fogging systems. It is the aftercare that is of vital importance if these cuttings are to root.

The optimum rooting-medium temperature is 18°–21°C (65°–70°F) with air temperatures around 21°C (70°F). The cuttings should be shaded by reducing the light levels to approximately 25 percent of average summer light conditions. Always check for fungal problems each day.

Rooting media can vary from nursery to nursery. Two parts peat and one part sharp sand or perlite is probably the most commonly used, or alternatively fine grade pine bark, peat and perlite, or bark and peat in equal proportions can be used. Grodan blocks (rockwool) are increasingly being used. A controlled-release fertiliser such as Osmocote (which remains active for six to nine months) is sometimes used to maintain nutrient levels in the cutting and the compost and to improve rooting performance. Alternatively, once rooting has occurred, a liquid fertiliser is used. The latter is preferred when high temperatures are regularly met, which may cause rapid release of the nutrients when granular fertilisers are used.

Cuttings are inserted into trays, cellular trays, or individual pots. The latter two options are best as they result in minimal root disturbance. Rooting takes place in about eight weeks, and it is most important for the survival of the cutting over the first winter that shoot growth is initiated as soon as possible. Do not disturb the cuttings until they have just started into growth in the following spring. In many instances apparently healthy cuttings fail to grow away the following year. The reason for this is obscure, but it is thought to have to do with nutrient balance within the plant.

Semi-ripe Cuttings

Evergreen species and cultivars such as *Magnolia grandiflora* and *M. delavayi* can be propagated successfully by semi-ripe cuttings taken during August or early September in southern England. Nodal cuttings 13.5 cm (5½ in.) long, with a heavy wound and their leaf blades reduced, are inserted into cellular trays, individual pots, or grodan blocks after being dipped in 0.8 percent IBA in talc. Similar protected structures, temperature regimes, and rooting media as for softwood cuttings are used here. Rooted cuttings remain in trays over the winter months and are potted up in the spring. If cuttings are inserted later in the autumn (October) they will generally callus in the autumn and root the following February for potting in March or early April.

LAYERING

Layering has long been a standard method of plant raising for all magnolias or where a small number of plants is required. It differs from other propagation methods in that it involves the development of adventitious roots on a stem that is still attached to the parent plant. Prior to layering, thoroughly cultivate the soil and work in liberal quantities of peat and sharp sand. During March,

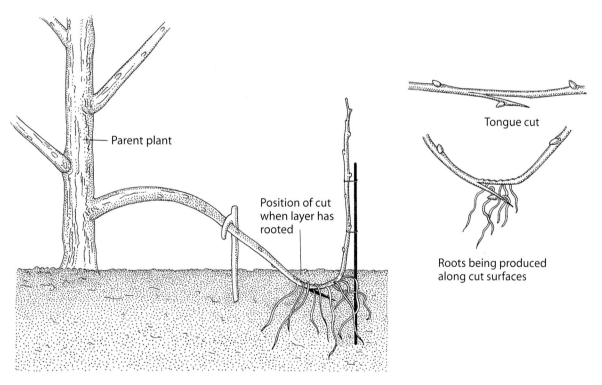

Simple layering. The tongue cut into the stem of the parent plant should be about 5 cm (2 in.) long. Bend the stem carefully at the tongue cut and peg it firmly into the ground, tying the stem to a cane. The bend in the stem at the tongue cut should be about 7.5 cm (3 in.) below the soil level. When the layer is well rooted, cut the stem as indicated. Drawing by Pauline Dean.

layer the shoots of the previous season's growth and make a tongue by cutting along the length of stem. Alternatively, layering can be done in October. This technique is particularly useful because, although *Magnolia* stems are reasonably pliable, they tend to be brittle when bent over to this degree. Dust the cut sliver with 0.8 percent IBA in talc. Then peg the layer firmly in the ground and tie up the stem with a cane.

Examine the layers after 12 months and, if they are well rooted, completely sever them from the mother plant. The rooted layer can then be lifted and containerised in October (18 months from time of layering). Alternatively it can be left until the following March or April (24 months after layering) and then containerised.

CHIP-BUDDING

Chip-budding has been recognised as a way of propagating open-ground trees since the 1930s, but it was not until David Knuckey presented a paper on his experiences with T- and chip-budding of magnolias onto pot-grown seedling rootstocks that *Magnolia* propagation moved forward.

Chip-budding is the substitution of the scion, consisting of a bud, rind, and sliver of wood, for a matching area of root-stock tissue. Stocks are seedling raised and potted up individually into 7.5–9.0 cm (3–3½ in.) square pots and are generally ready for budding 18 months after germination. The stocks are fairly closely (botanically) matched with the scions being budded (see the table on page 92).

The following procedure is used successfully by Hillier Nurseries of Winchester in chip-budding magnolias. First, stocks are lined out in a greenhouse controlled at a reasonably constant temperature of 15.5°C (60°F). The scion wood is collected during July and retained until everything is ready. Next, a chip-bud is married up with the stock and held in place by means of a 2.5 cm (1 in.) wide clear polythene strip. The polythene must be wound in such a way that it does not cover the bud or growth will be inhibited.

Bud takes are recognised quickly with the bud swelling and the leaf petiole abscising clearly within 10 days. As the scion grows away, the stock is cut back to just above the bud to promote the channelling of all the growth into the development shoot. By the end of October a shoot 7.5–10.0 cm (3–4 in.) long has been produced, which then goes dormant. All this time the polythene strip is left on

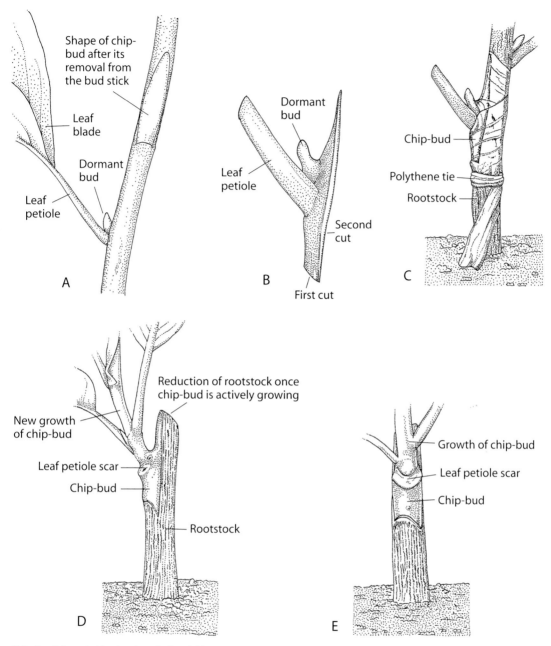

Chip-budding. A, The bud stick should be 15.0–22.5 cm (6–9 in.) long with 3–4 buds. B, The chip-bud should be about 3 cm (1¼ in.) long, and the leaf petiole about 2.5 cm (1 in.) long. C, The chip-bud is attached to the rootstock with a clear polythene tie about 2.5 cm (1 in.) wide. The polythene should not cover the bud or petiole or it will impede growth of the bud. It must hold the chip-bud firmly in place so that the union between stock and chip-bud is made. The top growth on the rootstock should be retained to encourage the flow of sap. D, Side view of the chip-bud three months after taking successfully, showing the growth of the chip-bud and reduction of the rootstock. E, Front view of the chip-bud three months after taking successfully. Drawing by Pauline Dean.

Matching stocks and scions for grafting and chip budding.

STOCK	SCION
M. campbellii subsp. *mollicomata* or *M. sargentiana* var. *robusta* or *M. sprengeri* or *M. ×soulangeana* if no other stocks are available	*M.* 'Albatross' * *M.* 'Caerhays Belle' *M. campbellii* and varieties *M. campbellii* subsp. *mollicomata* and varieties *M. campbellii* 'Charles Raffill' and Raffillii Group *M. dawsoniana* and varieties *M.* 'Eric Savill' * *M.* Gresham hybrids * *M.* 'Iolanthe' and Jury hybrids *M.* 'Michael Rosse' *M.* 'Princess Margaret' *M. sargentiana* var. *robusta* *M. sprengeri* var. *sprengeri* 'Diva' * *M. sprengeri* var. *elongata* * *M. ×veitchii* *
M. grandiflora	*M. delavayi* *M.* 'Porcelain Dove' * *M. ×thompsoniana* *
M. kobus or *M. acuminata*	*M. acuminata* subsp. *subcordata* * *M. cylindrica* * *M. kewensis* 'Wada's Memory' * *M. ×loebneri* * *M. ×proctoriana* * *M. salicifolia* *
M. obovata or *M. tripetala*	*M.* 'Charles Coates' * *M. fraseri* *M. macrophylla* *M. macrophylla* subsp. *ashei* *M. macrophylla* subsp. *dealbata* *M. officinalis* *M. officinalis* var. *biloba* *M. rostrata* *M.* 'Silver Parasol' *M. tripetala* *M. ×wieseneri*
M. wilsonii	*M. globosa* * *M. sieboldii* * *M.* 'Summer Solstice' *

* Also propagated by cuttings.

and the budded plants remain in a cool greenhouse at a temperature of 5°C (41°F). The three-month period from budding to dormancy is crucial to allow for sufficient scion growth to take place, which in turn ensures that the shoot breaks into growth the following spring and grows successfully. Another advantage of budding at this time of the year is the low level of sap exuded from cut surfaces.

The following spring successfully budded plants are potted into 18 cm (7 in.) pots with a peat, bark, and grit compost and a slow-release fertiliser added. Rapid growth follows, which can produce a plant of 1.5 m (5 ft.) in 15 months from budding.

The Saratoga Horticultural Foundation in California has developed a successful technique to T-bud selected forms of *Magnolia grandiflora* onto seedling rootstocks during April with a single stem plant ready for sale within six months. *Michelia* has also been budded onto *Magnolia grandiflora* seedlings. Soil-raised specimens of *M. acuminata* are often used as understocks in the United States and in Scandinavia because of their ability to grow in various soil types and for their hardiness qualities, which are thought to improve the scion's cold hardiness rating.

GRAFTING

Bench grafting has largely been superseded by budding as the latter technique enjoys several advantages: it is economic of scion wood, has a high overall percentage take, produces a more uniform plant, and requires less skill. Where grafting is practised, it is carried out between mid-August and March, depending on the variety and how it fits in with nursery working practices. Similar subjects are grafted to those that are budded (see the table).

Winter Grafting

Stocks are brought into growth during late January and maintained at a temperature of 10°–12°C (50°–54°F) some two to three weeks before scions are collected. A whip or side veneer graft is the best method here with the union taking place close to the roots of the stock plant. The stock and scion are bound together with a rubber grafting tie. The stock plant is headed back to 30 cm (1 ft.) above the union to "pull" sap upwards. Grafting wax is melted and applied to exposed cut surfaces to prevent moisture loss. Grafted plants are placed on an open bench with an air temperature of 8°–10°C (46°–50°F).

The plants slowly grow over the next two-month period. The stock can now be headed back to just above the union. An unsightly graft union often produces a poorly growing plant in later years unless scion rooting occurs. A technique has recently been developed to precallus the graft prior to root and shoot development. Known as hot pipe callusing, this process applies warmth to the graft union alone (20°–25°C [68°–77°F]), while the rootstock and scion are kept frost-free. This separate treatment enables the callus to form quickly within three weeks, at which point the grafted plant is potted and weaned so that it can grow away successfully. Peter Cave of Hamilton on the North Island of New Zealand continues to whip graft (instead of chip-budding) under polythene in July. Because of the prevailing climatic conditions an exceptionally large scion 30–38 cm (12–15 in.) is selected from last season's wood. The advantage of using a large scion is that a saleable plant can be achieved in nine months from grafting.

Summer Grafting

Summer grafting is usually carried out towards the end of July. The stocks are prepared by removing any side shoots or leaves that would interfere with the graft. Generally, the stocks are "dried" prior to bringing them into the greenhouse, so that the sap is not rising so vigorously and unites with the scion more readily. Half the number of leaves are left on the scion, which is prepared, tied, and placed in a high-humidity tent and shaded from direct sunlight. The stock and scion are bound with a rubber tie, and the stock plant is headed back to within 30 cm (12 in.) of the graft. Successful grafts are gradually hardened off and maintained in a greenhouse over winter to be potted up the following spring. The stock can only be headed back once the scion is growing actively.

TISSUE CULTURE

Magnolia propagation by tissue culture is seldom seen, with only one or two specialist companies like Briggs Nursery of Olympia, Washington, and Notcutts of Woodbridge, Suffolk, practising this technique. Most magnolias are easy enough to raise by conventional techniques; however, where material is limited to make cuttings, buds, or grafts, then tissue culture comes into play. One further enquiry needs to be clarified and that is how plants raised by this method perform alongside a plant that has been raised by conventional methods. In other genera, such as *Rhododendron* and *Kalmia*, plants raised by tissue culture are either difficult to establish or their habit of growth is not typical. I cannot answer either of these questions as this technique for raising magnolias is still in its infancy. *Magnolia acuminata* subsp. *subcordata* 'Miss Honeybee', *M.* 'Yellow Lantern', *M.* 'Elizabeth', *M.* 'Sayonara', *M.* ×*kewensis* 'Wada's Memory', *M. fraseri*, and *M. virginiana* are some species and hybrids raised by tissue culture.

PLANT BREEDING

The number of *Magnolia* hybrids available for planting has increased rapidly in the 1990s. Many of these hybrids have been chance seedlings such as *M.*×*loebneri* 'Leonard Messel', *M.* 'Princess Margaret', and *M.* ×*kewensis* 'Wada's Memory' and have become firm favourites. Many have resulted from deliberate crosses. Phil Savage of Bloomfield Hills, Michigan, is among the most accomplished *Magnolia* hybridisers. Over many decades he has perfected the art of collecting pollen and transferring it onto a receptive stigma.

It is not my purpose to discuss basic procedural details of plant breeding as

Magnolia 'Sayonara'. This early Gresham hybrid produces large white goblets with a staining of rich purple at the base of the tepals. It generally grows as a multistemmed large shrub or small tree. Photo by Kihun Song.

these aspects are more than adequately covered in other books. Instead, I will highlight some key points Phil Savage suggests you follow when hybridising magnolias.

For early flowering species such as *Magnolia campbellii* and *M. kobus*, collect several flowers around the middle of the day. Flowers of *M. grandiflora* and *M. virginiana* can be collected early in the morning. Remove all the tepals and then the gynoecium either with a knife or thumbnail. Place the flowers upside down on white paper, together with the name of the plant. The following day, pollen should have fallen onto the paper. Transfer this pollen into an envelope. Label and seal the envelope, then place it in a sealed jar with silica gel in a refrigerator at 3°–4°C (37°–39°F).

Determining whether the stigma is receptive is the secret of successful *Magnolia* hybridising and can only be achieved by careful observation and knowledge of the genus. Select flowers that are within a day or two of opening. Around midday, with a sharp knife or secateurs, cut a receptive bud (one that is down to its last perule). Slice off the pointed flower top, leaving a hole a few centimetres wide into which you can just see the gynoecium. The stigmas will be curled back with the upper surfaces glistening. Slice a corner off the envelope containing the desired pollen and insert a brush. Once pollen grains are on the brush, insert the brush into the top of the bud and move it around, dusting pollen onto the receptive stigmas. Remove the brush. Tie the bud tightly closed, and label the cross with the date and parentage. Place a fine plastic mesh over the flower bud, allowing potential seed to develop unhindered.

Magnolia kobus 'Two Stones'. August Kehr, a well-known *Magnolia* breeder, often uses colchicine to induce polyploidy. This tetraploid has incredible flowers resembling a gardenia in shape and poise. Photo by Jim Gardiner.

POLYPLOIDY

Polyploid magnolias have been known for more than 50 years. The work of E. K. Janaki Ammal at the Royal Horticultural Society's Garden, Wisley, in the 1950s first drew attention to the procedure to "create" more interesting hybrids. When Janaki Ammal carried out her work, she did so with an aqueous solution of colchicine, an alkaloid extracted from *Colchicum autumnale*, the autumn crocus.

August Kehr of Hendersonville, North Carolina, uses 1 gramme of colchicine in 200 cc of water to make a 0.5 percent stock solution, which is kept at 3°C (37°F). DMSO (dimethyl sulphoxide) is added (1 cc) to improve the penetration of colchicine into the plant tissue. The solution is sprayed over the seedling magnolias at the seed leaf stage each day until the true leaves are visible. An 18-hour-day regime at 24°C (75°F) is maintained during the process. Polyploid plants generally exhibit darker, broader, more "crinkled" leaves and are heavier in texture. Tepals too are thick in texture, which enables the flower to last longer.

CHAPTER FIVE
Pests and Diseases

M AGNOLIAS that grow outside the warm temperate and subtropical parts of the world are comparatively free of pest and disease problems. Those that are troublesome are mentioned below. In warmer climates, however, including the southern United States, a wider range of pests and diseases is seen. As with weed killers, much of the information on control measures applies primarily to the British Isles. Always check your own country's regulations first and seek advice from your local advisory service on identification of the pest or disease and method of control.

PESTS

Slugs

Slugs feed at night and are particularly active during warm humid evenings. Young magnolias are especially vulnerable to slug attack during the first year of planting. If the slugs are left unchecked, they can virtually defoliate the plants. In subsequent years, when the plants are established, comparatively light damage is done. Several control measures are available, most of which can only be used on a small scale. A solution of potassium permanganate, aluminium, and copper sulphate can be watered into the soil around the plant to control slugs for several months. Pellets containing methiocarb are effective for a few days only when scattered in the vicinity of the plants, but young children and cats should be kept away from treated areas. Other "safe" control measures include sinking shallow dishes containing beer to soil level, or trapping slugs by laying old cabbage leaves, grapefruit skins, and so forth within the vicinity of the plant to be protected. Collecting slugs during the early evening and dropping them into a bucket containing a strong salt solution is another method of reducing the population.

Glasshouse Red Spider Mite

Magnolias grown under glass or polythene are susceptible to infestations of red spider mite, which can be particularly severe between July and September if left unchecked. Natural predators help control populations of red spider mite, provided early action is taken. One widely used natural predator is *Phytoseiulus persimilis*. When natural predators are introduced early

Previous pages: A dull spring morning at the U.S. National Arboretum in Washington, D.C., is brightened by the colourful display of *Magnolia ×soulangeana*, showing the diversity of flower colour and outline of the plant. Photo by John Gallagher.

in the year and at regular intervals throughout the spring and summer, then control is achieved. The spread of glasshouse red spider is restrained by frequent spraying of water to keep humidity levels high. Chemical control is feasible, though products for the amateur gardener are restricted and give poor results.

Magnolia Scale

Weakly growing trees in North America are particularly prone to heavy infestations of magnolia scale, a brown varnishlike scale insect about 12 mm (½ in.) in diameter with a white waxy covering. It produces large amounts of honeydew. All newly acquired plants should be checked for the presence of scale and treated with an appropriate insecticide prior to planting. Non-persistent contact insecticides can be applied to coincide with the emergence of crawlers, which are generally seen in August or early September. A winter wash can be applied to deciduous species in early spring immediately prior to new growth to control the adults.

Magnolia Leaf Miner

Plants in the southern United States are prone to attack by this pest, which is also known as sassafras weevil. Adults feed on leaves and flowers, giving the tree a "tattered" appearance, while larvae mine through young leaves, giving the tree a "scorched" look. Adults overwinter on leaf litter below the tree and fly into tree canopies in the spring and feed on young growth. Larval activity is seen in late May and June. A systemic insecticide may be used successfully; however, availability needs to be checked at the local advisory service.

Deer and Rabbit

Both deer and rabbit damage young plants during scent marking or by gnawing. The best deterrent is a fence 2 m (6½ ft.) tall, and, in the case of rabbits, netting buried and extending outwards at right angles for about 15–23 cm (6–9 in.) under the soil surface.

Opossum

These New World marsupials have been introduced into New Zealand, where they are regarded as the most significant pest of magnolias. They readily strip bark, which is considered a delicacy! A 30 cm (1 ft.) wide metal strip placed around the trunk will prevent "possums" from climbing into magnolia crowns. Trapping is considered an alternative.

DISEASES
Cankers
Stem cankers attributed to *Phomopsis* are occasionally found. Canker on cuttings in mist benches has been blamed on *P. syringae* (lilac blight), but it occurs so infrequently that it is not a problem.

Magnolia Leaf Spot
Irregular spotting on leaves, especially of *Magnolia grandiflora*, occurs chiefly in warm humid climates. It is caused by *Phyllosticta magnoliae* and is not considered a problem.

Honey Fungus
This very common fungal disease in gardens today, caused by *Armillaria mellea*, affects a wide range of woody plants and is especially prevalent in wet areas. It is a secondary infectant entering plants that are in stress because of old age, drought, waterlogging, frost cracks in the bark, or damage caused by tools or lawnmowers. Magnolias are highly resistant to this disease. I have come across only two plants that had succumbed to the fungus. Once a young plant is under stress, however, the plant's vigour is considerably impaired when this fungus strikes, and the leaves become smaller and often look chlorotic. Large specimens decline over several years. There is no known cure. Complete removal of the stump is essential.

Phytophthora
This group of parasitic fungi is soil borne and is becoming an increasing problem when young plants have been planted in poorly drained soils. A rapid decline of the plant is noticed, either in whole or in part. Always ensure correct planting procedures are in place and that the soil is well cultivated prior to planting.

Verticillium Wilt Diseases

Although no record appears of this disease affecting magnolias in the British Isles, several cases are recorded of *Verticillium albo-atrum* affecting magnolias in North America. Apart from the brown-black discolorations that run in the conducting elements, the distinguishing feature of this disease is that sections of the crown or even complete sides of the tree die quite suddenly. *Verticillium* wilt is very difficult to tackle in this situation. If the affected specimen is very small, a soil drench of a fungicide at fortnightly intervals is worth trying.

Magnolia Virus

Mottled line patterns, rings, and oak-leaf patterns are occasionally seen on magnolias. They are thought to be caused by the cucumber mosaic virus.

DISORDERS

Cold-weather-induced Chlorosis

Chlorosis is often seen during spring on young, actively growing leaves during cold spells. Leaves of both deciduous and evergreen species lose their colour and become very pale green, sometimes white. This colour remains on the plant for the rest of the season.

Lichens

These composite organisms are part fungus and part algae and exist where nutrients are scarce. They are mainly grey or green in colour and are particularly evident in high rainfall or high humidity areas, where air circulation is not good. A phenolic emulsion approved for controlling overwintering aphids applied in December or January is recommended on deciduous plants and can be applied once every four years. Lichens are not a significant problem.

CHAPTER SIX
Magnolia Species

Magnolia delavayi. Photo by Dr. Helmut Orth.

A s THIS volume is a gardener's guide to the hardier magnolias, this chapter and the next focus on species and hybrids that are cultivated primarily in the British Isles, most of North America, northern Europe, South Korea, and New Zealand. These hardier magnolias represent only a small number of the 128 species in the genus. In the discussion of each plant, I have tried to provide information on the plant's origin and where it is found in the wild; a brief horticultural description of its habit, flower, and leaf; and its garden worthiness, cultural requirements, and hardiness.

In this chapter and the next, shrubs are grouped by size as follows: small shrubs are 1.0–1.5 m (3–5 ft.) tall; medium, 1.6–3.0 m (6–10 ft.) tall, and large, more than 3 m (10 ft.) tall. Similarly, trees are grouped by size also: small, 4.5–9.0 m (15–30 ft.) tall; medium, 10–18 m (33–60 ft.) tall; and large, more than 18 m (60 ft.) tall.

Magnolia acuminata
CUCUMBER TREE

Magnolia acuminata is a large, elegant, fast-growing deciduous tree widely distributed in North America from Lake Erie in Canada through western New York, Oklahoma, and Arkansas to Louisiana and northern Florida. Its introduction to the British Isles is well documented. Peter Collinson, a Quaker linen draper from Peckham in London, was a garden enthusiast to whom like-minded people in North America sent seeds and plants. Among these was John Bartram, a Quaker farmer, amateur physician, and self-taught botanist from Pennsylvania, who in July 1743 set out on a long journey from Pennsylvania to Lake Ontario. He kept a journal of this journey, three copies of which were sent to Collinson. Two of these copies were taken by French privateers and thus never reached Collinson. The third, which was published by Collinson in 1751 under the title *Observations . . . made on his travels from Pensilvania [sic] to the Lake Ontario*, documents the discovery of *M. acuminata*. Its seeds were included in a selection of 100 species of seeds (mainly trees) that Bartram sent in several boxes to Collinson, who then distributed them to his patrons, including the dukes of Richmond, Bedford, and Norfolk, and Lord Bute, who supplied the Dowager Princess of Wales with plants for Kew. Each box was initially priced at five guineas, which soon increased to ten. *Magnolia acuminata* duly flowered for Collinson at Mill Hill on 20 May 1762.

In cultivation *Magnolia acuminata* develops into a large tree of upright pyramidal outline that broadens with age. In the British Isles it grows to nearly 30 m (100 ft.), but it reaches its greatest height in the southern Appalachian Mountains of North America. The largest specimen on record is 38 m (125 ft.) tall with a spread of 18 m (60 ft.) and was found in the Great Smoky Mountains National Park in Tennessee. In the wild the plants show considerable variation in habit, from majestic straight-stemmed columnar trees to multistemmed large shrubs or small trees. As a consequence, they vary in growth rate from 30 cm (12 in.) to 75 cm (30 in.) a year. The bark is a light brown to grey and often exfoliates. Two geographic variants, subsp. *ozarkensis* and subsp. *ludoviciana*, named for their glabrous leaves or large flowers and tomentose leaves, have been sunk under the species name. Charles Sargent described subsp. *ludoviciana* from plants collected in West Feliciana, Louisiana, during 1914–15. The flowers were up to 10 cm (4 in.) long.

Magnolia acuminata has ovate green leaves up to 25 cm (10 in.) long and about half as wide. They are slightly downy on the underside, especially along the midrib. The plant gets its specific name from the shape of the leaves, which taper to a point at the apex in the form termed "acuminate." In autumn the foliage colour varies considerably, depending on the clone, from a dull dark brown to a bright butter yellow. The erectly held, slightly fragrant flowers are rather small and insignificant, 7.5–10 cm (3–4 in.), and are cup-shaped with 9–12 tepals. They occur on leafy shoots from late May to July (from early April in its habitat). In colour they are a mixture of glaucous green and yellow, but specific colour forms can be found varying from a blue through to a yellow.

A distinctly yellow-flowered form, *Magnolia acuminata* f. *aurea*, has been collected from the Carolinas, Tennessee, Georgia, and

Magnolia acuminata. The flower colour of this species varies from the yellow 'Fertile Myrtle', a selection used in breeding programmes by Phil Savage, to the glaucous green 'Philo', and blue specimens. Here the northern form displays a distinctive glaucous greenish blue during the early summer. Photo by John Tobe.

possibly Alabama. This yellow coloration of the flower was thought to be a potential gene source to raise a yellow-flowered hybrid on leafless stems. In 1977, the Brooklyn Botanic Garden patented 'Elizabeth', a hybrid between *M. acuminata* and *M. denudata*. For further information on *M.* 'Elizabeth', please refer to *M. acuminata* hybrids in chapter 7. *Magnolia acuminata* has also been hybridised with *M. liliiflora* to produce *M. ×brooklynensis* (see chapter 7).

The popular name, cucumber tree, refers to the shape and colour of the fruits when they are young. These turn from bright green to red in autumn and are 7.5 cm (3 in.) long, but are not produced in sufficient quantity or size to rank as an ornamental feature. The species is also known as Indian bitter, described originally by François Michaux because a fusion of whisky with half ripe seed cones produced an extremely bitter liquid that was taken as a "preservative against autumnal fevers."

Magnolia acuminata, probably the hardiest *Magnolia* species, is hardy to U.S. hardiness zone 4 in North America. The hardiest forms probably come from plants found in New York State. In North America the species is widely planted because of its ability to grow in a wide range of its soils, including alkaline ones, but it is not tolerant of drought. In its native environment it grows in deep, rich, moist soils with other deciduous trees such as *Acer saccharum* (sugar maple) and *Quercus alba* (white oak). The timber is light and durable, close-grained, and of a light yellow-brown colour. It was formerly used by the North American Indians to make canoes and wooden bowls and is now used for flooring and cabinet work.

Magnolia acuminata is often used as an understock onto which selected species or cultivars are grafted, particularly in the United States, where grafting magnolias is practised. In Scandinavia, where several magnolias are grown on their extreme limits of hardiness, *M. acuminata* is used as an understock as it is thought that it improves the scion's cold hardiness ability.

Several clones of *Magnolia acuminata* are cultivated for their habit, hardiness, leaf and flower colour and shape.

'Busey', a tree from Urbana, Illinois, has spreading branches and very good autumn leaf colour. It was selected by Professor Joe McDaniel.

'Fertile Myrtle', an exceptionally "fecund" seedling found in northern Ohio by Phil Savage of Bloomfield Hills, Michigan, is used extensively in breeding programmes. August Kehr of Hendersonville, North Carolina, has named colchicine-treated 'Fertile Myrtle' seedlings 'Laser' and 'Patriot' as more vigorous than the parent. 'Laser', with 16 sets of chromosomes, and 'Patriot' with 8 are being used for breeding programmes and not in their own right.

'Golden Glow', an upright-growing free-flowering tree, comes from the Great Smoky Mountains. It was selected by Frank Galyon of Knoxville, Tennessee.

'Klassen' is a fast-growing large-flowered form from Urbana, Illinois. It was selected by Professor Joe McDaniel.

'Koban Dori' (Golden Plate Bird) is a good yellow-flowered clone 5.0–7.5 cm (2–3 in.) in diameter with six tepals. It was introduced by Nakamura in Japan.

'Moegi Dori' (Yellow-Green Bird) is another yellow-flowered clone introduced by Nakamura in Japan. It is similar in size and shape to 'Koban Dori' but flowers later in mid-May.

'Philo' has blue-green flowers with good autumn colour. This tree produces a good seed harvest and was selected by Professor Joe McDaniel from farmland near Philo, Illinois.

'Seiju' (Blue Eternity) is a tree grown for its iridescent blue-green flowers, which on opening reveal bright yellow inner tepals.

Magnolia acuminata 'Koban Dori'. This yellow-flowered form was selected by Nakamura in Japan and widely circulated by Otto Eisenhut from his nursery in Ticino, Switzerland. The name means "golden plate bird." Photo by Dr. Helmut Orth.

Magnolia acuminata 'Moegi Dori'. Among several interesting, yellow-flowered forms selected by Nakamura in Japan, this clone flowers during early May. The name means "yellow-green bird." Photo by Dr. Helmut Orth.

Magnolia acuminata subsp. *subcordata*

Magnolia acuminata subsp. *subcordata* is very variable in habit, from a slow-growing large spreading shrub to a medium-sized tree of upright growth. An American subspecies, it has a restrictive distribution, in the southern states of Georgia, Alabama, the Carolinas, and Florida. It was discovered near Augusta, Georgia, by André Michaux (or perhaps his son François) between 1787 and 1796 and was sent to France in 1803. Two Scots, John Fraser and John Lyon, who were collecting at the same time and more or less the same area as Michaux, reportedly introduced the subspecies into the British Isles some two years earlier, in 1801. *Magnolia acuminata* subsp. *subcordata* was known only by these introductions until 1910, when Louis A. Berckmans stumbled on a group of shrubs between 1.2 m (4 ft.) and 1.8 m (6 ft.) tall in dry oak woodland some 29 km (18 mi.) south of Atlanta, Georgia.

Many plants in cultivation are slow growing, large spreading shrubs, but several trees between 12 m (40 ft.) and 15 m (50 ft.) tall can be found. The leaves are 15 cm (6 in.) long and up to 10 cm (4 in.) wide, generally elliptic in shape (rarely cordate as the name implies) and pubescent on the underside. The shoots are also pubescent for a short distance behind the main growth bud. Tulip-shaped flowers, up to 12 cm (5 in.) wide, are borne on leafy shoots during late May and June and sometimes into early July, but are never profusely produced in the British Isles. The colour varies from a pale to a canary yellow, often with reddish lines on the inner tepals. The fruits are reported to be smaller and a brighter red than those of *Magnolia acuminata*.

Magnolia acuminata subsp. *subcordata*. Although it was discovered at the end of the eighteenth century, not until 1910 was this subspecies rediscovered near Atlanta, Georgia. Plants in the British Isles vary in size to medium-sized trees, but are generally large shrubs, as is this specimen in the collection of Ambrose Congreve near Waterford, southern Ireland. Photo by Jim Gardiner.

Magnolia acuminata subsp. *subcordata* is, like *M. acuminata*, tolerant of alkaline soils. The soil must, however, be moisture retentive; only then can good growth be expected up to 38 cm (15 in.) per year. A warm sunny site is also required. In North America, this subspecies is hardy to U.S. hardiness zone 7.

Several clones are seen in cultivation. For information on the related hybrids, see *Magnolia acuminata* subsp. *subcordata* hybrids in chapter 7.

'Ellen' is grown primarily for its variegated foliage, but it also has yellow flowers. It was introduced into cultivation by Al Fordham of the Arnold Arboretum, Jamaica Plain, Massachusetts.

'Miss Honeybee' is frequently seen and has pale yellow flowers with lime-green running down the outer tepals. It develops into a large shrub or small tree and is reasonably hardy. Because it is a southern form, however, is prone to early autumn frosts. It was introduced in the early 1970s by J. Merrill Nursery of Painesville, Ohio.

'Mr. Yellowjacket' is a new clone with "brilliant canary-yellow to orange-yellow" flowers seen during June and again later in the year. It was selected by Dick Figlar from a small round-headed tree, 7.5 × 9.0 m (25 × 30 ft.), growing in Montvale, New Jersey.

'Skylands Best' flowers during May or early June and again in late summer. It is a compact, attractively shaped pyramidal tree selected by Dick Figlar.

Magnolia amoena
TIENMU MAGNOLIA
BEAUTIFUL MAGNOLIA

This small deciduous tree is native to the Tienmu Mountains in northwest Zhejiang Province, eastern China, and is found at altitudes of 700–1000 m (2300–3300 ft.) in broadleaf forest. Although it was described in 1933 it was a long time before it was introduced into cultivation by the Arnold Arboretum in 1986 from a small seed batch sent by the Shanghai Botanic Garden. It is found in a few collections primarily in the United States and Great Britain, so its ultimate height, spread, and performance can only be quoted from descriptions.

Magnolia amoena grows 8–12 m (26–40 ft.) tall. The green oblong leaves are 10–15 cm (4–6 in.) long and up to 5 cm (2 in.) wide; they are downy along the veins on the underside of the leaf. The precocious pale pink flowers are slightly fragrant and cup-shaped to 5 cm (2 in.) tall. Three of the nine tepals are erect and six are reflexed, with the stamens purplish red in colour. The fruits are 5 cm (2 in.) long and cylindrical in shape.

Charles Tubesing of the Holden Arboretum, Ohio, and a former president of the Magnolia Society, saw *Magnolia amoena* flowering for the first time during the spring of 1998. The scions had come from the Hangzhou Botanic Garden. Tubesing (personal communication) reported, "The small flowers were quite distinctive with six reflexed tepals surrounding three upright. They had a strong fragrance that was unlike any other magnolia I am familiar with and difficult to describe."

This species shares its geographic range with *Magnolia cylindrica*, *M. denudata*, and *M. officinalis*, so it is anticipated to be of a similar hardiness. Prior to its introduction, many considered it the pink form of *M. denudata*, which is also found in northwest Zhejiang.

Magnolia biondii

This rare medium-sized deciduous tree is native to central China through southern Gansu, western Henan, western Hubei, northern Hunan, Shaanxi, and eastern Sichuan at altitudes varying from 400 to 2400 m (1300–7900 ft.) in open woodland. Despite early initial herbarium collections by Augustine Henry between 1885 and 1888, and Ernest Wilson in 1907, who described a specimen from Hubei as "a shapely tree with many rather slender and spreading branches and a wealth of leaves," *Magnolia biondii* was not introduced to the West until 1977 when Yu Chen Ting found it in the Fu-Niew Mountains of Henan Province. The opportunity arose through the enthusiasm of August Kehr of the Louisiana State University, where Ting had been a student. Ting knew of E. H. Wilson's annoyance that *M. biondii* was the only Chinese magnolia that he failed to introduce into cultivation. A native of Henan Province, Ting brought seed to the United States, where it was equally divided between the Arnold Arboretum in Massachusetts and Professor Joe McDaniel in Illinois.

In cultivation *Magnolia biondii* is both a single-stemmed and multistemmed tree, ultimately to 12 m (40 ft.). It grows up to 45 cm (18 in.) per year. The leaves are oblong to elliptic, 10–18 cm (4–7 in.) long by 4–7 cm (1½–2½ in.) wide, dark green above and glabrous beneath once fully expanded. Flowers appear on leafless branches from mid-February and March, depending on site and season.

The nine tepals are white with a purple stripe running more or less the length, being broader at the base. They are about 5 cm (2 in.) long, slightly fragrant, and splay out to 10 cm (4 in.) wide. The fruit is cylindrical, slightly twisted to 12.5 cm (5 in.) long, and on ripening in September is bright red in colour.

In the wild *Magnolia biondii* is reported to withstand temperatures to –25°C (–13°F), while Kehr reports that partially opened flowers are unaffected by temperatures of –2°C (28°F). This species grows in various soils, but prefers a rich, moisture-retentive, mildly acid soil. Its timber is used for furniture manufacture and building, while the flower buds are used medicinally to ease pain such as headaches.

A magnolia garden was established within the Nanyue Arboretum, Hunan Province, by the Chinese forestry bureau in 1980, to ensure the continued existence of this rare species in China. During a 1998 field trip to Henan Province, Sun Weibang of the Kunming Botanical Garden looked at specimens of *Magnolia biondii*, the flower buds of which are used extensively in Chinese traditional medicine (xinyi). Many of the oldest trees are thought to be 200 years old and up to 20 m (66 ft) in height, with one tree 400 years old. Numerous plants in this population vary in tepal number (9–12), size, shape, and colour (from creamy white, creamy yellow with purple spotting at the base, to purple), especially in the three outer tepals.

Magnolia campbellii

This large deciduous tree is native to the Himalayas from eastern Nepal, Sikkim, and Bhutan to Assam, and is most common between 2400 m (8000 ft.) and 3000 m (10,000 ft.). It is an aristocrat among the *Magnolia* species. The English plant collector Frank Kingdon Ward, in *Plant Hunting on the Edge of the World* (1930), paints a vivid picture of this plant and its habitat in Sikkim:

> The road cleaves to the face of the cliff, winding round and round, ever ascending towards the distant snows, while the valley fades beneath us. At last the air grows colder, for it is only March, and we reach the zone of oaks and rhododendrons. Everything is padded in moss; long wisps of it swing from the branches of the trees. A thin mist floats ghostlike through the dripping forest. Suddenly round a corner we come on that

first magnolia in full bloom. It is just below us and we look right into the heart of the tree, spouting with blossom. The site overwhelms us. After that we see scores of trees, some with glowing pink, others with ivory-white flowers. From our giddy ledge we look down over the wide waves of the forest beating against the cliff, where the magnolia blooms toss like white horses, or lie like a fleet of pink water lilies riding at anchor in a green surf.

The "queen of magnolias" was named after Archibald Campbell, by Sir Joseph Hooker in 1855. Campbell was the political resident in Darjeeling, close to where Hooker had seen hillsides awash with pink. It was, however, William Griffith, who first found *Magnolia campbellii*—in fact the white form, in 1838. Before he could publish it, Hooker had described the pink form. Griffith was the assistant surgeon of the East India Company, based in Madras, and later became surgeon to the embassy in Bhutan. During his assignments he travelled extensively in the region. In 1924 the species was introduced into the United States from the London nursery firm of Stuart Low Company whose nurseries at Enfield and Jarvis Brook, Sussex were better known for their orchids. Plants were sent to San Francisco where they flowered for the first time in 1940.

In cultivation *Magnolia campbellii* is variable in habit. It is a single-stemmed plant when young, but quickly branches to become a tree of broad pyramidal outline. Some older trees have a sprawling habit, not tall but extremely wide—an advantage to the gardener, who is able to look down into the blooms. Many trees in the southwest of England in particular are broad, multistemmed trees. In cultivation, plants have reached 21 m (70 ft.) tall in southwest England; in the wild, plants more than 37 m (120 ft.) tall have been reported from Bhutan. Many fine mature specimens are often found in temple gardens; both Maurice Foster of Kent and Philippe de Spoelberch of Belgium saw specimens in Bhutan that were 21 m (70 ft.) tall with trunks approximately 1.8 m (6 ft.) in diameter. The growth rate in young trees is often quite vigorous and 90–120 cm (3–4 ft.) per year is not uncommon.

The green leaves are 20–25 cm (8–10 in.) long by 7.5–12.5 cm (3–5 in.) wide and elliptic in shape. The undersides are coated with fine flattened hairs, especially along the midrib and main veins. The young leaves start appearing just as the last flowers have fallen, and are generally bronze tinted. The flower buds are also distinctive for their hairiness and conical shape. Flowers appear on leafless branches from February to the end of March, depending on site and season. In New Zealand, where there are so many good specimens of *Magnolia campbellii* in both islands, flowering begins in late June in North Island and continues to mid-August in South Island. The flowers are slightly fragrant.

The 12–16 tepals are usually clear pink in colour, but they can vary from pure white, as in the case of *Magnolia campbellii* var. *alba*, to crimson. In the wild the white and pink forms vary in numbers depending on the location. Throughout Nepal and Bhutan, the white form is very much in evidence. Similarly, Frank Kingdon Ward reported very few pink forms above Gangtok, capital of Sikkim, which he said were "very rare and local," while the white form was much in evidence. The white "colour" is regarded as sacred while the pink is not, which possibly accounts for the white form being more common. Maurice Foster of Kent, when he visited Bhutan in 1990, saw only the white or cream-coloured form; however, "on closer examination some of the white flowers had an inconspicuous purple stain at the base of the sepal, with a thin line of purple extending part way up the centre of the sepal reverse." He described, in the journal of the Magnolia Society (1996), flowers of one magnolia having yellow buds opening "a touch yellower than Elizabeth." Visions of a yellow-flowered hybrid, similar in shape and size to *M. campbellii*, conjured pictures in his mind at the time! Until the 1970s, the white form was not common in cultivation, but the introduction of white-flowered forms collected by Roy Lancaster, Tony Schilling, and Geoffrey Herklots from Nepal has gone some way to redress the balance.

As the flowers of both colours expand, they become bowl-shaped, with the outer tepals often reflexing like saucers to 25 cm (10 in.) wide. The inner tepals remain upright, enclosing the stamens and stigmatic column. Cut specimens brought into the house often open out fully like giant water lilies, presumably because of the significant rise in temperature.

Seed-raised *Magnolia campbellii* from the wild takes up to 30 years before flowering begins. (If taken from gardens, they will be hybrids and flower in less than 10 years.) For this reason selected clones are grafted or chip-budded onto *M. campbellii* subsp. *mollicomata* as a rootstock. These generally flower in less than half the time, usually from 10 years.

Being among the earliest magnolias to flower, *Magnolia campbellii* is susceptible to frosting of the blooms, which bleaches out the colour. For this reason it is important to site the plant where it will suffer least from frost. A sheltered yet sunny site with adequate frost drainage is especially useful here. If a walled site is to be considered, the north wall should be chosen. The heat from the west wall will cause the buds to burst too early, making them more likely to become frosted. In North America, *M. campbellii* and its allies are hardy roughly to U.S. hardiness zone 7. The species is surprisingly wind tolerant, with many trees suffering only from minor branch breaks in the hurricane-force winds that swept southeast England during the great gale of October 1987 and subsequent storms in 1990, especially in the southwest of England.

Variability of flower colour of the pink form has led to several named clones, available from specialist nurseries.

'Ambrose Congreve' is a form with claret-red flowers. It was selected from a group of trees growing in Mount Congreve, Waterford, southern Ireland.

'Betty Jessel' comes from the same tree as 'Darjeeling', but seed was raised and grown in the garden of Sir George Jessel at Goudhurst in Kent. Like 'Darjeeling', this clone is among the last forms of *Magnolia campbellii* to come into flower during April, and sometimes as late as May, and is remarkable for its colour, which is close to crimson. It is also interesting for the deepest colouration to be on the upper surface and not the lower, as is normally the case. The flowers are 25 cm (10 in.) in diameter. Because of this clone's propensity to flower late, it is suited to "colder" gardens where it flowers more reliably.

'Darjeeling' is an exceptionally dark pink or wine-coloured form. It was propagated vegetatively from a tree growing in the Lloyd Botanic Garden, Darjeeling, India, and named by Hillier Nurseries of Winchester.

'Hendrick's Park' flowered for the first time in 1971 with deep rich pink flowers, that appeared 35 years after seed germinated. The clone was named for its colour and hardiness by Gossler Farms Nursery of Springfield, Oregon, from a plant growing in Hendrick's Park, Eugene, Oregon.

'Landicla' and the distinctly coloured 'Piet van Veen' are other British clones.

'Queen Caroline' has deep red-purple flowers. This clone was received as a scion from the Calcutta Botanic Garden in 1904 and planted by the Victoria Gate of the Royal Botanic Gardens, Kew. The flowers are 23 cm (9 in.) in diameter and rich red-purple on the outside and paler within.

For information on hybrids of *Magnolia campbellii,* please refer to *M. campbellii* hybrids, *M. ×veitchii,* Blumhardt hybrids, and Jury hybrids in chapter 7.

Magnolia campbellii 'Darjeeling' and *M. campbellii* (Raffillii Group) 'Sidbury'. *Magnolia campbellii* has generally finished flowering when its cross (the Raffillii Group) with its eastern sister comes into flower during late March or early April. The dark flowers of 'Darjeeling', a remarkable clone for its colour and lateness of flowering, can be seen (in the foreground) at the same time as the flowers of 'Sidbury' (in the background) in the garden of Sir Peter Smithers at Vico Morcote. Photo by Sir Peter Smithers.

Magnolia campbellii var. *alba*

Magnolia campbellii var. *alba* was introduced first into the British Isles in 1926 to Caerhays Castle in Cornwall, from Darjeeling. As well as extolling the virtues of *Magnolia campbellii*, Frank Kingdon Ward was equally descriptive when seeing *M. campbellii* var. *alba* for the first time in Sikkim: "Gaze down in wonder on the dark forest, lit by thousands of milk white glowing cups, hung like beacons on bare trees, and be silent."

The white form is quite distinct from its pink sister in many respects. For one thing, the white form tends to leaf out a lot later than the pink—quite often in mid-May. It blooms at an earlier age—12–15 years when raised from seed versus the up to 30 years with the pink form—but later by two weeks when compared with the pink. The leaves tend to be larger—up to 30 cm (12 in.) long by 15 cm (6 in.) wide—but also with silky indumentation on the underside, which is almost a glaucous green in colour. Last, the flower buds are larger, with the tepals more heavily textured than the pink. The cup-shaped flowers have 12 tepals and are 20–25 cm (8–10 in.) wide.

A few named clones of *Magnolia campbellii* var. *alba* have arisen in Caerhays and Chyverton, both in Cornwall. These bear the name of the garden in which they flowered.

'Ethel Hillier' has large white flowers and a soft pink centre. It was introduced by Hillier Nurseries.

'Nancy Hardy' is very similar to 'Ethel Hillier'. This large free-flowering tree has large white flowers flushed pink that appear from mid-April. The flowers, to 35 cm (13½ in.) wide, have 12 tepals that are each 15 cm (6 in.) long. This clone was first exhibited in 1984 from a plant growing at Sandling Park, Hythe, Kent, the home of Carolyn Hardy and her late husband Alan.

'Strybing White', the most distinct form of *Magnolia campbellii* var. *alba*, was named by Eric Walther, former director of the Strybing Arboretum in San Francisco. The outer tepals are completely drooping instead of being a flat like a saucer. Unlike plants of Cornish origin, this clone was raised from seed received from G. Ghose and Company of Darjeeling.

Previous pages: *Magnolia* 'Princess Margaret' with *M. campbellii* var. *alba*. Looking north towards Locarno, Switzerland, across Lake Maggiore is the superb setting to see magnolias in the garden of Piet van Veen at Vira Gambarogno, Switzerland. Photo by Dr. Helmut Orth.

Magnolia campbellii subsp. *mollicomata*

This large deciduous tree, the eastern form of *Magnolia campbellii*, comes from southeast Tibet (Xizang Zizhiqu), northern Myanmar (Burma), and western Yunnan. George Forrest, the Scottish plant collector, found it in 1904, growing at an altitude of 3000 m (10,000 ft.) as "a plant of the open forests, growing singly or in twos and threes together, and always on the western flanks of those ranges where the monsoon rainfall is the greatest." During the 1980 Sino-British expedition to the Cang Shan, western Yunnan, Roy Lancaster found scattered individuals, all but one of which had been felled, either for timber or to strip the bark for its medicinal properties. All those that had been felled were regenerating and the one seen standing was in flower at the beginning of May. Frank Kingdon Ward also found this subspecies growing in the Seinghku Valley in northern Myanmar, where he saw trees more than 30 m (100 ft.) tall.

Magnolia campbellii subsp. *mollicomata*. The eastern form of *M. campbellii* can be a paler pink when it flowers, yet is more floriferous than its western counterpart and flowers later. It readily sets seed, especially in southwestern England, and often forms important windbreak plants amongst the more traditional oak, beech, sycamore, and pine. Photo by John Gallagher.

In cultivation, *Magnolia campbellii* subsp. *mollicomata* grows in much the same way as its western sister, but its crown has a tendency to spread from an early age. The leaves are similar in outline to those of *M. campbellii* and have the same flattened hairs on the undersides. One of the main botanical distinctions between the two forms is the shape and size of the flower buds; those of subsp. *mollicomata* are larger, oblong in shape, and have hairy internodes on flowering stems, while those of the species are glabrous.

Horticulturally, subsp. *mollicomata* takes less than half the time of *Magnolia campbellii* to flower from seed, with 10–14 years on average. Its flower shape is sufficiently distinctive: subsp. *mollicomata* always has a beautiful cup-and-saucer shape, the outer tepals remaining horizontal and the inner tepals forming a bulbous dome. The size of its open flowers is comparable to flowers of *M. campbellii*. The flowers of subsp. *mollicomata* are rose or rose-purple in bud immediately prior to opening, revealing a bright pink "saucer." Reginald Farrer saw beautiful white-flowering forms in northern Myanmar (Burma), though no two trees were seen to have the same coloured flowers. Flowering time is April, significantly later than *M. campbellii*, and consequently missing many early frosts. Fruiting is not normally an attraction with *M. campbellii* but it is with subsp. *mollicomata*, which bears long, bright red fruits in early autumn. These are often collected and sown either for planting or to be used as a root-stock onto which other tree magnolias are grafted or budded.

Subspecies *mollicomata* has several distinct clones.

'Bernie Hollard' is a New Zealand clone that was named after the owner, who built up significant collections of woody plants in his garden to the south of Taranaki (Egmont) National Park on North Island. The flower is a rich pink in colour with a rose-lavender tone to the inner tepals.

'Maharajah', a seedling originally from W. B. Clarke Nursery of San Jose in 1954, was named by Todd Gresham of Santa Cruz, California, in 1964. It has a large 28 cm (11 in.) white cup-and-saucer-shaped flower with purple shading at the base of the tepals. Gresham said it had "no muddy magenta shading but a pure and very exciting colour, new to me in magnolias."

'Maharanee', like 'Maharajah', originated in 1954 at the W. B. Clarke Nursery of San Jose and was named by Todd Gresham of Santa Cruz, California, in 1964. The cup-and-saucer-shaped flower is slightly smaller that of 'Maharajah' at 20–25 cm (8–10 in.) and is pure white.

'Mary Williams' is a seedling from Caerhays Castle that first flowered in 1954. It has rose-purple flowers.

'Peter Borlase' is a chance seedling named after the person who raised it, the former head gardener of Lanhydrock in Cornwall. In 1967 it was planted within the western shelter belt with nine other open-pollinated seedlings. The flower is a deep reddish rose-pink in colour with a pale bar through the centre of the tepal. It is slightly smaller in size at 15–20 cm (6–8 in.) in diameter.

'Lanarth' is distinctive enough to warrant separate botanical ranking within the *M. campbellii* complex. It was collected by George Forrest in 1924 from northwest Yunnan Province, China, on the Salween–Kiu Chiang Divide in open thickets at an altitude of between 3000 m (10,000 ft.) and 3350 m (11,000 ft.). Only three seedlings were raised; these were named after the English gardens where they were planted—Lanarth and Wer-

rington in Cornwall and Borde Hill in Sussex. Both Cornish gardens were owned at the time by the Williams family (Mr. M. P. Williams at Lanarth and Commander A. M. Williams at Werrington), who affectionately knew the plant as "the magnolia with the telephone number"—a reference to the George Forrest collection number, 25655, which had five numbers like British phone numbers at the time.

'Lanarth' can be distinguished from other members of the species in several ways, of which only a half dozen of the most easily recognisable are mentioned here. The original 'Lanarth' exhibits vigorous growth with a fastigiate habit. The leaves of 'Lanarth' and subsp. *mollicomata* are similar in length, but those of 'Lanarth' are very much broader, oblong-obovate in shape, and thicker in texture, giving them a wrinkled appearance; they measure 23–25 cm (9–10 in.) long by 15 cm (6 in.) wide. The flower buds of 'Lanarth'

Magnolia 'Albatross' (left) and *M. campbellii* subsp. *mollicomata* 'Peter Borlase'. Peter Borlase, the former head gardener at Lanhydrock, displays (1992) two magnolia aristocrats from that Cornish garden while attending a study day at Trewithen. *Magnolia campbellii* subsp. *mollicomata* 'Peter Borlase' is distinctively bicoloured. Photo by Jim Gardiner.

Magnolia campbellii subsp. *mollicomata* 'Lanarth'. The flower colour, among the most sensational flower colours, was likened by G. H. Johnstone in *Asiatic Magnolias in Cultivation* (1955) to that of "a vintage port." This clone was introduced by George Forrest from northwest Yunnan Province, China, in 1924. Of the three seedlings raised, two were grown on—one in Lanarth and the other in Werrington, both famous Cornish gardens. Plants of both were propagated by Hillier Nurseries and flowered at the Hillier arboretum in Hampshire for the first time in 1975. Photo by John Hillier.

Magnolia campbellii subsp. *mollicomata* 'Borde Hill'. When George Forrest introduced seed of this plant, three seedlings were germinated and were grown by eminent British gardeners M. P. Williams and A. M. Williams of Lanarth and Werrington in Cornwall and Colonel Stephenson Clarke at Borde Hill in Sussex. The original tree at Borde Hill died before it flowered; however, G. H. Johnstone successfully propagated this plant and in turn distributed propagation material to Hillier Nurseries. Photo by John Hillier.

are much larger and flatter, and although the cup-and-saucer shape of the flower is typical of *M. campbellii* subsp. *mollicomata*, the colour or 'Lanarth' flowers, an incredible lilac-purple-red, is most distinctive. 'Lanarth' flowers at the same time as *M. campbellii*, while subsp. *mollicomata* flowers later. Last, budded propagules of 'Lanarth' show a markedly different growth response compared with *M. campbellii* and *M. campbellii* subsp. *mollicomata*: they are reluctant to grow. Seedlings, however, exhibit a vigour similar to that of the parent tree and come remarkably true.

'Werrington' flowered for the first time either in 1941 or 1943. When 'Lanarth' flowered for the first time in 1947 (on 7 April), 'Werrington' flowered a fortnight later. The flower colour is remarkable—a dark lilac-purple or magenta spread evenly over the tepals—and is generally seen during March in the south of England, or earlier, especially when planted against a wall, where, with this added protection, flowering can be seen as early as February. The flower is 23–25 cm (9–10 in.) in diameter and has 12–14 tepals.

Hillier Nurseries grafted 'Lanarth' and 'Werrington' and planted them against the wall of Jermyns House in Hampshire. This propagule of 'Lanarth' flowered for the first time in 1975.

'Lanarth' has been crossed with *M. liliiflora* (see Jury hybrids in chapter 7). *Magnolia campbellii* subsp. *mollicomata* has been crossed with *M. campbellii* and other species and hybrids. For further information on these, please refer to *M. campbellii* hybrids in chapter 7.

Magnolia campbellii Raffillii Group

Charles Percival Raffill of the Royal Botanic Gardens, Kew, in 1946, and Sir Charles Cave of Sidbury Manor, Devon, during the 1920s, working independently, both crossed the eastern with the western form of *Magnolia campbellii*. The resulting cross produced flowers that combined the bright pink colour of *M. campbellii* with the graceful cup-and-saucer shape of *M. campbellii* subsp. *mollicomata* and that appear slightly later in the season (similar to subsp. *mollicomata*). The 12 tepals, arranged like those of subsp. *mollicomata* are a rose-pink in colour, fading to white on the upper surfaces.

All members of the Raffillii Group are vigorous, growing 60 cm (2 ft.) or more each year and ultimately growing into medium-sized to large trees depending on their planting situation. They are similar in hardiness rating, but perform better than *Magnolia campbellii* when planted in the drier conditions found outside the southwest of England

Seedlings of *Magnolia campbellii* × *M. campbellii* subsp. *mollicomata* that were raised at Sidbury Manor, the home of the late Sir Charles Cave, started to flower in the late 1930s, thus predating the work of Raffill at Kew. 'Sidbury' is the only named seedling of this group and has strong pink flowers similar to Raffill's crosses. Raffill raised about 100 seedlings, which were widely distributed to gardens primarily in the south and west of England.

The first of Raffill's seedlings to gain recognition was one sent to the gardens of Windsor Great Park, where it flowered 13 years after the seedling stage. It was subsequently named 'Charles Raffill' after the originator of the cross and went

Magnolia campbellii Raffillii Group. Charles Raffill, assistant curator at the Royal Botanic Gardens, Kew, crossed the eastern and western forms of *M. campbellii* in 1946. Seedlings were then distributed to many gardens, including the Royal Horticultural Society's Garden at Wisley, as shown here. Photo by Jim Gardiner.

on to receive a Preliminary Commendation in 1961, an Award of Merit in 1963 after one of the coldest and longest winters on record during the twentieth century, and a First Class Certificate in 1966. The flowers are 23 cm (9 in.) in diameter, have 12 tepals, and are pink-purple on the outside with white flushed pink on the inside.

Other seedlings in this group include 'Kew's Surprise', which flowered for the first time at Caerhays Castle considerably later than *Magnolia campbellii* (Raffillii Group) 'Charles Raffill' because it was planted close to beech trees and grew less vigorously. It was exhibited on 4 March 1967 and received

Magnolia campbellii (Raffillii Group) 'Charles Raffill'. Photo by Jim Gardiner.

Magnolia campbellii (Raffillii Group) 'Charles Raffillii'. The first seedling of Raffill's cross (*M. campbellii* × *M. campbellii* subsp. *mollicomata*) flowered at Windsor Great Park in 1961 and was named after the originator of the cross. Photo by Jim Gardiner.

a First Class Certificate on its first showing. It displays most sensationally the cup-and-saucer effect. 'Wakehurst' is another named seedling growing at Wakehurst Place in southeast England. Raffillii Group hybrids are in many ways preferred to *Magnolia campbellii* because they are more reliable in flower when grown in colder gardens.

Magnolia enthusiasts in North America have continued this hybridisation programme. *Magnolia campbellii* 'Eric Walther' is reported to be of this parentage and has rose-pink flowers. It was named after the first director of the Strybing Arboretum in San Francisco where it is planted. It was obtained in 1965 from the San Francisco nursery firm of V. Reiter Jr.

Magnolia campbellii (Raffillii Group) 'Kew's Surprise'. This clone exhibits seedling variation in flower colour from pale to warm pink and bicoloured. Photo by John Gallagher.

Magnolia cylindrica

Magnolia cylindrica comes from Anhui, northern Jiangxi, northern Fujian, and western Zhejiang Provinces in eastern China. It was discovered by Ren-chang Ching on the Wa Shan at an elevation of 1280 m (4200 ft.) in 1925 and was named by E. H. Wilson in 1927. It did not reach Western gardens until 1936, when the late Mrs. J. Norman Henry of Gladwyne, Pennsylvania, received seed from the Lu Shan Botanic Garden in Jiangxi Province, China. Seeds sent to gardens in the British Isles at the same time failed to germinate. Mrs. Henry's seed, however, germinated and eventually became a tall upright-growing tree to 15 m (50 ft.). Scions from it were distributed to the University of Washington Arboretum in Seattle and to the late Sir Harold Hillier in about 1950. Hillier also received scions in 1951–52 from F. M. Kluis Nursery of Pompton Lakes, New Jersey (late of Boskoop).

Two or three distinct forms of this species are in cultivation. The one more generally seen in the United Kingdom is a slow-growing tree of a spreading and arching habit often as broad as it is tall. The specimen in the Hillier Gardens and Arboretum is 9 m (30 ft.) tall and wide after 35 years (1997). This is the so-called Hillier cylindrica and most commonly seen in British gardens. To distinguish it from other forms, the cultivar name of 'Pegasus' has been given it by Roy Lancaster. The leaves vary in size to a maximum of 15 cm (6 in.) long by 7.5 cm (3 in.) wide. They are dark green above and smell of aniseed when crushed. The candle-like flowers are 10 cm (4 in.) long and pure white with delicate rays of pale pink at the base of the six tepals. They open in April and show a remarkable tolerance to frost. A specimen at Chyverton in Cornwall is reported to have suffered no damage when exposed to ground frost at −12°C (10°F), although it had already broken bud. The plants

Magnolia 'Pegasus'. At one time this plant was named *M. cylindrica,* referring to the bright red cylindrical fruiting cones, which are seen during October. Photo by Jim Gardiner.

themselves also come through severe weather virtually unscathed. During late September and early October, the 10 cm (4 in.) long, bright red cylindrical fruiting cones that give the plant its specific name are an attractive feature.

The clone grown in America, again from the Lu Shan introduction via nurseryman Gus Krossa who received seed at the same time as Mrs. Henry, is very upright and treelike in appearance and more than 15 m (50 ft.) tall. The flowers are smaller and candlelike to 7.5 cm (3 in.) long with the pink markings not so clearly discernible.

The status of the Lu Shan introduction (that is, 'Pegasus'), the Mrs. Henry, and the Krossa introductions as species or hybrids has been questioned. Once magnolias are planted in gardens, invariably they have the opportunity to hybridise, whereas in the wild generally they would not. Professor Joe McDaniel

Magnolia 'Pegasus'. The name of Hillier Nurseries is known throughout the horticultural world as the most famous supplier of woody plants to gardens both large and small. *Magnolia cylindrica* was obtained by the late Sir Harold Hillier from Mrs. J. Norman Henry of Pennsylvania, and became one of the "star" attractions of the Hillier Gardens and Arboretum, where after 35 years (1990) a wide-spreading small tree some 9 m (30 ft.) tall and wide can be found. This cultivar is quite distinct from the recently introduced Chinese form of *M. cylindrica* and so has been renamed by Roy Lancaster in 1998. Photo by Jim Gardiner.

has suggested that the plants originating from the Lu Shan Botanic Garden were in fact hybrids with *Magnolia denudata*, as almost certainly it had been planted close by in this garden situation.

In the early 1980s, Shanghai Botanic Garden distributed seed of *Magnolia cylindrica* collected in the mountains of Chang-Hua in western Zhejiang at an altitude of 900 m (2953 ft.). One of those who received seed was plantsman Roy Lancaster of Chandlers Ford in Hampshire. A single seedling germinated and was planted in his garden in 1984. Like the North American clone, it grew quickly with a strong central leader, developing into a small, potentially medium-sized upright-growing tree. The flowers are smaller than those of the Hillier cultivar and "lacking the grace, charm, and substance of the other." The young wood of the Shanghai clone is a grey-green as opposed to brown in 'Pegasus' and leafs out very late, often into May. Further introductions during the late 1980s from Anhui Province have been made by the Chinese Academy of Forestry.

'Bjuv', a clone of *Magnolia cylindrica,* flowered for the first time in the garden of Karl Flinck in Bjuv, Sweden. Flinck obtained it as seed of *M. cylindrica* collected in China for the Arnold Arboretum. The flower has six tepals distinctly stained along the outside with red-purple, dense at the base but extending to the tip. This clone was registered by Philippe de Spoelberch in 1995.

All clones of *Magnolia cylindrica* as well as *M.* 'Pegasus' grow well in a rich, moisture-retentive acid soil in light dappled shade. They are quite hardy, to U.S. hardiness zone 5, though there are instances of this species surviving –30°C (–22°F) in eastern North America (U.S. hardiness zone 4). For information on hybrids of *M. cylindrica,* see chapter 7.

Magnolia dawsoniana

Magnolia dawsoniana, named in honour of Jackson T. Dawson, superintendent of the Arnold Arboretum, was first found by Père Jean Pierre Armand David in Boazing (now the small independent state of Mupin), western Sichuan in 1869. It was not introduced to the West until 1908, when E. H. Wilson discovered the species between 1900 m (6500 ft.) and 2100 m (7000 ft.) in western Sichuan near Kangding (Tatsien-lu) and sent the fruit to the Arnold Arboretum in Jamaica Plain, Massachusetts. Seedlings were raised along with Wilson's other Chinese species, but the young plants were too tender for the Boston area's harsh winter, with many plants dying back. In 1913 Professor Charles Sargent, director of the Arnold Arboretum, took the bold step of sending this species along with Wilson's other magnolia introductions to Léon Chenault, who ran the famous nursery at Orleans, France. Chenault successfully grafted Wilson's collection and distributed plants to Kew and later to several other gardens in the British Isles. One of these was Rowallane in Northern Ireland, where *M. dawsoniana* flowered for the first time in Britain in about 1932.

Magnolia dawsoniana grows into a small to medium-sized tree of a broad pyramidal outline, with a "twiggy" network of branches and distinctive fissured bark. Rates of growth vary, averaging from 30 cm (1 ft.) to 60 cm (2 ft.) per year. The shiny, dark green, leathery leaves are roughly oval in outline, up to 15 cm (6

Magnolia dawsoniana. The tepals of this magnolia, among the most distinctive Asiatic species in flower, soon droop after opening and hang limply, rather like prayer flags. The species was named after Jackson T. Dawson, superintendent of the Arnold Arboretum, Massachusetts. Photo by John Gallagher.

in.) long by 5.0–7.5 cm (2–3 in.) wide, and have distinctive net-veining on the upper and lower surfaces. Very numerous, white, suffused with a rich rosy red, faintly fragrant flowers are produced on leafless stems towards the end of March, in April, and often into early May. The nine horizontally held tepals up to 12.5 cm (5 in.) long are more attractive prior to opening as they hang limply when they are fully open.

Several clones of *Magnolia dawsoniana* are available.

'Chyverton Red', a more spectacular colour form, is named after the famous

Magnolia dawsoniana 'Valley Splendour'. This clone is one of the first tree magnolias to flower and one of the largest trees in the collection at the Savill and Valley Gardens of Windsor Great Park, which has one of the finest collections of magnolias in the British Isles. Initially started by Sir Eric Savill, the gardens continued to be planted at a prodigious pace under the guidance of John Bond, keeper of the gardens until 1997. Photo by Jim Gardiner.

Cornish garden where it flowered for the first time in 1968, some 23 years after raising. On first opening, the flowers are bright crimson; the colour seems to become more pronounced during cold weather. The blooms are remarkably frost tolerant and last for about six weeks. During 1969 Chyverton experienced an air frost to –5°C (23°F) during the end of March without any flowers being affected. Some authorities consider 'Chyverton Red' not to be a true form of the species but a hybrid with *Magnolia sprengeri* var. *sprengeri* 'Diva'.

'Clarke' has pink flowers deepening towards the base of the 10 cm (4 in.) long tepals. Introduced by W. B. Clarke Nursery, San Jose, California, this clone is highly regarded in western North America because of its freedom of flowering, which is seen year after year, and for its hardiness.

'Lanarth' is an Award of Merit clone exhibited on 21 March 1939 by M. P. Williams of Lanarth, Cornwall. The 10 cm (4 in.) tepals are rose blush pink with fuchsia purple seen towards the base of the outside of the flower. This 'Lanarth' is not to be confused with *M. campbellii* subsp. *mollicomata* 'Lanarth'.

'Valley Splendour' has masses of deep pink flowers. It grows in the Valley Gardens, Windsor Great Park, and flowers during the second half of March.

Today most plants of *Magnolia dawsoniana* are either grafted or budded, thus considerably reducing the time for flowering to start. The average is 10 years from propagation. Like most magnolias, this species needs a moisture-retentive soil to flourish. It prefers a soil on the acid side of neutral, but is surprisingly tolerant of alkaline sites. Plenty of space in full sun is also needed for this plant to develop its full potential. In North America it is hardy to U.S. hardiness zone 7, although 'Chyverton Red' is thought to be hardier than the species.

Magnolia delavayi

This imposing evergreen tree was discovered northwest of Dali in Yunnan Province, China, by the French missionary and plant collector Père Jean Delavay in 1886. Thirteen years later Ernest Wilson introduced it into cultivation. Wilson collected seed during the autumn of 1899 from southern Yunnan, where plants were growing in sandstone and limestone formations among *Lithocarpus* (tanbark oak) scrub and *Pinus armandii* (Chinese white pine).

In cultivation *Magnolia delavayi* grows into a broad-spreading, multi-stemmed large shrub in the south and southeast of England, or in southern

France and northern Italy into a small to medium tree that can reach 12 m (40 ft.) in spread. It rarely has a stem, branching more or less from ground level. The elegant, ovate, matt green leaves are up to 36 cm (15 in.) long and 20 cm (8 in.) wide and are among the largest leaves of temperate evergreen trees. The leaves are held fairly rigidly on the tree, so it is difficult for the viewer to appreciate fully the glaucous underside, which contrasts well with the upper surface. As the leaves of some clones unfurl, they are a distinctive dull deep mahogany green in colour that persists for a week or two prior to opening.

The flowers are a disappointment, lasting for about two to three days. They open during the early evening, and are cup-shaped with the inner tepals still in the upright position. They are ivory-white in colour, fragrant (most noticeably so at night), and when fully open are 18 cm (7 in.) wide. These reflex for a short time over two nights. The flowers are seen sporadically from July to September in the British Isles, but May and June in China. During the mid-1990s, Sun Weibang of the Kunming Botanical Garden, Yunnan Province, introduced a red-flowered form from the Hua-Fu Mountains, Mon-Din County, where it grows in mixed woodland of *Magnolia delavayi* and *Manglietia insignis*. Raised from seed, *M. delavayi* flowers after 10 years when about 3.7 m (12 ft.) tall. It does not normally fruit in the British Isles but in California large red fruiting cones are sparsely produced.

Magnolia delavayi is surprisingly frost tolerant considering that it comes from an altitude of 1100–2200 m (3600–7200 ft.) in China; it shows no adverse effects to −14°C (7°F) in the British Isles (U.S. hardiness zones 7–8). It may be grown in various situations—used as a wall shrub or as a free-standing tree in an open woodland setting, where it is seen to advantage. Magnificent specimens can be seen in the south of France and northern Italy (Villa Taranto). During prolonged periods of severe winter weather, tip dieback or even defoliation can occur, but in most in-

Magnolia delavayi red form. During the mid-1990s, Sun Weibang of the Kunming Botanical Garden introduced this red-flowered form into cultivation. It was found growing in the Hua-Fu mountains in mixed woodland, with *M. delavayi* and *Manglietia insignis*. Photo by Sun Weibang.

stances regeneration occurs. Plants growing at Windsor that were exposed to marginally lower temperatures than −14°C (7°F) were completely defoliated and did not really recover.

A remarkably wide range of soils suits this species, from a thin chalk to a rich, acid, moisture-retentive loam (where it is most at home).

Magnolia denudata

YULAN
LILY TREE

Magnolia denudata is native to the central Chinese provinces of Anhui, Zhejiang, Jiangxi, and Hunan, where it grows in moist woodland. Buddhist monks have been cultivating this species for centuries and planted it extensively in their temple gardens. The earliest records indicating the significance of this plant to the Buddhists goes back to the T'ang dynasty (A.D. 618–907), when the flower was regarded as a symbol of openness and purity. At this time, the Buddhist monks were taking their religious opinions to Japan, and almost certainly took the yulan with them.

The monks must also have distributed this species around China as well. George Forrest saw *Magnolia denudata* on the Yunnan-Burmese border between the Salween and Mekong Rivers in the ancient city of Yungchang:

> In Yunnan, quite a few species of Magnolia are cultivated and are seen most often as ornamental plants in the grounds surrounding many of the larger temples and guild houses. All are decorative, and one of the most charming effects I can remember is of an avenue of exceedingly well grown

Magnolia denudata. Buddhist monks have cultivated this species for well over 1000 years. It can be traced back as far as the T'ang dynasty, when the flower was regarded as a symbol of openness and purity. Photo by Jim Gardiner.

trees of *M. conspicua* in full bloom in the grounds of one of the large
guild houses in the city of Yungchang-fu. In late January or February....
I have seen plants smothered in bloom. Flowers appear much before
the foliage, and are 15.0–17.5 cm (6–7 in.) in diameter, fragrant, and of
a clear ivory white.

In several Chinese cities today *Magnolia denudata* has been planted as a
street tree and in temple gardens. Mike Robinson of East Sussex visited China
in 1997 and saw *M. denudata* seedlings ranging in flower colour from ivory to
yellow to clear pink. The clear pinks were seen in Shanghai Botanic Garden
and Xian and both looked like *M. denudata* 'Forrest's Pink'. The yellow was also
seen in Xian at the entrance to the Big Goose Pagoda and was the same colour
as 'Elizabeth' as it bursts into flower. Sun Weibang of Kunming Botanical Garden, Yunnan Province, has grown a *M. denudata* with a beautiful clear yellow
flower.

Sir Joseph Banks introduced the species to the British Isles in 1780, almost
certainly from a cultivated source, but it remained uncommon in cultivation for
many years. One famous early specimen was grown by Sir Abraham Hume at
Wormleybury in Hertfordshire; in 1826 it measured 6 m (20 ft.) tall and carried
more than 900 blooms. At Goldsworth Nursery in Woking, Surrey, a specimen
known to have been planted in 1815 was 10.5 m (35 ft.) tall and wide after about
130 years.

In cultivation *Magnolia denudata* is often seen as a multistemmed shrub or
broad-spreading, small tree; it often takes more than a hundred years to grow to
9 m (30 ft.) tall and wide. The green obovate (sometimes elliptic-obovate) leaves
are up to 15 cm (6 in.) long and 7.5 cm (3 in.) wide and have a fine coating of
hairs on the underside. The species flowers young—plants of only three or four
years old flower prolifically. It is also early flowering—from February to April,
depending on the climate and the geographic location. The lemon-scented
blooms consist of nine tepals forming erect chalices, 7.5–10.0 cm (3–4 in.) long,
of pure white flowers that light up the garden at sunrise and sunset. The first
flush of flower is particularly effective during a frost-free period, as the blooms
are often spoiled by frost, which results in browning of the tepal margins. This
particular trait apart, the plant can tolerate exceptionally harsh conditions; in
North America it is hardy to U.S. hardiness zone 5. As well as white, western

forms of *M. denudata* can also be pink or pink flushed. The brown fruiting cones, 12.5 cm (5 in.) long, open to reveal bright red seeds.

Magnolia denudata prefers a rich, moisture-retentive soil on the acid side of neutral. Like several other Chinese species, it tolerates alkaline conditions provided the soil does not dry out during the summer months. It should be given a sunny site or one in a light dappled shade.

The tepals of *Magnolia denudata* are considered to be a delicacy. Dipped in flour and fried in oil until they are crisp, they have a slightly sweet taste. The bark is used medicinally as a treatment for the common cold.

Debate has raged in the botanical world over the naming of this species; many authorities have considered that it should correctly be called *Magnolia heptapeta*. *Magnolia denudata* (1791), although it had an unsatisfactory description, was adopted by Rehder and Wilson in 1913 and is regarded as the accepted name. *Magnolia conspicua*, long time regarded as the "proper" name, and *M. heptapeta*, recently thought of as such, have also been dismissed as "inadequate and false." In 1987, Frederick Meyer of the U.S. National Arboretum and Elizabeth McClintock of the University of California proved *M. denudata* of Desrousseaux (1791) to be the earliest applicable name for the species.

With its variation in flower colour and size, the species inevitably has several named clones. Phil Savage of Bloomfield Hills, Michigan, has a hypothesis that if *Magnolia denudata* is raised from seed, seedlings that flower between 6 and 10 years are almost certainly hybrids with *M. ×soulangeana* or *M. liliiflora*, whereas if they flower between 10 and 16 years then they will be pure bred. Inevitably, unless there has been a deliberate cross, uncertainty will exist over whether it is the species or a hybrid. Where there is uncertainty, the plants will be regarded as "clones."

Magnolia denudata is one of the parents of the all-important *M. ×soulangeana* (see chapter 7) and *M. ×veitchii* (see chapter 7), and more recently, of 'Elizabeth' and other yellow-flowered hybrids (see under *M. acuminata* hybrids in chapter 7). For information on other hybrids, please refer to *M. denudata* hybrids in chapter 7.

The following clones are the most commonly seen.

'Forrest's Pink' is a beautiful clean pink in colour with 9–11 tepals that are flushed with deeper pink at the base of the flower. In habit it is a single-stemmed or multistemmed, small upright-growing tree. This seedling was raised in the 1920s at Caerhays in Cornwall and thought to have originated from one of George Forrest's seed collections. It appears that this clone's performance is reliant on temperature. When grown in the southeast of England the colour is generally disappointing. When grown in Cornwall or by Sir Peter Smithers at Vico Morcote, Switzerland, where spring temperatures are generally warmer, then it performs far better. Sir Peter has been consistently impressed with this clone over the past 20 years as being a "clearer, truer pink" than the best of the *M. ×soulangeana* cultivars, having none of the purplish tints they possess.

'Gere' is a beautiful ivory-white clone found by Professor Joe McDaniel in an Urbana, Illinois, cemetery. It flowers at the same time as the last of the *M. ×soulangeana* cultivars and is very similar to Wada's Japanese clone. McDaniel named it after "the name on the nearest tombstone!"

'Purple Eye' is a large white-flowered cup-shaped clone with a purple flush both on the inside and the outside of the base of the nine tepals. It originated in a batch of seedlings grown by J. C. Williams of Caerhays Castle and sent to Peter Veitch, whose firm, Robert Veitch and Sons of Exeter, named and distributed it. The flowers are larger but less floriferous than the normal white clone, and are seen a few days later. This clone is also more vigorous.

On opening, 'Sawada's Cream' has bright butter-yellow tepals that fade to a creamy white, while 'Sawada's Pink' has pink in the opening flowers. Both are used by Phil Savage of Bloomfield Hills, Michigan, in his breeding programmes and were obtained from Ken Sawada of Overlook Nursery, Semmes, Alabama. Sawada raised 'Sawada's Pink' from Japanese seed, which he had listed as *Magnolia denudata* var. *purpurascens*. Both clones set seed readily.

Magnolia denudata 'Purple Eye'. A particularly large flowered form, 'Purple Eye' exhibits a purple flush at the base of the nine tepals. Photo by John Hillier.

Magnolia fraseri

EAR-LEAVED MAGNOLIA
MOUNTAIN MAGNOLIA
FRASER'S MAGNOLIA
FISHTAIL MAGNOLIA

This small to medium-sized tree is native to the rich woods of the southern Appalachian region of eastern North America and is found in the states of Georgia, Alabama, Louisiana, West Virginia, Texas, South Carolina, and northwest Florida. It is named after John Fraser, a Scot from Inverness-shire who went to London in 1770. Fraser made several collecting trips to North America in the 1780s and brought back the species to England in either 1784 or 1786. André Michaux introduced it to France in 1789. It was William Bartram, son of John, who had first discovered the species, in South Carolina in 1776.

Magnolia fraseri is a fast-growing medium-sized tree that reaches a height of 18 m (60 ft.), but has been known to be taller. It often has multiple stems. It is found in the stream valleys and creeks to an altitude of 1350 m (4400 ft.) and is often seen among the taller specimens of *Acer rubrum* (red maple) and *Quercus alba* (white oak). The narrowly obovate-oblong, sea-green leaves up to 30 cm (1 ft.) long and 12.5 cm (5 in.) wide are most distinctive, with auriculate lobes at the base that give rise to the tree's common name of fishtail magnolia. The leaves are characteristically crowded towards the end of the branches, giving a "whorled" appearance. In autumn they turn a reddish brown colour.

This species is the first American species to flower, on leafy shoots during late May and June, but up to one month earlier in the

Magnolia fraseri. The fishtail magnolia, so-called because of the lobed base to the leaves, was introduced into the British Isles towards the end of the eighteenth century by John Fraser, after whom the species was named. It is the first American magnolia to flower, during late April or early May in the wild. Later in the season it has good autumn foliage colour. Photo by Jim Gardiner.

wild. The milky white to pale yellow flowers have eight tepals up to 10 cm (4 in.) long which splay out to about 20 cm (8 in.) wide. As they open, the flowers have a distinctive sweet scent. The fruiting cones are a decorative rosy red in colour and 12.5 cm (5 in.) long. Because seed germinates readily, this species is often used as an understock for grafting or budding. Even during the winter months the one-year-old shoots are quite decorative, their brown colour contrasting with the dark purple of the winter bud. Between 30 cm (1 ft.) and 60 cm (2 ft.) of growth is put on annually, with trees growing to approximately 9 m (30 ft.) in 20 years.

Magnolia fraseri is perfectly hardy, growing well in full sun in the British Isles, although it tolerates shady conditions, especially in its native environment. A rich, moisture-retentive, acidic soil suits it, although it is known to grow in deep, moisture-retentive, alkaline soils in North America. It is quite hardy; in North America it is hardy to U.S. hardiness zone 5.

Magnolia fraseri var. *pyramidata*

Magnolia fraseri var. *pyramidata* is one of America's rarest magnolias and is seldom seen in cultivation outside its native environment. It was introduced into the British Isles by John Lyon of Gillogie, Forfarshire (now Angus), Scotland, in 1811. It was amongst a consignment of plants collected in the Carolinas, Georgia, and Florida, brought over in cases in good condition and disposed of by public auction at Chelsea. It is found in southwestern Georgia, the panhandle of Florida, southern Alabama, and southeastern Mississippi. Smaller than *M. fraseri*, it is a tree to 11 m (36 ft.) tall. Like *M. fraseri* its leaves are clustered towards the end of the branches, but in keeping with its height it also has smaller leaves, 23 cm (9 in.) long and about 10.0–12.5 cm (4–5 in.) at their widest. The

Magnolia fraseri var. *pyramidata*. One of America's rarest magnolias, this variety differs from the species in its stature, which is smaller, and, most noticeably, in the shape of its leaves, which are kite-shaped. Photo by John Tobe.

creamy white flowers too are smaller, 12.5 cm (5 in.) wide, and are seen in April and May in its native habitat. Bright red pyramidal fruiting cones are seen in July and August.

Magnolia globosa

This species is found as a large shrub or small tree, at altitudes between 2400 m (8000 ft.) and 3400 m (11,000 ft.), over a wide geographic range, from eastern Nepal in the west to northwest Yunnan, China, in the east. Distinctive botanical differences exist between the eastern and western forms, which in cultivation are known as the Indian form and the Chinese form.

The Chinese form was introduced into cultivation in July 1919 by George Forrest, who found it in the Tsarong region of southeast Tibet (Xizang Zizhiqu). Plants seen by Forrest were shrubs or small trees up to 6 m (20 ft.) tall, with young shoots densely clothed with rust-coloured down. The species was originally described as *Magnolia sarongensis*. The Indian form was introduced from Sikkim by J. Cromar Watt of Aberdeen in 1930; it flowered in 1937. Watt first saw it at Tonglu at 3000 m (10,000 ft.), "the magnificent white oval buds standing erect on leafless branches, and the stem silhouetted against a background of Kangchenjunga's snows." Given mild protected sites in cultivation it becomes treelike in habit, growing to 7.5 m (25 ft.), with young shoots green and glabrous. The foliage is oval, up to 25 cm (10 in.) long by half as wide, silvery grey between the veins on the Chinese form and golden on the Indian. The Chinese form starts into growth considerably earlier than the Indian.

In cultivation, the creamy white flowers, about 7.5 cm (3 in.) wide, are produced on leafy shoots in June and early July. They are held either nodding or almost horizontal, which partially exposes a rich rose-red ring of stamens. They do not fully open, forming egg-shaped cups of nine tepals held in three whorls (which accounts for the Nepalese name, "the hen magnolia"). The flowers are fragrant, most noticeably in the evening. The fruiting cones are reddish brown, pendulous, and up to 6 cm (2¼ in.) long. The Indian form has green, glabrous young shoots, glabrous petioles, reddish gold on the underside of the leaf, ash-brown-coloured wood, and comes late into growth. The Chinese form, on the other hand, has a dense pubescence on the young shoots, felted petioles silvery grey on the underside of the leaf, reddish fawn-coloured wood, and comes very early into growth.

The Indian form is considerably hardier than the Chinese, the latter being suitable only for the mildest localities. Even the Indian form is considered the least reliable of the four pendulous-flowered species with specimens in Cornwall, southern Ireland, and southwest Scotland performing well. The Chinese form, even in Cornwall, does not perform well, coming into leaf up to one month earlier. Both forms are best grown in a sheltered, shaded environment in a rich, leafy, moisture-retentive soil. The Indian form is hardy to U.S. hardiness zone 7.

Magnolia grandiflora
SOUTHERN MAGNOLIA
BULL BAY

This "elegant aristocrat of American trees" is a large, handsome tree of southeastern United States, from North Carolina south to central Florida and west to eastern Texas and Arkansas. It grows only within a few hundred miles of the Atlantic Ocean or the Gulf of Mexico. It can be found along the bluffs of the Lower Mississippi River and on the borders of river swamps and ponds, where it grows with *Quercus nigra* (water oak), *Liquidambar styraciflua* (sweet gum), and *Nyssa sylvatica* (sour gum, tupelo). It can be seen growing as a large forest tree, but is also found as scrub amongst the sand dunes overlooking the Gulf of Mexico. It was commonly planted in front of early homesteads in the American South, often with the lower branches pegged down so that they rooted as layers. This practice not only provided replacement plants, but also made the tree virtually impregnable against the prevalent hurricane-force winds. This magnolia is a symbol of the American South, being the state flower of Mississippi and Louisiana, as well as a symbol of the Confederacy.

Magnolia grandiflora was first introduced into European gardens during the 1720s, when the English, French, and Spanish introduced it. The story of its introduction to the British Isles is discussed in chapter 1, "The Story of the Magnolia." The species has since become one of the most popularly planted evergreen plants around the world in warm temperate and subtropical areas.

In its native environment *Magnolia grandiflora* reaches 27.5 m (90 ft.) tall. In the southeast of England, 12 m (40 ft.) is the most that can be expected, but sites in the south of France or Italy especially bordering on the Riviera produce specimens as large as those found in North America. One of the largest seen is the specimen on the Borromean island of Isola Madre in Lake Maggiore; it is about 18 m (60 ft.) tall by 12 m (40 ft.) wide.

In cultivation, *Magnolia grandiflora* is variable in leaf, flower, shape, and size. Leaves are generally oval in shape, up to 25 cm (10 in.) long and less than half as wide, and tapered at both ends. They are leathery in texture, dark glossy green above, and often have a thick, red-brown felt-like indumentum beneath. The large creamy white flowers have a lemon fragrance and are of a size in keeping with the majestic foliage—often up to 36 cm (15 in.) wide. They vary in the number of tepals (9–15) and last only for two to four days. On the first day they are cup-shaped, on the second, saucer-shaped. The flowers appear during the late summer and early autumn in the British Isles, while in North America they are

Magnolia grandiflora. The southern magnolia is found in a wide range of habitats in the southeastern United States, from forests to sand dunes overlooking the Gulf of Mexico. Photo by John Tobe.

generally seen from May or June through to September. The fruiting cones are an ornamental feature in warmer environments, and are orange-red and up to 12.5 cm (5 in.) long. *Magnolia grandiflora* seldom bears fruiting cones in the British Isles, needing the heat of its native country to produce them. Seedling-raised trees begin to flower from 12 years old; vegetatively propagated plants flower earlier, from five years.

This species is among the most temperature-tolerant of temperate broad-leaved evergreen plants (to U.S. hardiness zone 6). It can grow happily in tropical climates but is able to withstand temperatures down to −24°C (−12°F), depending on the variety, for short periods of time. In the British Isles, prolonged periods at −14°C (7°F) defoliate young plants (other than those noted for their tolerance of low temperatures), but mature plants are unscathed. In its native environment, this species lives with temperatures down to −12°C (10°F). It tolerates a wide range of soil types—almost anything except a thin, dry, alkaline soil sustains it—and it grows happily in sun or semi-shade.

Magnolia grandiflora has more than 100 clones, originating not only in North America but also in the British Isles and France. The following represent some of the more popular named forms, together with some of the more recently named clones. They also illustrate the variation within the species. Most of the named plants are European clones such as 'Angustifolia', 'Exmouth', 'Gallisson-niere', and 'Goliath'. Many plants in North American gardens are of seedling origin and are unnamed. Since the 1970s *M. grandiflora* has been increasingly propagated from cuttings, thus offering gardeners plants whose habit, leaf shape and colour, flower size, and growth response can be predicted.

'Angustifolia' is distinct for its narrow lanceolate leaves, to 20 cm (8 in.) long by 11 cm (4½ in.) wide, which are glossy green above with a light cinnamon colouring beneath that disappears with age. This clone is said to have originated in France in 1825 and to have arrived in Britain via Caledonia Nurseries of Guernsey, Channel Islands.

Magnolia grandiflora. The "elegant aristocrat" of American trees is probably the most widely planted evergreen tree worldwide. Seen here is a first-day flower in Washington, D.C. Photo by Ken Robertson.

'Bracken's Brown Beauty' is distinguished by its dense pyramidal habit, prolific flowering, and attractive brown indumentum on the underside of the foliage. The leaves are 12.5 cm (5 in.) long, but the flowers are only 12.5–15.0 cm (5–6 in.) wide. This clone is quite hardy to –29°C (–20°F). It was discovered by Ray Bracken in his nursery in Easley, South Carolina, in 1968 and registered in 1987.

'Charles Dickens' is a broad-spreading clone with very large flowers up to 30 cm (12 in.) in diameter and broad green leaves that have a distinctive pale appearance on first opening. It was introduced into cultivation by Jewel Templeton, who found it growing in the garden of Charles Dickens in Franklin County, Tennessee. It has very large bright red fruit.

'Claudia Wannamaker' has an upright pyramidal habit with small elliptical leaves up to 17.5 cm (7 in.) long by 5.0–7.5 cm (2–3 in.) wide and with small "miniature" flowers 9 cm (3½ in.) wide, about one-third the size of typical grandiflora flowers. It flowers more or less continuously over a five-month period from May in the southern United States, where it is widely planted in shopping malls and at Disney World at Orlando, Florida. It was selected by Johnny Brailsford of Shady Grove Plantation and Nursery, Orangeburg, South Carolina, who named it after his cousin.

'D. D. Blanchard', a compact, upright-growing clone, has dark glossy green leaves with an intense copper-coloured indumentum on the underside of the leaf. The original tree grew in the backyard of Mr. D. D. Blanchard of Wallace, North Carolina, in the early 1960s. 'D. D. Blanchard' is a registered trademark of Robbins Nursery, Willard, North Carolina, from where this plant is available.

'Edith Bogue' is a broad-spreading vigorous clone with narrow dark green leaves, whose attribute is its hardiness: it is well suited to cooler climates. The former director of the Morris Arboretum, John M. Fogg, reported that this clone survived two severe winters in Philadelphia, with temperatures as low as –31°C (–24°F). It originated as a seedling in Florida and was sent to the garden of Miss Edith Bogue of Montclair, New Jersey, in 1920.

'Emory' is an exceptionally fastigiate clone, whose dark green leaves have a rich brown indumentum. It has bowl-shaped flowers of medium size. The original tree at the Louisiana State University Hilltop Arboretum was 27.5 m (90 ft.) tall and only 3.6 m (12 ft.) wide.

'Exmouth', the oldest English clone, was introduced in the early eighteenth century and takes its name from the Devonshire town where Sir John Colliton grew it. It is vigorous and erect in growth and has elliptic leaves that are waxy green above with a reddish brown indumentum beneath that disappears with age. The flowers are extremely large and occasionally have up to 20 tepals; they appear from a very early age. This clone is the one most frequently planted against walls.

'Ferruginea' is an erect form of compact habit that has a rich rust-coloured indumentum on the underside of the leaf. The flowers are typical in size and are produced freely when the plant is growing in a sunny site. It is often recommended for chalky soils.

'Gallissonniere' is a pyramidal clone with russet-brown indumentum on the underside of the leaf. It was imported into France by the Baron de la Gallissonniere between 1741 and 1749 and is now among the most popular European clones being grown. It is the "tailored" grandiflora of Italian nurseries.

'Goliath', an extremely popular clone in the British Isles, is of bushy habit with oval leaves up to 20 cm (8 in.) long and virtually no indumentum on the underside of the leaf. It produces globular flowers, up to 30 cm (12 in.) wide when fully open, over a long period from July to November (in the British Isles) and from an early age. It was sent out by Caledonia Nurseries of Guernsey, Channel Islands.

'Little Gem' is a slow-growing compact tree of distinctive columnar habit, which according to reports was only 4.25 m (14 ft.) tall and 1.2 m (4 ft.) wide after 16 years. The leaves are elliptic in shape, 12.5 cm (5 in.) by 5 cm (2 in.), dark green above with a good rust-coloured indumentum beneath. The medium-sized flowers are cup-shaped with a tendency to remain this shape as opposed to opening saucer-like on the second day. This clone is a heavy bloomer seen over a long flowering period from April to August in the southern United States. It was selected in 1952 by Steed's Nursery of Candor, North Carolina, and is really only suitable for warmer climates as tip dieback is common in more temperate growing conditions.

'Majestic Beauty' is an upright-growing pyramidal clone with very large dark green leaves and large flowers that are often seen from May to July in the southern and western United States. It was selected by Monrovia Nursery, Azusa, California, in 1963.

'Monland', a distinctly broad oval-shaped clone, is broader than it is tall. It has narrow, dark glossy green leaves with a long petiole. The flowers are large, 25–30 cm (10–12 in.), with 12 tepals and are seen profusely over a long period. Remontant flowering is far more evident in hybrids than in the species. The sterility of the seed of the plant and the number of tepals lead people to think this is in fact a hybrid with *Magnolia virginiana*. 'Monland' was discovered by Bob Eiland of Charmwood Nursery, Millbrook, Alabama, growing near Wetumpka, Alabama, in the late 1960s. It was introduced by Monrovia Nursery, Azusa, California, in 1987. The name is an acronym of Monrovia and Eiland, and the plant is marketed as *Magnolia* hybrid Timeless Beauty™ 'Monland'.

'Nannetensis' is a large flowering clone often with extra tepals giving it the

Magnolia grandiflora 'Gallissonniere'. One of many clones of *M. grandiflora* identified by its habit, 'Gallissonniere' is also among the most widely cultivated clones, especially in Europe. Here it is seen in the northern Italian town of Azzate, south of Varese. Photo by Dr. Helmut Orth.

appearance of being double. It was introduced into Europe by the Delaunay Nursery of Angers, France, in 1865. The name comes from Namnetes, the Roman name for the city of Nantes.

'Ruff', a vigorous upright-growing clone, has possibly the darkest golden brown-red indumentum on the underside of any *Magnolia grandiflora* clone. It was named after Wallace Ruff of Eugene, Oregon, and introduced by Gossler Farms Nursery of Springfield, Oregon, in 1973.

'Russet' is a compact upright pyramidal clone to 12 m (40 ft.) in California. It has medium-sized dark glossy green leaves with rich russet-orange-brown indumentum on the underside of the leaf. The 20 cm (8 in.) flowers have 16 tepals and are extremely fragrant. This clone was selected by Mausell van Rensellaer in 1952 from southern California and introduced by the Saratoga Horticultural Foundation in 1965.

'St. Mary' grows quite distinctively into a large bushy shrub with waxy, rich green wavy margined leaves. The particularly dark indumentum on the leaf underside disappears with age. The porcelain-white flowers are freely produced from an early age, are cup-shaped, and about 15 cm (6 in.) across. This American clone was named by W. B. Clarke Nursery of San Jose, California, after the Glen St. Mary Nursery, Florida, from which it was purchased in 1939. It was the first clone of *Magnolia grandiflora* named and selected in the United States.

'Samuel Sommer' is one of the finest selections. When young it has a sturdy, erect growth and is characterised by an ascending branch habit. It has large, very glossy, green leaves above and an excellent golden rusty-brown indumentum on the underside. The flowers, with 12 creamy white tepals, are exceptionally large, even from an early age—30 cm (12 in.) across initially, reaching up to 39 cm (15 in.) across in favoured locations on well-established plants. The flowers are cup-shaped, which on the second day flatten to a bowl shape and will be seen like this for five or six days. Neil Tre-

Magnolia grandiflora 'Goliath'. One of many clones of *M. grandiflora* differentiated by their leaf and flower shape, 'Goliath' produces globular flowers. Photo by Dr. Helmut Orth.

seder reports this form survived tornado winds and temperatures of −12°C (−10°F) at Reinhardt College in Georgia. It was raised by the Saratoga Horticultural Foundation and named after the president of the Board of Trustees when it was first offered for sale in 1961.

'Symmes Select' is a compact-growing clone that flowers reliably over a long period. The rich dark green leaves have undulating margins and a good brown indumentum. John Symmes of Cedar Lane Farm, Madison, Georgia, selected and introduced this clone from a batch of seedlings he raised. The seedlings came from Westview Cemetery, Atlanta, Georgia.

'Victoria' has a rich rusty red indumentum on the underside of the dark green foliage. It is particularly hardy, withstanding −24°C (−12°F). Its origins are unknown. One possibility is that it was imported from Exbury to Victoria, British Columbia, by Layritz Nursery. Alternatively, it may have been imported into North America from England under its own name.

'Workman' is a very compact growing clone with small deep green undulating leaves. The small cup-shaped flowers are 11 cm (4½ in.) in diameter and are seen over an extremely long season from April to December in the southern United States. This clone was selected in southern Louisiana and introduced by Ken Durio of Louisiana Nursery, Opelousas.

Magnolia grandiflora has been hybridised with *M. virginiana* to produce the Freeman hybrids (see chapter 7).

Magnolia kobus

In cultivation *Magnolia kobus* is most frequently seen as a small to medium tree initially pyramidal in outline, becoming broad spreading with age. It is common throughout the forests of Japan as well as on the isolated volcanic island of Cheju-do (Quelpart Island), off the south coast of South Korea. It was first introduced into North America during the winter of 1861 by George Hall of Rhode Island, who passed it on to Parsons Brothers, nurserymen of Flushing, Long Island, as *Magnolia thurberi*. It was almost certainly collected from plants growing on the island of Honshu. Seeds from plants growing in Sapporo on the island of Hokkaido were later sent to the Arnold Arboretum in 1876 by William Clark, the first president of the Massachusetts Agricultural College. Not until about 1879 was this species introduced into the British Isles, when Charles

Maries, an English plant collector, brought back seed to be grown at Veitch's Coombe Wood Nursery.

With such a widespread distribution this species can vary considerably in habit, from a large multistemmed shrub to a fine tree some 23 m (75 ft.) tall. Many authorities regard the robust tree form found in forests on the island of Hokkaido and the Japan Sea side of northern Honshu as *Magnolia kobus* var. *borealis*, but George Johnstone in 1950 and Stephen Spongberg in 1976 and 1998 both rejected this view on the grounds that there are no clear-cut characteristics distinguishing the forms. Growth rates vary considerably, with young and vigorous trees growing as much as 75 cm (2½ ft.) a year.

The winter buds are quite distinctive, being very downy. The leaves are up to 15 cm (6 in.) long by 7.5 cm (3 in.) at their widest point and are elliptic-obovate in shape. Both the leaves and the young stems emit a distinctive smell of aniseed when crushed, but this is not nearly so distinctive as with *Magnolia salicifolia*. The white flowers (often with a hint of pink at the base of the tepals) appear on leafless shoots from early March to early April, depending on site and season. The flowers have nine tepals. The three outer ones are shorter, about 2.5 cm (1 in.), and generally fall as the flower opens. The six inner tepals are generally 10 cm (4 in.) long, and the flowers retain a vase shape to maturity. Occasional trees produce flowers that open completely, but these are probably hybrids of *M. kobus* (such as *M. ×loebneri* and *M. ×kewensis*). The flowers are frost sensitive: because the first flush of flower also happens to be the main flush, a frost of only a few degrees (to −3°C [26°F]) can have a disastrous effect, with the tepals becoming completely browned. The fruiting cones are not particularly attractive; initially green, they eventually turn russet-brown. They are about 7.5–10.0 cm (3–4 in.) long and appear distorted in shape, revealing bright red seed. *Magnolia kobus* produces seed quite freely, especially when grown near other plants of the same or a closely related species.

Plants raised from seed are often used for understocks in the nursery trade, as this species grows well in various soil types and conditions including those with an alkaline pH. It does not do well, however, in thin, dry soils, presumably because its home is in moisture-retentive, humus-rich sites in Japan. Apart from the flowers, the plant is particularly hardy, surviving temperatures as low as −34°C (−29°F), or U.S. hardiness zone 4.

The wood is soft, close-grained, and a light yellow in colour. In Japan it has been used for making matches as well as kitchen utensils. The bark is used in medicinal preparations by the Ainu of Japan as a cold cure.

Magnolia kobus is very variable in the time it takes to flower. Raised from seed, it flowers 7 to 30 years after germination; however, vegetatively propagated material flowers within 10 years of propagation. It has been crossed with *M. stellata* to produce *M. ×loebneri* (see chapter 7), *M. salicifolia* to produce *M. ×kewensis* (see chapter 7), and others (see *M. kobus* hybrids in chapter 7).

'Esveld Select' is an upright-growing small tree with slightly larger flower than *Magnolia kobus* and later in the season. The young leaves as they unfold are mahogany-red in colour and are seen continuously throughout the season. This clone was introduced by Dick van Gelderen of Boskoop.

'Two Stones' is an interesting tetraploid from August Kehr. This pure white 10 cm (4 in.) gardenia-like flower has 10–12 strap-shaped tepals arranged horizontally with a central cup of 15 or so tepals arched over the central boss. I have only seen young plants flowering towards the end of April in South Korea. This effect on a larger bush will, I am sure, have considerable appeal.

Magnolia kobus 'Janaki Ammal'. This colchicine-induced clone was named for a geneticist who was employed by the Royal Horticultural Society at Wisley during the 1950s. Photo by Jim Gardiner.

Magnolia kobus—The Wisley Clones

In the early 1950s, E. K. Janaki Ammal, a geneticist, was investigating chromosome numbers of various woody plant genera, including *Magnolia*, for the Royal Horticultural Society at Wisley. Included in the study was the investigation of the impact of colchicine on *M. kobus* seedlings. Several original plants (all polyploid) can still be found, primarily on Battleston Hill. All are vigorous, multistemmed small trees more than 6 m (20 ft.) tall and wide. All have an abundance of flowers, which open successively and are seen over several weeks; however, they vary in the number of tepals per flower. Another feature of these polyploids is the crinkled nature of many of the leaves—evident on both sides of the leaf and in most instances wider than normal. August Kehr considers the length-to-width ratio of leaves a distinguishable characteristic of polyploids. The length-to-width leaf ratio of *M. kobus* 'Norman Gould', for example, varies between 1.43 and 1.56 whereas that of *M. kobus* is generally 1.75.

'Janaki Ammal' is found within yards of 'Norman Gould' and matches it for vigour and floriferousness. It varies only in that the 8–9 tepals are narrower and more crinkled than those of 'Norman Gould' and open more fully.

'Norman Gould' has a pure white cup-shaped flower with 8–9 tepals. The 10 cm (4 in.) long broad tepals have a hint of pink at their base and are seen during the end of March. The flowers are produced in abundance and within a few years when plants are raised from cuttings. This clone was named after the man who served as the Royal Horticultural Society's botanist between 1931 and 1960.

Magnolia liliiflora
MU-LAN
WOODY ORCHID

This species, named woody orchid because of its orchidlike flowers borne on woody stems, is a medium-sized to large shrub with an open, sprawling habit. It has been cultivated in China, Korea, and Japan for centuries, but it is considered native only to the warm temperate regions of eastern and central China (Zhejiang, Fujian, and Hubei Provinces). Ernest Wilson and George Forrest sent back herbarium specimens of the species between 1900 and 1925. Several of these were undoubtedly collected from cultivated sources in and around temple gardens. Forrest recorded flowers as "pinkish white, veined a deeper shade . . . lipped creamy white, flushed deep reddy purple at the base, fragrant."

Planting *Magnolia liliiflora* in temple gardens is not solely the preserve of China and Japan. In South Korea too this species is widely planted and many beautiful clones are seen. Interestingly, the fragrance referred to by George Forrest of a plant collected on the Salween Divide (1924–25 Expedition) is not often regarded as a significant characteristic of this species. When it is found, however, as was the case in South Korea (Toksan Provincial Park), a most delicate tea rose scent was noted and may well be a quality worth considering for future breeding programmes.

The species was introduced to the British Isles by the third Duke of Portland many years before, in 1790, from a cultivated plant growing in Japan. It is a slow-growing, multistemmed shrub. Once established it grows up to 30 cm (1 ft.) per year in favourable locations. Specimens of up to 3.5 m (12 ft.) tall and wide can be seen, and are upwards of 20 years of age. The dark green leaves are generally elliptic to obovate in shape and 18 cm (7 in.) long by 10 cm (4 in.) wide. When young they are downy on the underside but by the middle of the season the downiness is visible only along the midrib.

Magnolia liliiflora. The mu-lan has been widely cultivated for centuries in China, Japan, and Korea, and frequently in temple gardens. The numerous clones vary in colour (from pink to the darkest of purples), size and shape of tepals, and how the tepals reflex. The specimen seen here grows in Toksan Provincial Park, South Korea, and has the delicate scent of a tea rose. Photo by Jim Gardiner.

The 10.0–12.5 cm (4–5 in.) vase-shaped flowers vary in colour from pink to the darkest purple on the outside and from white to purple on the inside. The six inner tepals initially hold their shape, though they reflex like a water lily, giving additional poise to the flower. The tips of the tepals are variably pointed, with some clones more rounded than others. The three outer tepals are small and calyxlike and are often a purplish brown-green colour. The plants flower over a long period generally during mid-April, May, and into June depending on the site and season, but in all instances providing a succession of flower over a long period prior to and during the unfurling of the foliage. Sporadic flowers also appear later in the season, during late

June or even July and August. This flowering period is brought forward by several weeks when considering plants in the southern United States and California.

Several clones are in cultivation, though this may be misleading as some may indeed be backcrosses with *Magnolia liliiflora* or hybrids with *M. denudata* or *M. ×soulangeana* cultivars. By inference the current range of *M. liliiflora* forms available has been selected over time, with plants from cultivated sources coming through for use.

'Darkest Purple' has rich purple narrow tepals and has also been used by the U.S. National Arboretum and Frank Galyon of Knoxville, Tennessee, in breeding programmes.

'Holland Red' has rich purple-red flowers, with the colour on the inside of the broad 6–8 tepals similar to the outside. The flowers have a distinct spicy fragrance.

'Nigra' is very commonly grown in the British Isles. It has very dark purple candles in bud, which on opening reveal a purplish white, lightly veined inside and a dark red-purple on the outside of the six tepals. It was introduced from

Magnolia liliiflora 'Nigra'. The most widely grown clone of *M. liliiflora* in the British Isles, 'Nigra' is seen at its most vibrant during warm spells at the end of April, or more generally during May. Photo by Clive Morris.

Japan by John Gould Veitch in 1861 and is sometimes referred to as *Magnolia ×soulangeana* 'Nigra'. A few clones in the British Isles referred to as *M. liliiflora* 'Nigra' vary in the level of purple colouring on the inside of the tepals.

'O'Neill' is an American introduction distributed by Professor Joe McDaniel from a plant growing at the home of Mabel O'Neill, Champaign, Illinois. This very distinct clone has narrower tepals than 'Nigra' and more of them, generally 7–9. They are slightly larger and are a rich red-purple in colour on the outside and a pretty pink-purple with darker veins on the inside. In a conversation with McDaniel, Todd Gresham indicated that he used a superior *Magnolia liliiflora* clone and not the usual 'Nigra' when carrying out his hybridisation work. The assumption is that he may well have used 'O'Neill'.

'Reflorescens' was used by William Kosar of the U.S. National Arboretum to produce the group of hybrids known as the "Eight Little Girls." Apart from its ability to repeat flower (as do many of the other clones), the quality for which this plant is named is unclear to me.

It is evident from visiting temple gardens in South Korea that several clones exist that are quite distinct from clones generally grown in the West. Through

Magnolia liliiflora 'O'Neill'. Professor Joe McDaniel found this clone in the garden of Mabel O'Neill at Champaign, Illinois. It is the most widely cultivated clone in the United States. Photo by Jim Gardiner.

the good offices of Ferris Miller (Min Pyong-gal), a number will be introduced gradually into the collections at the Chollipo Arboretum prior to being imported to Western collections.

Magnolia liliiflora and its forms are excellent subjects for the smaller garden, either as lawn specimens or as border plants. They generally like a sheltered yet sunny position in a moisture-retentive soil on the acid side of neutral. 'Nigra' and 'O'Neill' are hardier forms, to U.S. hardiness zone 6, while *M. liliiflora* is hardy to U.S. hardiness zone 7. In the British Isles 'Nigra' is regarded as the most satisfactory choice for cultivating because of its extra vigour, extended flowering period, and availability. 'O'Neill', however, is slowly becoming better known and will, in time, make more of an impact.

Magnolia liliiflora is an extremely important parent and probably the most influential species in *Magnolia* breeding programmes. It has been used extensively, most famously in work on *M. ×soulangeana* (see chapter 7), but more recently it has been widely used in North America to produce the small de Vos and Kosar hybrids often referred to as the "Eight Little Girls" (see chapter 7) , *M.* 'Galaxy' and *M.* 'Spectrum' (see under *M. liliiflora* hybrids in chapter 7), new cultivars from New Zealand (see Jury hybrids in chapter 7), the Gresham hybrids (see chapter 7), and others (see *M. liliiflora* hybrids in chapter 7). *Magnolia liliiflora* 'Nigra' was crossed with *M. kobus*, producing 'Marillyn' (see under *M. liliiflora* hybrids in chapter 7).

It has been known by several synonymous names, including *Magnolia purpurea*, *M. discolor*, and, most recently, *M. quinquepeta*. Frederick G. Meyer and Elizabeth McClintock (1987) have come down in favour of *M. liliiflora* Desrousseaux (1791) as the earliest applicable name.

Magnolia macrophylla
BIG LEAF MAGNOLIA

Magnolia macrophylla has a restricted distribution in the southeastern United States, being found in Georgia, Alabama, Mississippi, and Louisiana, and northwards to western Virginia, Kentucky, Arkansas, and Ohio. It was first discovered by André Michaux in the mountains of South Carolina in 1759 and was introduced into the British Isles in 1800.

In its native habit it is a small to medium-sized tree from 7.5 m (25 ft.) to 15 m

(50 ft.) tall, varying in habit from a single erect to a multistemmed spreading crown. In the British Isles it seldom reaches a height of more than 12 m (40 ft.). This species is very remarkable for its sensational foliage—the largest of all the *Magnolia* species—which in its native habitat can attain up to 100 cm (40 in.) long by 45 cm (18 in.) wide. Climatic conditions in the British Isles do not allow such sizes to be reached, but the leaves can still be 60 cm (2 ft.) long. Despite their size, the leaves have a rather flimsy, papery appearance; they are green above and a silvery chalky white beneath. They are oblong-obovate in shape with an auriculate base.

The fragrant flowers can be even larger than those of *Magnolia grandiflora*. Initially cup-shaped and then reflexing to 30–45 cm (12–18 in.) wide, they are composed of six fleshy tepals, creamy white in colour and often with some purple spotting towards the centre of the flower. The three outer tepals are greenish in colour and smaller than the six inner tepals. They are seen during May in North America and generally mid-June and July in the British Isles. These giant flowers have been said to "shine out through the forest in spite of the huge leafy parasols on which they nestle." *Magnolia macrophylla* does not flower prolifically in the British Isles because of the comparatively cool summer temperatures. The fruits are conelike, up to 7.5 cm (3 in.) long, and reddish pink fading to a pale brown in colour.

This rare tree is found either individually or in small groups in sheltered woodlands, especially in ravines and river valleys, along with *Liquidambar styraciflua* (sweet gum), *Liriodendron tulipifera* (tulip tree), and *Quercus texana* (southern red oak). Rich, deep, moisture-retentive soils either just on the acid or the alkaline side of neutral are best for this species, which requires also a sunny yet sheltered site so that the flamboyant foliage display is not severely reduced.

Provided effective ripening of the wood takes place, *Magnolia macrophylla* is quite hardy, in North America to U.S. hardiness zone 5. Far too often growth in the British Isles continues well into the autumn, causing frosting of the new growth to hamper the tree's development. The tree also needs hot, humid summer days, which tends to restrict its planting sites, to make good growth.

Phil Savage has raised hybrids of *Magnolia macrophylla* (see chapter 7). Several clones are in cultivation.

'Sara Gladney' has pure white flowers and was selected at the John James Audubon Foundation at Gloster Arboretum, Mississippi.

Magnolia macrophylla. Growing in sheltered locations often as an understory tree, the big leaf magnolia lives up to its name with huge leaves that can be 100 cm (4 ft.) long. The flowers are said to "shine out through the forest in spite of the huge leafy parasols on which they nestle." Photo by John Tobe.

Professor Joe McDaniel of Urbana, Illinois, selected 'Whopper' in 1974. When fully opened all nine tepals have the purple spots on the white flowers, which can be up to 48 cm (19 in.) wide.

Magnolia macrophylla subsp. *ashei*

Magnolia macrophylla subsp. *ashei* is one of America's rarest magnolias. It is found in the lowlands of northwest Florida, in Leon County, but also in the southernmost counties of Alabama and Mississippi, where it attains a height of 6 m (20 ft.). *Ostrya virginiana* (American hop hornbeam), *Stewartia malachodendron* (silky camellia), *Illicium floridanum* (purple anise), *Kalmia latifolia* (mountain laurel), and *Aesculus pavia* (red buckeye) grow with it. Subspecies *ashei* can be distinguished from *M. macrophylla* by its habit. The leaf size is smaller, and the flowers are smaller and vary from 12.5–30.0 cm (5–12 in.), though both are scented and appear in May. They can be pure white or spotted, often red in subsp. *ashei*, with flowering time from seed being much quicker at 3 years against 12–15 years. The fruit is much shorter and not so round.

'Weatherley' is an exceptionally good-flowering form introduced by Ken Durio of Louisiana Nursery, Opelousas.

This subspecies is found in a few collections in Europe and the British Isles, including the Hillier Arboretum. Although it is regarded as tender, it has not suffered when exposed to temperatures down to −14°C (7°F). George Johnstone introduced it into the British Isles in 1949 and flowered it some four years later.

Magnolia macrophylla subsp. *dealbata*

Magnolia macrophylla subsp. *dealbata* is a small to medium-sized single fastigiate or more generally multistemmed tree and is the only deciduous magnolia in central America. It grows in the forests of the southern and eastern central mountain ranges in the states of Oaxaca, San Luis Potosi, and Veracruz with *Liquidambar* (sweetgum) and *Quercus* (oak) species at an altitude of between 1200 m (4000 ft.) and 1500 m (5000 ft.) where it is seen in both sun and shade. The leaves are up to 70 cm (28 in.) long, similar in shape to those of *M. macrophylla*. The flowers are a creamy white colour but lack the purple to purple-red blotch of both *M. macrophylla* and subsp. *ashei*. Like *M. macrophylla*, subsp.

Magnolia macrophylla subsp. *ashei*. The fragrant flowers are slightly smaller than those of *M. macrophylla* and can be pure white or spotted with red. The leaves are marginally smaller but nevertheless impressive. Photo by John Tobe.

Magnolia macrophylla subsp. *dealbata*. In Mexico where this subspecies is found, the flowers are used to decorate the churches during Easter celebrations. The photograph shows the pure white flower; it lacks the red-purple blotching often seen in the species or in subspecies *ashei*. Photo by Jim Gardiner.

dealbata has a sweet scent. The distinguishing feature that reportedly separates the two is the presence of stylar beaks on the follicles. Subspecies *dealbata* flowers midway between *M. macrophylla* (12–15 years) and subsp. *ashei* (3 years) at about 7–9 years, when trees are about 6 m (20 ft.) tall, though a plant at the Hillier Gardens and Arboretum flowered in a pot and others from the Russell introduction have flowered after five years.

During Easter each year, these magnolia trees are pruned by the Mexicans who use the flowers to decorate their churches. When boiled, the leaves are used medicinally as a poultice and applied to sore tendons. Subspecies *dealbata* was the first magnolia to be printed in European literature. Francisco Hernandez, the court physician to King Philip II of Spain, was sent in 1570 to explore "New Spain" (Mexico) and described this magnolia in *Plantarum Historia Mexicana* in 1631.

Subspecies *dealbata* was introduced into the British Isles by Sir Harold Hillier during the 1970s and again by James Russell in the early 1980s. It is thought to be reasonably hardy, being similar to subspecies *ashei*. Until comparatively recently this taxon was regarded as a species in its own right. Dorothy Johnson (now Callaway) of the L. H. Bailey Hortorium, Cornell University, Ithaca (1989), and more recently John Tobe of the Florida Department of Environmental Protection, Tallahassee (1993), both proposed its subspecific status.

Magnolia nitida
GLOSSY MAGNOLIA

This erect-growing evergreen shrub (in cultivation) or ultimately a small tree (in the wild) is native to northwest Yunnan Province, northern Myanmar (Burma), and southeast Tibet (Xizang Zizhiqu). It was discovered by George Forrest in 1917 on the Mekong-Salween Divide in northwest Yunnan at an altitude of between 3000 m (10,000 ft.) and 3350 m (11,000 ft.), and subsequently in southeast Tibet (Xizang Zizhiqu) and northern Myanmar. Reginald Farrer also found the species in 1919 in northern Myanmar around Hpimaw, in "a frontier outpost bordering northwest Yunnan where it was growing at 2500 m (8000 ft.) on the fringes of the forest with a bitter winter and a complete absence of ripening heat or light in the summer."

Two forms appear in cultivation; one is a large, cone-shaped shrub, the other a small columnar tree to about 9 m (30 ft.). It is commonly known as the glossy magnolia for its beautiful elliptic foliage, which is up to 11 cm (4½ in.) long and 5 cm (2 in.) wide. In an article entitled "Chinese Magnolias in Cultivation," George Johnstone (1950) wrote:

> It has the most lovely foliage, the leaves being more highly polished than any evergreen leaf that I know of—better than the best hollies. The young growth is bronze, also very highly polished. The leaf has a silver edge to it. If you hold it up, so that the sun is behind it, you will see that silver edge all the way round each leaf.

Magnolia nitida takes about 15 years to flower from seed. The flowers are fragrant, ivory or cream coloured, to 7.5 cm (3 in.) wide, with nine inner and three outer tepals that appear during March and April on shoot tips. The best forms are those of a pale primrose-yellow colour with a purple streak down the outer tepals (the cone-shaped shrub). The seed is also particularly attractive; in colour it is a beautiful shade of orange, within a striking grass green 7.5 cm (3 in.) long seed cone.

Until this species is seen in flower, the first thought is that it must be a *Michelia* species. Once the terminal flower buds are seen, however, it is unmistakably a *Magnolia* species, as all *Michelia* flower buds grow from the leaf axils.

In the British Isles *Magnolia nitida* is hardy only in localities that provide it with adequate shelter and frost protection. It has been grown successfully in a few gardens in Cornwall and at Ventnor on the Isle of Wight. Colonel Stephenson Clarke grew plants against the south and east wall at Borde Hill in Sussex. The microclimate of the south wall proved too hot and dry, whereas the protection of the east wall enabled it to thrive until the winter of 1939. In New Zealand a good specimen is growing in the garden of Mark and Abbie Jury at Tikorangi on the western side of North Island. It is probably hardy to U.S. hardiness zone 9, although there have been recent reports of plants having survived temperatures of −12°C (10°F), which put it in U.S. hardiness zones 7–8.

A rich, moisture-retentive, preferably acid soil in dapple shade would suit this rare species.

Magnolia obovata

This fast-growing deciduous tree is found in the forested mountainous regions of the Russian Kuril Islands and southward through the Japanese islands of Hokkaido, Honshu, Shikoku, and the Ryukyus, where it grows with many other broad-leaved deciduous trees. Along with *Magnolia kobus*, its natural distribution is probably the most northerly of all *Magnolia* species.

Magnolia obovata was first introduced to the West in 1865, when it was sent to the United States. Not until 1877, however, did it come to Europe, when it was introduced to Germany. There are various dates when it was thought to have been introduced to the British Isles beginning from 1878; however, it must have flowered, possibly for the first time, in 1893, when it was awarded a First Class Certificate by the Royal Horticultural Society when exhibited by James Harry Veitch.

Magnolia obovata. This large tree produces a fine display of richly scented white flowers during midsummer. Unfortunately, few flowers are close enough to the ground for their scent to be fully appreciated. On a still summer's evening or early morning, however, the fragrance is strong enough to fill the atmosphere for a considerable distance away from the plant. The species is also highly regarded for its autumn foliage colour, which is a rich brown. Photo by Jim Gardiner.

In cultivation this magnolia develops into a medium-sized to large upright-growing tree, though it grows considerably larger in the forests of Hokkaido, Japan, where specimens more than 30 m (100 ft.) tall have been found. The leaves are obovate in shape and can reach 46 cm (18 in.) long by 20 cm (8 in.) wide when planted in a favourable site. As the young leaves unfold, a fine pubescence creates a silvery green colour on the underside of the leaf, which with age changes to a grey-green. The white flowers appear on leafy shoots during June and early July and are richly scented. The nine inner fleshy tepals are generally cup-shaped when they open, but become saucer-shaped, up to 17.5–20.0 cm (7–8 in.) wide, and are white in colour, ageing to a creamy white. The three outer tepals are shorter, reflexed, and reddish brown or pink in colour. The stamen filaments are a bright crimson, which provides an eye-catching combination of colour. A few trees have been noted to have distinctly pink flowers. This species flowers from a comparatively early age, at 10–15 years. The heavily scented blooms of midsummer are followed by richly coloured scarlet fruits, approximately 18 cm (7 in.) long, during September and early October. By mid-November these become light brown in colour.

In the south and southwest of England, *Magnolia obovata* is a fast-growing tree forming a broad-spreading crown. It grows 60–90 cm (2–3 ft.) a year when young, especially if situated in a sunny yet sheltered site in a rich, moisture-retentive, slightly acid soil. It is surprisingly hardy, to U.S. hardiness zone 5 in North America.

The timber is soft, close-grained, and pale yellowish brown in colour. It is used extensively in Japan for furniture and cabinet work.

'Lydia' is an upright-growing small, potentially medium-sized tree selected for its narrow crown. The fragrant lemon-scented flowers are 15.0–17.5 cm (6–7 in.) wide with six cream white inner tepals and three pink-flushed outer tepals and are seen in June. This clone flowered for the first time after 15 years from germination. It fruits freely, and the fruits are rich maroon in colour. 'Lydia' was selected by Polly Hill from seedlings sent by Tsuneshige Rukujo in Japan, and named after her youngest granddaughter.

'Pink Flush' is probably the clone grown at the Royal Horticultural Society's Garden at Wisley in the 1950s. Francis Hanger, former curator, introduced *Magnolia obovata* seedlings from Exbury, Hampshire, and this colour form arose from one of these seedlings. Plants from this raising were also given to Sir Eric Savill at Windsor for planting in the Savill and Valley Gardens. One of these seedlings, a pink form, was exhibited at the Royal Horticultural Society's Show at Vincent Square, London, where it was given an Award of Merit.

Magnolia obovata has been crossed with another Japanese species, *M. sieboldii*, to produce an extravagantly scented shrub *M. ×wieseneri* (see chapter 7). It has also been crossed with *M. tripetala* to produce *M.* 'Silver Parasol' (see under *M. obovata* hybrids in chapter 7), with *M. globosa* to produce *M.* 'Summer Solstice' (see under *M. globosa* in chapter 7), and *M. wilsonii* to produce *M. ×gotoburgensis* (see chapter 7), and with others (see *M. obovata* hybrids in chapter 7).

David Hunt, the editor of *Magnolias and Their Allies* (1996, pp. 9–20), and R. K. Brummitt, the leading specialist on nomenclatural matters at the Royal Botanic

Gardens, Kew, and secretary of the Committee of Spermatophyta, assessed all the evidence for and against the name *Magnolia obovata* and its synonym, *M. hypoleuca*. They came out in favour of *M. obovata*, thus revoking the decision of the late J. E. Dandy, of the department of botany at the British Museum, in 1973, to install *M. hypoleuca* over *M. obovata*, which had been the accepted name since 1913.

Magnolia officinalis

This fast-growing, medium-sized tree is known almost entirely from cultivated plants in the central Chinese provinces of Hubei, Sichuan, Guizhou, and Guangxi. It was first discovered by Augustine Henry, an Irishman who went to China in 1880 as a medical officer and assistant inspector of customs for the Imperial Chinese Maritime Customs Service. He became interested in plants because one of his assignments was to compile a report on the drug plants used by the Chinese. This started a correspondence with the Royal Botanic Gardens at Kew that led to several important plant discoveries and introductions, including *Magnolia officinalis*, which he found growing in eastern Sichuan in 1885. The species was introduced into cultivation by Ernest Wilson in 1900 when he was on a Veitch expedition to western Hubei and later, when he was collecting for the Arnold Arboretum, from areas to the north and south of Yichang (Ichang) in western Hubei, an important town on the Yangtze River.

The species is rare in cultivation in the British Isles, whereas *Magnolia officinalis* var. *biloba* is more commonly seen. The type may be restricted to Cornish gardens and other collections in the south and southeast. It was often confused with the closely related *M. obovata*, from which it differs by its pubescent young shoots (glabrous in *M. obovata*), yellowish grey young wood (purple-brown in *M. obovata*), and flat-topped fruit (cone-shaped in *M. obovata*).

The leaves are obovate in shape to 46 cm (18 in.) long by 20 cm (8 in.) wide, green above and slightly glaucous beneath. The underside is also covered with fine down, especially noticeable on the midrib. The leaves tend to be concentrated towards the end of the branchlets (as in *Magnolia obovata*), producing a rufflike effect, and are rather papery in texture. The creamy white flowers are produced on leafy shoots, are cup-shaped, about 14 cm (5½ in.) wide with 9–15 tepals, and quite fragrant, with a rather antiseptic scent. In the British Isles they are seen during mid-May (May in China and North America), but are not produced in sufficient quantity to be a visual attraction. The fruiting cones are about 7.5 cm (5 in.) long, flat-topped, generally oblong, and red in colour but quickly turn a dull purple-brown.

The Chinese know this species as the hou-po or hou-phu tree and grow it extensively for its bark and flower buds, which have prized medicinal qualities. When boiled the bark yields an extract, the alkaloid magnocurarine (toxic at high concentrations), which is taken internally as a cure for coughs and colds and as a tonic and stimulant during convalescence. An extract obtained from the flower buds, which is called Yu-po, is esteemed as a medicine for women. Once the bark has been stripped, the tree dies, which probably accounts for its disappearance from its native habitats.

Magnolia officinalis var. *biloba*

More commonly seen than the species, *Magnolia officinalis* var. *biloba* was first described by Ernest Wilson in 1927 and is native to the southeastern provinces of Hubei, Jiangxi, Zhejiang, Fujian, and Hunan. It was introduced into cultivation by Sir Harold Hillier from seed received from the Lu Shan Botanic Garden in 1936 when five seedlings were raised. It is a fast-growing, medium-sized to large tree of an upright stature that puts on about 46 cm (18 in.) of growth per year in favoured locations. The leaf is of a similar size, shape, and character to that of the type, but is distinct in that it has a deep notch at the tip, which gives it a bilobed appearance. This character comes true when plants are raised from seed. A pressed pubescence is also present on the underside of the bilobed leaves.

Magnolia officinalis var. *biloba*. The bilobed leaf form of *M. officinalis* is the one more commonly seen in the British Isles. It was introduced into cultivation by the late Sir Harold Hillier, who obtained seed from the Lu Shan Botanic Garden in 1936. Photo by Jim Gardiner.

In cultivation this variety grows in similar situations to *Magnolia obovata*, in a rich, moisture-retentive, acid soil in a sunny site sheltered from strong winds. In North America it has been reported as growing successfully in Michigan, which indicates a similar hardiness rating to *M. obovata* (U.S. hardiness zone 5).

Magnolia rostrata

This open-branched large deciduous tree comes from a restricted area in northwest Yunnan, southeast Tibet (Xizang Zizhiqu), and northeast Myanmar (Burma). The Scottish plant collector George Forrest and Englishman Reginald Farrer had both seen it either in northwest Yunnan or in northern Myanmar during 1917 and 1919 respectively, between 1500 m (5000 ft.) and 3900 m (12,800 ft.). There was great confusion and consternation when it was first introduced. When Forrest and Farrer first saw the plant, they erroneously combined the fruiting material with its beaked carpels, quite unlike anything else, with the flowers of *Magnolia campbellii*, seen as big as "tay-kettles, abundant in every shade from pure white to a deep and rather magenta rose." What seemed to have happened was that Sir William Wright Smith prepared a scientific description based on Forrest's fruiting and flowering specimens, but citing Farrer's also in *Notes from the Royal Botanic Garden, Edinburgh*, vol. 12, pp. 213–215 (1920). The first whisper of doubt circulated around the horticultural world in 1927, when J. E. Dandy of the British Museum examined all available material. He recognised the leaves and fruiting cones as indeed a new species, but it was quite impossible for it to have precocious flowers (that is, flowering before the leaves) and they could only come out after the leaves had unfurled. Thus *M. campbellii* and *M. rostrata* had been confused in the forest, with the former flowering in February and the latter in May or June. The mixup is quite easily done, as the habits of both are similar when the plants are not in leaf.

Magnolia rostrata is very much a tree of mixed forest, being a large single-stemmed tree with few side branches, making it rather gaunt in appearance. In cultivation it tends to produce a single leader with few short stubby side branches or two or three competing leaders. The obovate-oblong leaves are coppery green in colour until they are fully expanded, measuring up to 50 cm (20 in.) long by 20.0–22.5 cm (8–9 in.) wide. As they appear from the bud scales they are folded longitudinally, with the undersurface facing outwards. The surfaces are densely covered with a chestnut-coloured felt, which remains on the underside on the midrib and main veins, while in between the leaf is quite glaucous. The leaves, which are "parchmentlike" in texture, are grouped at the end of the branchlets and tend to tear even before they have attained their ultimate size. An interesting characteristic of *M. rostrata* is the persistence of the petiole rings on trunks of about 25–30 years.

The flowers have 11 tepals, of which the 8 inner tepals are fleshy, creamy white in colour, and conelike, while the outer three reflex and assume a pinkish tinge on he upper surface, and greenish white beneath. The flowers are fragrant and said to be melon-scented, and open in June or July. The outer reflexed tepals are up to 12.5 cm (5 in.) long, while the cone of inner tepals is similar, being 14 cm (5½ in.). Frank Kingdon Ward, on seeing *Magnolia rostrata* in the Mishmi Hills in the Assam Himalaya, indicated that "he was not prepared for such undistinguished flowers . . . being rather small and white or off white not

Magnolia rostrata. This species from Yunnan and Tibet was initially confused with *M. campbellii.* When eventually seen in flower, it was somewhat of a disappointment. Kingdon Ward was not prepared for such "undistinguished flowers." The species prefers the mild, sheltered gardens of southwestern England and Scotland and southern Ireland. It is seen here at Mount Congreve, Ireland. Photo by Jim Gardiner.

to be compared with those of *M. campbellii* and did little or nothing to enhance the beauty of the foliage." His comments were justified only after the species flowered for the first time in the British Isles in 1935.

The fruiting cones are held erect "like candles on a Christmas tree." They are 12.5 cm (5 in.) long with masses of bright red seeds, the smallest in the genus. What is quite distinct about the fruiting cones are the carpels, which are beaked and become curved and spinelike.

In the British Isles this species is grown in sheltered gardens in the southwest, southern Ireland, and southwest Scotland, in a sunny position. It can probably be more widely cultivated as fresh sources of seed become more readily available.

A fine specimen has grown at Glenarn, Helensburgh, Strathclyde, for many years. Others grow at Trewithen and Trengwainton in Cornwall and Mount Congreve in County Waterford, Ireland. Interestingly, this species was also grown at the Hillier Gardens and Arboretum in Hampshire, where in 1974 it was exhibited for its foliage at one of the Royal Horticultural Society's shows at Vincent Square.

Magnolia salicifolia
JAPANESE WILLOW LEAF MAGNOLIA

Magnolia salicifolia varies in habit from an erect, large shrub to a broad-spreading, medium-sized tree. It is found growing in oak and beech forests at moderate elevations—between 490 m (1600 ft.) and 1340 m (4400 ft.)—on the Japanese islands of Honshu, Shikoku, and Kyushu. Japanese willow leaf magnolia was introduced almost simultaneously to North America (in 1892) by Professor Charles Sargent, director of the Arnold Arboretum, and to the British Isles (in 1893), by the English nurseryman James Harry Veitch. Both men were collecting in Japan, on Mount Hakkoda in northern Honshu, and both sent back quantities of seed to their respective establishments. Sargent's seed germinated, Veitch's did not, although he obtained seedlings a year later from Sargent, presumably from this same source. The Yokohama Nursery Company sent a plant from a different source to Kew in 1906.

The tree forms are generally upright-growing, becoming pyramidal in shape

Magnolia salicifolia. Although it is not as flamboyant as other *Magnolia* species, the willowleaf magnolia flowers reliably each year over several weeks with the flowers tolerant of a few degrees of frost. The flowers and the foliage are scented, the foliage particularly so when rubbed between the fingers. The scent is that of aniseed. Photo by Jim Gardiner.

and increasing by up to 60 cm (2 ft.) per year. They can be single-stemmed or multistemmed and reach 15 m (50 ft.) or more in sheltered environments in the south of England. The foliage gives off a most distinctive scent. The leaves and young shoots, when crushed, smell of aniseed and lemon verbena. The leaves are oblong lanceolate or elliptic in shape and up to 14 cm (5½ in.) long by 5 cm (2 in.) wide. They are green above and glaucous green below. The fragrant, pure-white flowers, often with a pale pink streak at the base of the tepals, open during mid-March and early April on slender leafless stems from an early age. They generally consist of six tepals which, on opening, are held vertically before reflexing to the horizontal and tend to nod over as they open fully to 10.0–12.5 cm (4–5 in.) wide. The three strap-shaped outer tepals are about 3.8 cm (1½ in.) long. The fruiting cones are small and cylindrical in shape, to 7.5 cm (3 in.) long, and are seen in early October. They are rose-pink in colour but soon fade to dull brown.

A fastigiate multistemmed form was described by J. G. Millais in *Magnolias* (1927) as *Magnolia salicifolia* var. *fastigiata*; this appears similar in growth, habit, and flower size to *M. ×kewensis* 'Wada's Memory'.

'Jermyns', a large-flowering slow-growing, large shrub, has broad leaves that are distinctly glaucous on the underside. It is very similar in flower and leaf to *M. ×kewensis* 'Iufer', indicating it may well be a hybrid. It was introduced by Hillier Nurseries of Winchester and named after their arboretum near Romsey in Hampshire.

'Mount Hakkoda' is a much broader crowned tree that var. *fastigiata*, with large flowers that open about two weeks later than those of the type and with leaves 12.5 cm (5 in.) long by 6.3 cm (2½ in.) wide. This clone was formerly referred to as *Magnolia salicifolia* var. *concolor*.

'Van Veen' was named after Piet van Veen of Vira Gambarogno, Switzerland, and introduced by Otto Eisenhut. It was selected for its very fragrant flowers and fine bamboolike foliage.

Magnolia salicifolia prefers to be grown in a moisture-retentive, acid soil and in the British Isles can be grown in full sun or dappled shade. It is quite hardy and in North America is hardy to U.S. hardiness zone 5.

Magnolia ×proctoriana and *M. ×kewensis* have *M. salicifolia* as a parent. For further information on these, please refer to chapter 7.

Magnolia sargentiana
SARGENT'S MAGNOLIA

Magnolia sargentiana develops into a large, upright tree and is native to the Chinese provinces of northern and western Yunnan and Sichuan. The species was first discovered in 1869 by Père Jean Pierre Armand David, a French missionary and naturalist, near Mupin. David made three great journeys of exploration. The first, to Mongolia, was of little botanical importance. The second, between 1868 and 1870, was of great significance. It was the first scientific journey that was made through the great alps that border Tibet (Xizang Zizhiqu). From Beijing David travelled to Chongqing (Chungking) on the Yangtze River and then on to Chengdu (Chengtu), the capital of Sichuan. On 22 February 1869 he travelled to Mupin, the small independent state on the border of Tibet, where he made his headquarters and remained there until August of that year. In his third journey, between 1872 and 1874, he travelled from Beijing to Henan and Shaanxi Provinces, primarily in search of rare birds and animals, and from there southeast to Jiangxi and Fujian Provinces. During August 1873 he was diagnosed with "intermittent fever" (malaria) and became so ill that by November was given the last sacrament. He recovered, however, to eventually return to France via Shanghai in the summer of 1874.

Ernest Wilson re-discovered the species in 1903 and first collected seed in 1908. He never saw the species in flower. The Chinese who collected for him said the flowers were rose-red to rose-pink in colour and about 20 cm (8 in.) wide. Wilson found it growing in thickets and moist woods on and to the west of the Wa Shan in western Sichuan at an altitude between 1500 m (5000 ft.) and 2000 m (6500 ft.). He sent it to the Arnold Arboretum, Jamaica Plain, Massachusetts, where it was first raised in 1909. It was named after Charles Sprague Sargent, director of the arboretum.

Over the next few years a number of Wilson's Chinese magnolias were introduced to the Arnold Arboretum, but problems arose in keeping young plants alive, especially during the severe winters often experienced in eastern North America. Sargent decided to ship all these young plants to Chenault's Nurseries in Orleans, France, to be propagated. In a letter of 3 July 1913 to Léon Chenault, he proposed:

[To] send to you this autumn the entire stock of these plants with the understanding that you will propagate them as largely as possible and then after you have got up a stock of them, return to us a couple of plants of each species, reserving others for yourself.

Sargent's gamble paid off. Plant introduction records from the Royal Botanic Gardens, Kew, show that Chenault must have distributed a plant of *Magnolia sargentiana* immediately after receiving the consignment from the Arnold Arboretum. He also distributed grafted plants to Kew in 1918.

Magnolia sargentiana grows very large. Wilson reported seeing a tree 24 m (80 ft.) tall whose trunk 1.8 m (6 ft.) from the ground was 3 m (10 ft.) in girth and was clean for 5 m (16 ft.) before the branches commenced. The branches were very numerous and wide-spreading, forming a massive head of flattened-oval contour. In the southwest and south of England large rather spindly and twiggy trees of 15 m (50 ft.) or more can be found; these are about 40 years old. The glossy green leaves are extremely variable in shape and up to 18 cm (7 in.) long by 10 cm (4 in.) wide. They are generally obovate and are rounded or occasionally notched at the apex. The underside is grey-green in colour and is covered with downy hairs.

The flowers are slightly frost tender as they tend to shed their protective perules during the autumn and winter. The 10–12 tepals are a deep pink colour on the outside and a very pale pink on the inside. The 20 cm (8 in.) flowers, which open during March and April, hang down like "the fringe of a tassel until the tepals recurve upwards and outwards," similar in fact to *Magnolia dawsoniana* but differing primarily in having more tepals than *M. dawsoniana*, 10–12 as opposed to 9–10. In the British Isles the flowers are sparingly produced and do not put on a good show. They have a subtle, almost medicinal fragrance. Seedlings take up to 25 years before they start to flower but budded plants flower between 10 and 15 years. The fruiting cones are cylindrical, between 10 cm (4 in.) and 12.5 cm (5 in.) long, and initially a dark red colour.

Magnolia sargentiana prefers a sunny site with other woodland plants and needs a moist, humus-rich, acid soil. It is quite hardy, despite its exotic appearance, roughly equating with U.S. hardiness zone 7. Plants and flowers are not particularly wind tolerant and require protected sites if they are to thrive.

Magnolia sargentiana var. *robusta*

Magnolia sargentiana var. *robusta* is sufficiently distinct to merit individual attention. Ernest Wilson saw this plant in fruit but not in flower during his fourth and last expedition to China in 1910. He discovered it on the Wa Shan in western Sichuan, some 48 km (30 mi.) to the east of where he collected *M. sargentiana*, growing at an altitude of 2300 m (7600 ft.). It was one of the plants that Sargent handed over to Chenault for propagation. To a horticulturist's eye, this variety is distinctly different from the species in habit, in flower size and quantity, in time taken for the plants to produce flowers, and in tolerance to climatic conditions.

In cultivation in the south and southwest of England, *Magnolia sargentiana* var. *robusta* forms a wide-spreading, bushy tree to about 12 m (40 ft.) tall and wide, with branching occurring a few feet above ground level. The leaves—generally found at the end of the shoots—are variable, being oblong-obovate, with many having a distinctive notch at the apex. They measure up to 20 cm (8 in.) long by 9 cm (3½ in.) wide and are grey-green on the underside, pubescent at first becoming glabrous. The flowers are seen in large numbers, the sickle-shaped buds opening slightly earlier than those of *M. sargentiana* to reveal beautiful flowers up to 30 cm (1 ft.) wide with 12–16 rich rose tepals deepening to rose-crimson at the base and pale pink to white on the inside. They vary in colour of flower from clone to clone, from white to pink to a rich rose-purple. Those that are white-flowered are regarded as *M. sargentiana* var. *robusta* 'Alba'. They open in a nodding position, but as they unfold bend over to present their full faces. In *Trees and Shrubs for the Milder Counties* (1948), W. Arnold Forster wrote of seeing *M. sargentiana* var. *robusta* flowering for the first time at Caerhays in Cornwall:

> The flowers formed with 12 tepals are semi-pendulous at the ends of the spreading branches and in size appear to be about 20–30 cm (8–12 in.) in diameter, in colour pale rose-purple shading to pale pink at the tips. Looking up into the bloom, they appear like open parachutes of coloured paper, their beauty accentuated by black scales of unopened or partly opened buds.

The flowers are slightly fragrant, with a scent that has been likened to that of wintergreen. The plants flower from a comparatively early age, even if seedling raised, with upwards of 11 years being cited. A mature specimen in full flower, with the sheer weight of blooms bowing down the branchlets, is one of the most spectacular flowering trees. The fruits are larger and more prolific than those of *M. sargentiana*, being oblong in shape up to 20 cm (8 in.) long.

Whereas *Magnolia sargentiana* is comparatively intolerant of wind and frost, *M. sargentiana* var. *robusta* will stand up to greater levels of exposure and cold with no die back being seen. Flowers, however, will not tolerate frosty conditions but will tolerate temperatures to −10°C (14°F) when still in bud.

With the variation in flower colour it is inevitable that there are several named clones in cultivation. 'Blood Moon' has flowers that are larger and a darker crimson than those of any other clone. The original tree is found at the Strybing Arboretum, San Francisco, and was originally distributed by Edwards Nursery of Palo Alto, California.

'Chyverton Dark Form' and 'Chyverton Pale Form' were selected by Nigel

Magnolia sargentiana var. *robusta*. The flowers of this spectacular Chinese tree magnolia appear "like open parachutes of coloured paper." The "classical" shape and colour are captured here in the garden of Michael Galsworthy at Trewithen in Cornwall. Photo by Jim Gardiner.

Magnolia sargentiana var. *robusta* 'Blood Moon'. The original plant grows in the Strybing Arboretum in San Francisco and is noticeably hardier than the type. 'Blood Moon' is probably the darkest seedling of var. *robusta*. It is seen here in the collection of Otto Eisenhut in Ticino, Switzerland. Photo by Dr. Helmut Orth.

Holman of Chyverton, Zelah, Cornwall. The former has deep purple buds, while the latter has very large white to pale pink flowers.

'Marjorie Congreve', with very large pure pink flowers, and 'Multipetal' are two of fifty seedlings raised and growing at the garden of Ambrose Congreve at Mount Congreve, Waterford, Ireland. The latter lives up to its name, having 19–27 tepals per flower. The pale pink outer six tepals are cup-shaped, reflexing backwards, while the remainder retain an upwards poise similar to a gardenia. Sir Peter Smithers named this clone in 1983. Another multi-tepalled plant of *Magnolia sargentiana* var. *robusta* can be found at Broadleas, Devizes, Wiltshire, the home of Lady Anne Cowdray. This, however, has pale flowers with reflexing tepals similar in poise to *M. sargentiana*.

Magnolia sargentiana var. *robusta* is the parent of several fine hybrids (see chapter 7). Examples that are well worth growing are *M.* 'Princess Margaret' and *M.* 'Michael Rosse' (see under *M. campbellii* in chapter 7), *M.* 'Ann Rosse' (see under *M. denudata* in chapter 7), *M.* 'Mark Jury' (see Jury hybrids in chapter 7), and *M.* 'Treve Holman' (see under *M. campbellii* hybrids in chapter 7).

Magnolia sieboldii

This large, broad-spreading shrub is native over a wide geographic area, being found in the forests of Japan on the islands of Honshu, Shikoku, and Kyushu, and in Korea, southwest Manchuria, and the Chinese provinces of southern Anhui in the Hwang Shan, Fujian, and Guangxi, and cultivated in Lu Shan mountains of Jiangxi. Arthur deCarle Sowerby collected the species in southern Manchuria, where it grew in stream valleys throughout the hills surrounding Shenyang, probably the most northerly location of an Asiatic species. Ernest Wilson also found it, in 1918, in the forests of Korea. He reported:

> It delights in rocky, granite country and is specially happy by the side of forest streams. On the Diamond Mountains in northeast Korea, where the winter temperature is more severe than in Massachusetts, this lovely magnolia is a feature, and I have hopes of this Korean form being a better garden plant than the Japanese one now in cultivation.

The Magnolia Society on their 34th Annual Meeting in South Korea in April 1997 saw *Magnolia sieboldii* in the Chirisan National Park overhanging a boulder-strewn streamside at 900 m (3000 ft.). It was still leafless at the end of April.

This species is thought to have been introduced into the British Isles first to Veitch's Coombe Wood Nursery somewhere between 1879 and 1888 and then to the Royal Botanic Gardens at Kew, from the Yokohama Nursery Company, in 1893. It is a large shrub of a broad-spreading habit. Given ideal conditions (a moisture-retentive acid loam in semi-shade), it grows quite vigorously. J. G. Millais cited a plant in his garden in Sussex that measured 6.7 m (22 ft.) tall by 6.4 m (21 ft.) wide within 15 years, which must be quite exceptional. In less favourable locations up to 30 cm (1 ft.) of growth per year may be expected, with plants reaching 1.8 m (6 ft.) tall and wide after 10 years.

The leaves are obovate or elliptic in shape, 15–18 cm (6–7 in.) long by 12 cm (5 in.) wide, and are glaucous green and downy beneath, especially when young. The sheer beauty of the species is to be found in the nodding flowers, which are held sufficiently stiffly to "look you in the face" but can also be pendent, and are most prolific from late May to early June onwards for about six

Magnolia sieboldii. This species is sweetly scented with a wide geographic spread in China, Japan, and Korea. The Korean form, pictured here, has the most vivid magenta boss of anthers, while the Japanese clone is either yellow or rose-pink in colour. Photo by Jim Gardiner.

weeks. The flowers still show during late June and early July and sometimes again in early August. They are probably the purest white of all the magnolia flowers. The nine tepals, three of which are reflexed, are up to 10 cm (4 in.) wide. Those flowers that are pendent tend to have concave tepals, while those that are nodding are less so. The tepals contrast most vividly with the ring of stamens, which vary in colour from a yellow and rose-pink (both Japanese) to deep crimson, with the latter thought to be from Wilson's Korean introduction of 1918. The yellow form comes from Mount Yoshino in Nara Prefecture, Honshu, at 1370 m (4500 ft.). The flowers are fragrant, especially at dusk. Plants flower young, from five years old. Small pink fruiting cones, 7.5 cm (3 in.) long, can be seen during late September.

The flowers of *Magnolia sieboldii* are associated with the Japanese tea ceremony, which often consists of a single blossom with foliage in a simple container. The guests kneel or sit cross-legged on the floor so that the pendent flower in its container, when mounted on the wall, is seen from below.

The hardiness of this species has been questioned, with instances of dieback being reported. From my experience, the species is quite hardy in the British Isles when planted in suitable sites. Temperatures of −17°C (1°F), equivalent to U.S. hardiness zones 6–7, have not caused dieback. This hardiness has been substantiated in North America, where temperatures as low as −23°C (−9°F) have been quoted. *Magnolia sieboldii* has also been recommended as the most suitable magnolia for cultivation in Scandinavia. Here mature specimens have been known to withstand a temperature of −39°C (−38°F), with the ground frozen to a depth of 90 cm (3 ft.), for up a week. The plants suffered no adverse effects and flowered the following August. What affects flowering is when plants coming into leaf with visible flower buds are frosted. No flowering occurs during that season.

Opinions vary as to the soil type preferred by *Magnolia sieboldii*. Some claim it is a lime-hater, others that it is reasonably tolerant of lime. I see no reason why this species will not grow in alkaline conditions if provided a moisture-retentive soil and a sheltered semi-shaded site, although it will flourish more freely in acid soil.

Magnolia sieboldii has been studied by Ueda (1980) who concluded that the Japanese and Chinese form with rose-pink and yellow stamens with a more procumbent habit should be regarded as *M. sieboldii* subsp. *japonica*, while the Korean and Manchurian form should be known as *M. sieboldii* subsp. *sieboldii*. Korean plants appear to have the more prominent crimson stamens with flowers that are more open (not so concave) and nodding. They also appear to be more vigorous, with an open habit and not as compact as the Japanese clones. Korean clones are almost certainly hardier.

'Genesis', a colchicine-induced tetraploid, produces a tightly branched vigorous medium-sized shrub with flowers that are of a heavier texture than normal. It flowers over a long period from late May to early or mid-July in southern England. The flowers and leaves are typical of the Japanese form. This clone was raised by August Kehr of Hendersonville, North Carolina, and registered in 1985.

'Harold Epstein' is a semi-double to fully double form registered by August Kehr in 1993.

'Kwanso' is a fully double form with up to 36 tepals.

'Semi-Plena' is one of many multi-tepalled forms.

'White Flounces' is a double-flowered form with 16–24 tepals that are flat instead of cup-shaped. This seedling was selected and named by Harry Heineman of Scituate, Massachusetts.

Magnolia sieboldii 'Genesis'. This colchicine-induced clone from August Kehr of Hendersonville, North Carolina, flowers over a six- to seven-week period from late May in southern England. Photo by Jim Gardiner.

Magnolia sieboldii is also the parent of *M.* 'Charles Coates (see under *M. tripetala* in chapter 7), *M.* ×*wieseneri* (chapter 7), and other hybrids (see under *M. sieboldii* hybrids in chapter 7).

Magnolia sieboldii subsp. *sinensis*

This attractive broad-spreading large shrub is native to the Chinese province of western Sichuan, where Ernest Wilson first discovered it growing "amongst miscellaneous broad-leaved deciduous trees and shrubs, rhododendrons and silver firs at an elevation from 2130 m (7000 ft.) to 2740 m (9000 ft.) on and around

Magnolia sieboldii subsp. *sinensis*. Originally regarded as a species in its own right, this beautiful large shrub was introduced to Western gardens by E. H. Wilson in 1928. It is widely grown throughout the British Isles and is seen here at Branklyn near Perth, Scotland. Photo by Jim Gardiner.

the moist woodlands of the Wa Shan." It was one of the Chinese magnolias distributed by Professor Sargent to Léon Chenault for propagation. It did not arrive in the British Isles until 1928, as the introduction made earlier via Chenault's Nurseries was either *Magnolia globosa* or *M. wilsonii*.

In cultivation this subspecies grows into a rather straggly shrub to 6 m (20 ft.) tall and wide. It puts on 30–46 cm (12–18 in.) of growth per year when younger. The bark is a distinctive fawn colour. The leaves are obovate or elliptic in shape and rounded or acuminate at the apex. Measuring up to 21 cm (8½ in.) long by 13 cm (5 in.) wide, they have a distinctive dense coating of silvery silky hairs on the underside and along the topside of the midrib when young. They are tough and leathery with very "prominent" veins.

The fragrant flowers are pendent, initially cup-shaped, to 12.5 cm (5 in.) wide, and composed of nine tepals in three layers. In the British Isles they appear on leafy shoots in late May and early June and produce a secondary flush in August. The visual appeal of the flowers is enhanced, as it is in *Magnolia sieboldii*, by the dramatic colour contrast of the white tepals with the ring of crimson stamens. The fruiting cones are 7.5 cm (3 in.) long, pendant, and pale pink, turning to brown with age.

There has been much debate on whether this should be regarded as a species (*Magnolia sinensis*) or a subspecies of *Magnolia sieboldii*. Most recently Stephen Spongberg (1998) treated it as a subspecies, while Ueda (1980) suggested it should remain as a separate species. My assessment is that it should be treated as a subspecies. There is greater similarity between the Korean *M. sieboldii* and *M. sieboldii* subsp. *sinensis*, while the Japanese *M. sieboldii* subsp. *japonica* is distinctly different—small and more compact. Dick Figlar of Pomona, New York, has pointed out to me that Chen and Nooteboom (1993) confirmed his views that a little-mentioned character, the length of the pedicel (the node immediately beneath the perianth scar), differentiates *M. sieboldii* from *M. sieboldii* subsp. *sinensis*. The pedicel of the species is 0–2.8 mm long, while that of subspecies *sinensis* is 13–17 mm. The limited examples checked in Wisley concur with these findings.

Magnolia sieboldii subsp. *sinensis* is at home in either acid or alkaline soil, as long as it is moisture retentive and mulched regularly. Many regard it as best sited in full sun, but although this may be so in areas of high rainfall or high atmospheric humidity, dappled shade certainly suits it better in areas of low rainfall or high summer temperatures coupled with high light levels. It is hardy to U.S. hardiness zone 6.

'Findlay's Form', a selection found in Scottish gardens, has particularly large pendent flowers and a strong second flush during August.

'Grandiflora' is similar to 'Findlay's Form' and is found in several southwest English gardens.

'Ursula Grau' is a seedling with semidouble camellia-like nodding flowers, which are seen earlier than those of *Magnolia sieboldii* subsp. *sinensis*—in May. It has a strong second flowering in August.

Magnolia sprengeri

Two distinct forms of *Magnolia sprengeri* are grown today: the pink-flowered *M. sprengeri* var. *sprengeri* from western Hubei and eastern Sichuan at altitudes of 1310–1800 m (4300–6000 ft.), and the white-flowered *M. sprengeri* var. *elongata* from western Hubei at 910–1200 m (3000–4000 ft.).

One of the doyens of botanical exploration in China was undoubtedly Ernest Wilson, a Gloucestershire man, who trained at the Birmingham Botanical Gardens and attended evening classes at the Birmingham Technical School, where he won the Queen's Prize in Botany. In 1897 he left Birmingham to take up an appointment as a gardener at the Royal Botanic Gardens, Kew. He continued his botany studies by attending courses at the Royal College of Science. This enthusiasm for botany led him to leave Kew in 1898 to study at the Royal College full time. It was at this time, however, that the nursery firm of James Veitch and Sons of Chelsea asked Sir William Thiselton-Dyer, the director of Kew, to recommend a suitable plant collector to travel to China. Wilson was recommended and for a salary of £100 a year plus expenses he agreed to travel to China and collect for the firm. He made two expeditions for Veitch, from 1899 to 1902 and then from 1903 to 1905. It was on his first trip that he travelled to China via the United States, where he met Professor Charles Sprague Sargent, director of the Arnold Arboretum. Wilson recalled that his first meeting took place under the shadow of the large pig-nut hickory on Bussey Road in the arboretum.

> After the formal greetings he pulled out his watch and said, "I am busy now but at 10 o'clock next Thursday I shall be glad to see you." Good

Magnolia sieboldii subsp. *sinensis* 'Grandiflora'. This particularly large-flowered cultivar is widely planted in western England in Devon and Cornish gardens. Photo by John Gallagher.

Magnolia sprengeri var. *elongata*. Not often seen in collections this sister of the goddess magnolia is less flamboyant but deserves attention because of its flowers, which are like water lilies, and its upright growth habit. Photo by John Gallagher.

morning! I voted him autocrat of the autocrats, but when our next interview took place, I found him the kindliest of the autocrats.

This marked the beginning of Wilson's long association with Sargent and the Arnold Arboretum, until his death in 1930, initially as their collector during 1906–1908 and again in 1909–1911, then as assistant director, and later, on Sargent's death in 1927, as keeper.

On his first expedition to China, for which the primary objective was to find *Davidia involucrata*, Wilson collected seed of what turned out to be both forms of *Magnolia sprengeri*. In a manuscript that remained incomplete at the time of his death, Wilson wrote that he "sent seeds (W. 688) packed in earth but unfortunately mixed with them seeds of another magnolia having identical fruits but white flowers." Wilson at first thought he had found the wild type of *M. denudata*, which has 9 tepals instead of 12. These seeds, from plants found in September 1901 growing in woodland south of Yichang (Ichang) in western Hubei, went to Veitch's Coombe Wood Nursery, where a number germinated and were subsequently lined out.

When Sir Harry Veitch decided to retire in 1913, he closed the business. Wilson's herbarium material was sent to Kew and Veitch's plants were sold at the Coombe Wood Nursery site at Kingston upon Thames in Surrey. This group of magnolias collected under Wilson 688 had not flowered and were bought by J. C. Williams (Caerhays), the Honourable H. D. McLaren (Lord Aberconway—for Bodnant), and the Royal Botanic Gardens, Kew. Plants at Bodnant and Kew on flowering had white flowers, although the Bodnant plant has quite a distinct rose-pink to purple streak on the outside of the tepals, while the Kew plant was slightly smaller with hardly any pink. The leaves were similar in both instances. The Caerhays plant, when it flowered, was quite distinct with flowers of great beauty in rich pink approaching crimson. When flowering stems were sent to Kew to be featured in *Curtis's Botanical Magazine*, it was obvious this was a species new to cultivation. Otto Stapf, at the suggestion of J. E. Dandy of the British Museum, looked at herbarium material collected by Silvestri, an Italian missionary, which had been named and described by Renato Pampanini as *Magnolia sprengeri*. Thus the white-flowered form became *M. sprengeri* var. *elongata*, and Stapf described the Caerhays plant as *M. sprengeri* var. *sprengeri* 'Diva', the goddess magnolia.

Magnolia sprengeri var. *elongata* differs from *M. sprengeri* var. *sprengeri* 'Diva' in several ways. It is less vigorous, developing into a small multistemmed tree of between 6 m (20 ft.) and 9 m (30 ft.), depending on the site, with oblong-obovate leaves to 15 cm (6 in.) long and nearly 7 cm (2½ in.) wide, with hairs along the midrib. The flowers have 10–12 white or creamy white tepals that can be flushed or streaked with rose-pink to purple at the base; they are delicately held, opening like miniature water lilies to 12.5–15.0 cm (5–6 in.) wide. Although overshadowed by its more flamboyant sister, *M. sprengeri* var. *elongata* should not be overlooked. It is well suited to areas where space is limited.

Stephen Spongberg (1998) agrees that the white form is properly called *Magnolia sprengeri* var. *elongata*, but refers to the pink form as *M. sprengeri* var. *sprengeri*, and reserves the name *M. sprengeri* var. *sprengeri* 'Diva' for the original plant grown by J. C. Williams at Caerhays Castle.

Magnolia sprengeri var. *sprengeri* 'Diva' develops into a medium-sized, broad-spreading tree that can reach 15.25 m (50 ft.) tall in southwest England and have a spread in excess of 9 m (30 ft.). The green leaves, which unfurl as the last flowers start to fall, are obovate in shape, nearly 18 cm (7 in.) long by 11.5 cm (4½ in.) wide, and have a silvery pubescence, especially on the midrib on the underside of the leaf. The slightly fragrant 15–20 cm (6–8 in.) flowers appear during March and April and are a beautiful deep rose-pink or purple-pink on the outside and pale pink streaked with darker lines on the inside. The flowers are saucer-shaped, and the 12 tepals have a tendency to curl upwards and inwards at the tip. The flowers are prolifically produced and borne almost down to ground level. The original plant took 19 years to flower from seed, but grafted plants can be expected to flower in fewer than 10 years. In western North America, 'Diva' fruits readily, producing fruiting cones 15 cm (6 in.) long. The seed germinates readily and is often used as a rootstock. This magnolia flourishes in a moisture-retentive acid soil, in a sunny yet sheltered site. In the United States it is highly regarded because of its hardiness; it is reported to have withstood temperatures of –27°C (–18°F) in Michigan, which equates to U.S. hardiness zone 5.

Magnolia sprengeri var. *sprengeri* 'Diva' has produced several attractive seedlings differing in flower colour but regarded as the same taxon.

'Burncoose', a small to medium-sized tree, is similar in habit to the original but with 17.5 cm (7 in.) rose to red-purple flowers. The original plant is at Burncoose & South Down Nurseries, Redruth, Cornwall.

Magnolia sprengeri var. *sprengeri* 'Diva'. The goddess magnolia was the only pink-flowered seedling from the batch Wilson 688 sold at Veitch's closing down sale in 1913. It was purchased by J. C. Williams of Caerhays Castle in Cornwall. Photo by Jim Gardiner.

'Claret Cup', a small to medium-sized tree, has scented 20 cm (8 in.) saucer-shaped rosy purple flowers with inner surfaces paler and fading to white as the flower opens. The 12 or 14 tepals are arranged in three whorls of 4, with up to 6 in the inner whorl. Lord Aberconway exhibited a plant in 1963 growing at Bodnant.

'Copeland Court' is a small to medium-sized broad-spreading tree with 20 cm (8 in.) deep clear pink, shaded crimson flowers, paler within, with 12–14 tepals. This clone originated as a seedling given to Bishop Hunkin by George Johnstone, and planted in the grounds at Lis Escop, Truro. The grounds were sold to the Copeland family, who donated the property to the Truro Cathedral School as a hall of residence and renamed it Copeland Court.

'Eric Savill', a small to medium-sized tree, has 17.5–20.0 cm (7–8 in.) deep wine-red flowers with 12 tepals that are rich pink fading to pink inside. The outer tepals tend to flop. The original seedling, from Caerhays as *Magnolia sprengeri* var. *sprengeri* 'Diva', took 17 years to flower in the Savill and Valley Gardens and it was named after the creator of the garden by John Bond in 1982.

'Marwood Spring' is a small to medium-sized upright-growing tree. The 15 cm (6 in.) deep red-purple flowers have 12 tepals and are creamy white flushed purple on the inside. Seed was collected by Michael Hickson, head gardener of

Magnolia sprengeri 'Copeland Court'. This seedling of the goddess magnolia was given to Bishop Hunkin of Truro by George Johnstone of Trewithen, Cornwall. Photo by Jim Gardiner.

Knightshayes in Devon, from a plant growing in the garden of Norman Haddon, Porlock, Somerset. One of the resultant seedlings was given to James Smart of Marwood Hill Gardens, Barnstaple, Devon, and took 14 years to flower.

'Wakehurst', a sister seedling of 'Claret Cup', differs by having darker flowers. They are 17.5 cm (7 in.) in diameter, goblet-shaped, a rich purple on the outside, and rich pink on the inside with 10–12 tepals. Sir Henry Price of Wakehurst Place, Sussex, exhibited this clone in April 1948.

'Westonbirt' is a seedling of 'Diva' raised at Westonbirt, Gloucestershire, in the late 1950s from the original Caerhays plant. Some 40 years from planting, it has developed into a large upright tree approaching 24.5 m (80 ft.)—an astonishing rate of growth for this species. The flowers are a deep pink fading towards the tips of the 12 pointed tepals.

For information on hybrids of *Magnolia sprengeri,* see chapter 7.

Magnolia stellata
STAR MAGNOLIA

The star magnolia is the best known of all *Magnolia* species. It is a slow-growing, rather densely branched shrub (or, occasionally, small tree), which has been cultivated in Japan for centuries. It is native to the mountains of southern Honshu in the prefectures of Gifu, Aichi, and Mie at low altitudes of between 50 m (150 ft.) and 600 m (2000 ft.). It generally grows by the side of streams, by marshy areas near small lakes or ponds, or on hillsides above streams. In moist, marshy areas it grows as a multistemmed shrub, generally to 3 m (10 ft.) but can reach 6 m (20 ft.). On drier slopes, however, it grows as a single-stemmed small tree to 7 m (23 ft.). At low altitude it grows with *Mallotus japonicus, Clerodendron trichotomum,* and *Alnus* spp., but at higher altitudes in Gifu it is found with *Acer pycnanthum* and *Chionanthus retusus* (Chinese fringe tree). It is in this location, not far from Mizunami, that *Magnolia salicifolia* grows in close proximity. In these situations, the intermediate hybrid, *M. ×proctoriana,* can be seen.

The first confirmed introduction of this species into Western gardens was made by George Hall, who, in 1861, brought this species and *Magnolia kobus* back and passed them on to Parsons Brothers, nurserymen of Flushing, New York, for propagation. It is uncertain when or by whom *M. stellata* was intro-

duced into the British Isles. John Gould Veitch and Richard Oldham are reported to have sent plants back in the early 1860s, but more probably Charles
Maries, the English plant collector, introduced it (along with *M. kobus*) in 1877
or 1878.

In cultivation this species forms a dense, twiggy shrub that ultimately
reaches 6 m (20. ft.) tall. Growth varies, depending upon the selection and the
method of propagation. Grafted plants (generally onto *M. kobus*) increase at a
faster rate than plants produced by cuttings. Young rooted cuttings, once established, increase by approximately 30 cm (1 ft.) per year, but after five years
the rate of growth is slower.

The green leaves are elliptic to obovate in shape, measuring 10 cm (4 in.) long
by 5 cm (2 in.) wide. As this species has been cultivated by the Japanese for centuries, a wide diversity of flower size, number of tepals, and colour can be expected. Faintly fragrant flowers open in succession, on leafless stems, over several weeks from late March to early May, depending on site, situation, and
selection. Individual flowers vary in size between 7.5 cm (3 in.) and 10 cm (4
in.) wide, although a vigorous American selection has produced flowers that
can reach as much as 12.5 cm (5 in.) wide. The number of tepals varies enormously from 12 to 40. The colour is generally white or creamy white, though
several forms have a pink flush, especially when the flower first opens. A significant advantage is that the blooms are frost hardy, withstanding several degrees before discolouring. Plants found in the wild vary considerably in colour
from white to deep pink. The plants will flower from 18 months old.

Magnolia stellata needs a moisture-retentive soil in a sunny position if flowering is to reach its potential. It does best in acid soils, but grows in alkaline
soils provided regular mulching is carried out in the autumn or spring. It is quite
hardy, to U.S. hardiness zone 5. Some clones have a still greater frost tolerance;
'Royal Star', for example, withstands temperatures as low as −37°C (−35°F),
which are consistent with U.S. hardiness zone 3.

'Centennial' is an American selection raised at the Arnold Arboretum and
named during the arboretum's centennial year (1972). It is one of several seedlings raised from *Magnolia stellata* 'Rosea' obtained from Veitch's Coombe
Wood Nursery in 1900. Many seedlings were pure white; however, one was the
largest *M. stellata* clone seen. Robert Hebb, then assistant horticulturist at the

Magnolia stellata. The star magnolia is among the most popular for small gardens, producing a dense twiggy shrub that flowers consistently over several weeks. Photo by Jim Gardiner.

Arnold Arboretum, noted the more open flower habit and larger size—14 cm (5½ in.) wide—with 28–33 tepals per flower. It is similar to the British 'Water Lily', with up to 32 tepals, and is a vigorous-growing plant.

'Chrysanthemumiflora' is a clear pale pink multi-tepalled flower, with a darker pink line running the length of the outside of the tepals. Plants I have grown have up to 25 tepals per flower, with tepals appearing at all angles on the flower, from the vertical to the horizontal. This clone is a seedling of *Magnolia stellata* 'Rubra' selected by K. Wada of Yokohama, Japan.

Magnolia stellata forma *keiskei* is very similar to 'Chrysanthemumiflora', though slightly smaller with fewer tepals. It was named after Keisuke Ito, a nineteenth-century Japanese plant collector.

'Dawn', an American selection popularised by Harold Hopkins of Maryland in the 1970s, is described as a good pink with up to 45 tepals on mature plants. He first saw the plant, whose origins were unknown, growing in the garden of Charles McAfee in Bethesda, Maryland. It is rich pink in colour, almost double, and flowers 10 days later than most forms of *M. stellata* towards the end of

Magnolia stellata 'Centennial'. This clone was raised and named by the Arnold Arboretum, Massachusetts, to celebrate its centennial year in 1972. Photo by Jim Gardiner.

March or early April in eastern North America. It is unclear whether this clone, true to name, is in the British Isles. Plants in the British Isles do not conform to this description, either in colour or tepal number, but this may well be because they are as yet too young.

'Jane Platt' is an extremely floriferous rich deep pink flowered clone with up to 30 tepals. This vigorous plant was discovered in the garden of the late Jane Platt of Portland, Oregon, who grew it as *Magnolia stellata* 'Rosea'. Gossler Farms Nursery, Springfield, Oregon, named it 'Jane Platt' for its distinctiveness. Sir Peter Smithers of Vico Morcote, Switzerland, grows *Magnolia stellata* 'Rosea' fine variety, with 32 tepals. He obtained the plant from Wada in Japan and regards it as the finest *M. stellata* cultivar. It has a deep rich pink flower. David Clulow, when he lived at Tilgates in Surrey, grew these alongside one another and pronounced them to be the same clone.

'King Rose' or 'Rosea King' has beautiful soft pink buds opening white with a distinct pink flush to the flower as it opens. The flowers have between 25 and 30 tepals each. This clone was introduced from New Zealand.

Magnolia stellata 'King Rose'. This introduction from New Zealand has flowers that are a soft pink as they unfurl before fading to white. Photo by Jim Gardiner.

'Massey', also known as 'Dr. Massey' or 'Rosea Massey', is similar to 'Rosea' except that it has a darker pink line running over the length of the outside surface of the tepals.

'Rosea' is distinctly paler and smaller than either of the clones mentioned above and with fewer tepals. It has up to 13 flushed pink tepals that fade almost to white as the flower opens fully. Almost certainly the name 'Rosea' has been attributed to more than one clone. This clone was introduced into the United States and the British Isles simultaneously. The Domoto Brothers of Oakland, California, imported plants from Japan soon after 1885, while Veitch imported them into the British Isles in 1893.

Magnolia stellata 'Rosea' fine variety (synonym 'Jane Platt'). Probably the deepest pink of all the *M. stellata* cultivars, 'Rosea' was obtained from Wada's Nursery by Sir Peter Smithers. Photo by Sir Peter Smithers.

'Royal Star', a seedling of *Magnolia stellata* 'Waterlily', has pale silvery pink buds opening to a clear ice white flower with up to 25 tepals. The clone was introduced by John Vermeulen and Sons of New Jersey in 1959–60 from a Long Island seedling raised in 1947.

'Rubra' has several clones in cultivation. All have pale pink (deeper than 'Rosea') tepals, generally up to 14 in number, a characteristic pink-purple line along the back of the tepal, and a degree of scent to the flower. The original clone was introduced by Wada of Yokahama in Japan, while another clone came from F. M. Kluis of Boskoop. The latter has 14 narrow tepals and slightly larger flowers, up to 10 cm (4 in.) wide, and scented.

Neil Treseder in his *Magnolias* (1978) described three distinct American selections of *M. stellata* that bear the name 'Waterlily' (one word). Each is vigorous, carries pink-flushed flowers with more than 30 tepals, and flowers between one and two weeks later than other forms of *M. stellata*. They are all quite distinct from the 'Water Lily' (two words) cultivated in the British Isles, which has no trace of pink in the flower.

Magnolia stellata 'Water Lily'. Four distinct selections bear this name. The clone illustrated here is the one generally grown in the British Isles. Photo by Jim Gardiner.

Magnolia stellata has been hybridised with the closely related Japanese species *M. kobus* to produce *M. ×loebneri* (see chapter 7). It has also been hybridised with *M. liliiflora* to produce the de Vos and Kosar hybrids (see chapter 7) and with *M. salicifolia* to produce *M. ×proctoriana* (see chapter 7).

In May 1991 the Japan Association for Shidekobushi Conservation was established, linking the nine areas where *Magnolia stellata* is found growing in the wild. In two of these areas, surrounding Mizunami and Ena, several plants were transplanted to avoid losses where development of the native stands was taking place. In all locations the number of plants found in the wild is restricted. Evidence from Shidekobushi Conservation highlights the value of maintaining *M. stellata* as a valid relic species and emphasises the uniqueness of the distinct habitats in which plants of *M. stellata* are found growing. Stephen Spongberg in his latest revision (1998) confirms this status.

Magnolia tripetala

UMBRELLA MAGNOLIA

Magnolia tripetala is a small to medium-sized tree growing in the deep rich forests of eastern North America—in the Allegheny region from Pennsylvania southward through the Appalachian and Ozark Mountains, to Florida, Arkansas, Mississippi, and Missouri. It occurs in moist, humus-rich soils and is mainly found in protected ravines, along streams and swamp margins, and on lower mountain slopes to an altitude of 650 m (2200 ft.). It grows with many hardwoods, including *Liquidambar styraciflua* (sweet gum), *Acer rubrum* (red maple), *Liriodendron tulipifera* (tulip tree), and *Betula lenta* (sweet or cherry birch). It was first introduced into the British Isles in 1752, probably in one of John Bartram's consignments to Peter Collinson, who is believed to have first flowered this species at Mill Hill, London, on 24 May 1760.

This upright-growing tree seldom exceeds 12 m (40 ft.) in its native habitat and is often multistemmed, with upright shoots radiating from the base. In the British Isles it is vigorous, with established plants commonly growing 60–90 cm (2–3 ft.) per year. The green leaves, of a thick papery texture, are among the largest in the genus, up to 50 cm (20 in.) long and 25 cm (10 in.) wide; they are broadly oblanceolate, tapering to the apex and the base. This species gets its common name, umbrella magnolia, from the way in which the leaves cluster towards the end of branches. The creamy-coloured flowers are vase-shaped and in the British Isles appear on the ends of leafy shoots during late May and early June. They have 9–16 tepals (usually 12) and when open are up to 20 cm (8 in.) wide. Initially the flowers are held upright like candles, but soon splay open. The name *tripetala* is derived from the three outer reflexed tepals. The tepals are seen rather sporadically, which may not be a disadvantage as this is among the few *Magnolia* species with a disagreeable smell to its flowers, especially evident when brought into a room. The flowers are seen about eight years from seed. The conical fruiting cones are about 10 cm (4 in.) long. Their bright red colour makes them probably the most attractively fruited of the American species grown in the British Isles and can be regarded as this species's best asset.

Despite its tropical appearance, *Magnolia tripetala* is extremely hardy (to U.S. hardiness zone 4). It requires a sunny yet sheltered site and a humus-rich, moisture-retentive soil. The bark may be chewed like tobacco and is said to be a cure for smoking.

Two forms have been selected. 'Bloomfield' was selected by Phil Savage of Bloomfield Hills, Michigan, for it large flowers with up to 16 tepals reportedly of dinner-plate size, and for its leaves measuring 70 cm (28 in.) long by 30 cm (12 in.) wide. This clone was registered in 1974. 'Woodlawn' was selected by Professor Joe McDaniel for its large fruiting cones, which are 12.5 cm (5 in.) long by 5 cm (2 in.) wide and bright red in colour. It was registered in 1974.

Magnolia tripetala is a parent of several hybrids, including *M.* 'Charles Coates' (see under *M. sieboldii* in chapter 7*)*, *M.* ×*thompsoniana* (see chapter 7), and *M.* 'Silver Parasol' (see under *M. obovata* in chapter 7).

Magnolia tripetala. The American umbrella tree is probably the only scented *Magnolia* species that is not agreeable. It gets its name from the three outer reflexed tepals, which are seen clearly in this photograph. The bright red fruiting cones and autumn foliage colour are this magnolia's principal assets. Photo by John Tobe.

Magnolia virginiana
SWEET BAY MAGNOLIA
SWAMP BAY MAGNOLIA

Magnolia virginiana is found over an extremely wide geographic range in the coastal plain and Piedmont regions of eastern North America, between Massachusetts and New York in the North, Georgia and Florida in the South, and Texas, Arkansas, and Tennessee in the West. With such a wide distribution it varies considerably in habit from a large multistemmed deciduous shrub in northern locations to a small evergreen multistemmed tree of 9 m (30 ft.) in favoured locations in the South. The sites vary from wet, sandy, often acid soils along streams, swamps, and flatwoods to moist, rich, deep soils. In its tree form, this species grows with *Acer rubrum* (red maple), *Persea borbonia* (red bay), and *Gordonia lasianthus* (loblolly bay).

The sweet bay was the first magnolia introduced into the British Isles; it was sent to Bishop Compton's garden at Fulham Palace in 1687 by John Bannister.

The aromatic, rather pungent bark was used by Native Americans and early settlers rather like the *Cinchona* (quinine) for rheumatism and fever, or as a stimulant. The fruits were also put into brandy and used as a cure for coughs and other chest ailments.

In cultivation in the British Isles, the sweet bay magnolia is not a particularly strong grower and is generally seen as a straggly shrub or small tree increasing slowly each year. In its native habitat it often forms a small thicket by suckering. A range of forms has been tried in Britain, but none has been entirely successful. To make really strong growth *Magnolia virginiana* seems to need the hot, ripening summers of eastern North America.

The oblong to elliptic leaves are generally up to 12.5 cm (5 in.) long but can be up to 20 cm (8 in.) by 5.0–7.5 cm (2–3 in.) wide;

Magnolia virginiana. The sweet or swamp bay grows more or less the entire length of the United States, from Massachusetts to Florida, and can be deciduous or evergreen. It often grows in swampy ground with beautifully, sweetly scented flowers, for which it gets its common names. The flowers are seen over long periods of the summer months. Photo by Ken Robertson.

they are green above and glaucous white and quite downy beneath. (This characteristic accounted for one of the species's names, *Magnolia glauca*.) The flowers have a rich fragrance, once described as "one of the best outdoor scents—cool and fruity and sweet," but, in the British Isles at least, they make little visual impact. They are small, up to 7.5 cm (3 in.) wide, with 8 (sometimes as many as 12) creamy white tepals that green with age but last for two days only. In its native habitats *M. virginiana* flowers from June until mid-August; in the British Isles, even in southern climes, it flowers rather sporadically during August and September. Fruiting cones are seldom seen in the British Isles but in North America they are an ornamental feature, being crimson in colour with bright red seeds.

There are several clones of *Magnolia virginiana* in cultivation.

'Havener' is a large-flowered fragrant form with cream-coloured flowers showing a hint of pink. The flowers, 11 cm (4½ in.) wide, have up to 20 tepals. This clone was selected by Professor Joe McDaniel from a plant growing in Mt. Pulaski, Illinois.

'Mayer', a burly multistemmed shrub that flowers from an early age, was selected by Professor Joe McDaniel from a plant growing in Champaign, Illinois.

'Ravenswood' is a small multistemmed deciduous tree with very fragrant flowers to 7.5 cm (3 in. wide). It has 11 tepals. This clone was selected from the Ravenswood Park Swamp between Gloucester and Manchester, Massachusetts, the most northern natural population of *Magnolia virginiana*.

In the British Isles a wide range of soils, provided they are moisture-retentive and not hot and dry on the one extreme or waterlogged on the other, can sustain *Magnolia virginiana*. A sunny yet sheltered site is desirable. The northern deciduous forms are quite hardy, to U.S. hardiness zone 5.

Magnolia virginiana has been hybridised with several species. Noteworthy among the hybrids produced are *M. ×thompsoniana* (see chapter 7), and *M.* 'Freeman' and *M.* 'Maryland' (see Freeman hybrids in chapter 7).

Magnolia virginiana var. *australis*

Magnolia virginiana var. *australis* was described by Professor Charles Sprague Sargent of the Arnold Arboretum in 1919 from plants growing in the Carolinas, Florida, and eastern Texas. Professor Joe McDaniel, in an article published in the *Morris Arboretum Bulletin* (1966), detailed several differences between the species and this variety, which I will summarise here. Flowering and vegetative growth of var. *australis* are three to four weeks later than that of the species, starting in late May to early June in the southern United States. The flowers are lemon scented, have paler coloured pollen, and open at sunset, while those of the type species open during the afternoon. In habit the species is generally multistemmed and spreading while var. *australis* has one or two dominant erect growing stems. Generally var. *australis* is evergreen while the species has both deciduous and evergreen forms, but erring towards the deciduous. Finally, the type species is generally hardier than var. *australis*, though several clones of the latter are quite hardy.

Several clones of *Magnolia virginiana* var. *australis* are in cultivation.

'Henry Hicks', a small to medium-sized pyramidal-shaped evergreen tree selected for its hardiness, is claimed to withstand temperatures to −29°C (−20°F). It was selected by Professor Joe McDaniel from a seedling growing at the Scott Arboretum, Swarthmore College, Pennsylvania, and registered in 1967.

'Milton' is a small to medium-sized tree of an upright, almost columnar habit, with long narrow evergreen foliage. It is hardy to −23°C (−9°F) and was selected by Peter Del Tredici of the Arnold Arboretum from a plant growing at Milton, Massachusetts.

Magnolia wilsonii

WILSON'S MAGNOLIA

Magnolia wilsonii, named after its finder, Ernest Wilson, is a broad-spreading, large shrub that comes from the Chinese provinces of eastern Gansu, western Sichuan, northern Yunnan, and western Guizhou. Of its habitat, Wilson wrote:

> This magnolia is quite a common shrub in the woods of western Szechwan [Sichuan], especially around the town of Tachien-Lu [Kangding]. It is found at elevations between 2130 m (7000 ft.) and 2590 m (8500 ft.) on the edge of woods in thickets and more especially along mountain streams, growing with deciduous trees and shrubs, rhododendrons, silver fir, spruce, and hemlock fir. Usually it is a straggling bush anywhere from 3.0 to 4.5 m (10–15 ft.) tall and as much through . . . . It was

discovered by me in the summer of 1904 and introduced into English gardens by seeds which I sent to Messrs. Veitch in the autumn of that year.

These seeds must have failed to germinate, for it was a further 16 years before *M. wilsonii* was introduced into the British Isles. It was collected again by Wilson in 1908, this time for the Arnold Arboretum, which in turn distributed plants to Léon Chenault.

In cultivation this species develops into a multistemmed large shrub, but if judicious pruning is carried out from the beginning, it is possible to grow it as a single-stemmed small tree up to 6 m (20 ft.) tall, increasing by up to 60 cm (2 ft.) a year when young, or by epicormic shoots. *Magnolia wilsonii* can be distinguished at any time of the year by its very dark brown branchlets, which appear almost black after the first year of growth. The leaves are generally elliptic to lanceolate in shape and up to 18 cm (7 in.) long by 10 cm (4 in.) wide. The leaves are quite downy on the underside and are initially pale brown in colour, although they later take on a rather silvery appearance, but always maintain a line of light golden-brown hairs on the midrib.

The geographic variant of *Magnolia wilsonii* coming from the Cang Shan in northern Yunnan is known as *M. taliensis*. Originally collected by George Forrest and latterly seen by Roy Lancaster, it differs from *M. wilsonii* by having leaves that are less hairy beneath, being confined to the midrib, veins, and leaf stalk.

The fragrant flowers open to a cup shape during May and June, are about 10 cm (4 in.) wide, and are more often fully pendent but can also be nodding. Each flower consists of nine pure white tepals with a ring of rich rose-red stamens (not quite as stunning a combination as that of *Magnolia sieboldii*).

Magnolia wilsonii. One of the delights of walking through woodland gardens during late May is to see the pendent pure white blooms of Wilson's magnolia in full flower. The species was named after Ernest Henry Wilson, who was responsible for its introduction, along with five other *Magnolia* species from China. Photo by Jim Gardiner.

In western North America, with its higher prevailing temperatures, flowering takes place earlier, in March and April, and the blooms are often larger, up to 15 cm (6 in.) wide. The fruiting cones are cylindrical in shape and up to 10 cm (4 in.) long; they are pinkish during early October and gradually fade to a dirty brown by mid-November.

Magnolia wilsonii prefers a sheltered semi-shaded site and a moisture-retentive soil, which may be on either the alkaline or the acid side of neutral. In North America it is hardy to U.S. hardiness zone 7, but is not as hardy as *M. sieboldii* subsp. *sinensis* or *M. sieboldii* subsp. *sieboldii*, thereby restricting it to the Pacific Northwest.

'Highdownensis' was given to the late Sir Frederick Stern in a pan of unlabelled seedlings during 1927 by J. C. Williams of Caerhays Castle in Cornwall. When it first came into flower, Stern thought it was *M. globosa*; however, when it was exhibited at the Chelsea Flower Show in May 1937, it was thought to be a hybrid between *M. sieboldii* subsp. *sinensis* and *M. wilsonii* and accordingly named *M. ×highdownensis*. Stephen Spongberg regards it as belonging to *M. wilsonii*, because it is similar to specimens of the species collected in China and because in his opinion it falls well within the range of variation that might reasonably be encountered in cultivation of the species.

What is evident, however, is that whenever this plant is raised from seed, the resulting plants all come uniform and appear to be midway between *Magnolia wilsonii* and *M. sieboldii* subsp. *sinensis*. They have large fragrant, initially cup-shaped flowers that, when they open more fully, are nodding and then pendent. The flowers, composed of white tepals, are of a similar size to those of *M. sieboldii* subsp. *sinensis* and are between 12.5 cm (5 in.) and 15 cm (6 in.) wide. They occur over the same period those of as *M. sieboldii*, from late May to early July. The elliptic leaves to 23 cm (9 in.) long and 11 cm (4½ in.) wide have a hint of fawn hairs on the midrib and petiole. With so many plants, raised both from seed and vegetatively, in gardens in southern and western England being so similar, and certainly more vigorous than the "normal" *M. wilsonii*, it is appropriate to call this *M. wilsonii* 'Highdownensis'. J. E. Dandy gave a full description of this magnolia in the *Journal of the Royal Horticultural Society* (1950).

'Jersey Belle' was shown at the Chelsea Flower Show in 1983 by Mrs. V. Lort-Phillips. Floral Committee B considered it close to *Magnolia wilsonii* 'Highdownensis' and made no recommendation for award. Karl Flinck and Stephen

Spongberg suggested in an article in the journal of the Magnolia Society (1989) that this plant was a hybrid between *M. sieboldii* subsp. *sinensis* and *M. wilsonii* because of the habit and leaf shape (closer to *M. wilsonii*), because the seed parent was known to be *M. sieboldii* subsp. *sinensis*, and because the crinkled hairs on the underside of the leaf were like those of *M. sieboldii* subsp. *sinensis*.

My observations indicate the name *M. wilsonii* 'Highdownensis' should be maintained.

Magnolia wilsonii has been hybridised with *M. obovata* to produce *M.*×*gotoburgensis* (see chapter 7).

Magnolia zenii

This small deciduous tree comes from Jiangsu Province, eastern China, where it grows in mixed woodland at an altitude of 250–300 m (750–1000 ft.) on the Paohua Shan. It is a rare endemic first described by W. C. Cheng in 1933 and subsequently brought into cultivation at the Jiangsu Institute of Botany and Botanical Garden in Nanjing. It was named in honour of H. C. Zen, director of the China Foundation for the Promotion of Education and Culture.

Magnolia zenii was introduced into the West when Professor He Shan-an, director of the Jiangsu Institute of Botany, presented nine seeds to Stephen Spongberg, then of the Arnold Arboretum, and four to Theodore Dudley of the U.S. National Arboretum, both members of the 1980 Sino-American Botanical Expedition to China. Four of the nine seeds sown in February 1981 at the Arnold Arboretum germinated, as did two of those at the U.S. National Arboretum. The first plant to flower did so in 1988 when 3.5 m (11½ ft.) tall outside the Hunnewell Visitor Center at the Arnold Arboretum.

The very fragrant white flowers have rose-

Magnolia zenii. This rare species was introduced into Western gardens by Stephen Spongberg, currently director of the Polly Hill Arboretum, and Theodore Dudley of the U.S. National Arboretum, in 1980, when they were given seeds by Professor He Shan-an of the Jiangsu Institute of Botany. It flowered for the first time outside the Hunnewell Visitor Center at the Arnold Arboretum, Massachusetts, in 1988. Photo by John Gallagher.

purple streaks, marking the outside of the seven tepals to half their length. (The normal number is nine.) Each tepal is up to 8 cm (3 in.) long and pointed. The flowers on opening are candlelike, ultimately opening to an open tulip shape to 12.5–15.0 cm (5–6 in.) wide. In Boston they open during late March and April, which is more or less similar to the southern counties of the British Isles. Plants at Gossler Farms Nursery, Springfield, Oregon, open as early as February. The green leaves are oblong or oblong-obovate up to 16 cm (6½ in.) long and 7 cm (3 in.) wide. The seeds are scarlet, and generally each 7 cm (3 in.) long cylindrical fruit has two seeds in it.

This species is closely related to *Magnolia denudata*, differing in leaf shape and flower size. Both flowers have a streak of rose-purple running half the length of the tepals. This magnolia is hardy to U.S. hardiness zone 5.

CHAPTER SEVEN
Magnolia Hybrids

S INCE 1989, there has been an "explosion" of *Magnolia* hybrids being introduced into cultivation, many of which have found their way into gardens around the world. The list below is by no means comprehensive, so my apologies for not including your favourite hybrid! With the introduction of so many, however, careful selection is needed to ensure distinctiveness. The wide range now available creates an opportunity for magnolias to become increasingly popular to a wider audience, thereby promoting the genus as a whole.

Magnolia acuminata Hybrids

Magnolia hybridisation at the Brooklyn Botanic Garden has spanned some 40 years, with the first trials being carried out by Eva Maria Sperber in 1956. Along with Sperber a small team of researchers, including Lola Koerting and Doris Stone, worked at the Kitchawan Research Station, Ossining, Westchester County, New York. What was particularly interesting about their work was that for the first time an American species and an Asiatic species were used in the breeding programmes. *Magnolia acuminata* was selected as the seed parent for the following qualities which it was hoped would be inherited by subsequent generations: its yellow flower colour, exceptional hardiness, tolerance to a wide range of soil types, variable habit (from a large multistemmed shrub to a large tree), and foliage that is always a "clean" green and often colours a dull bronze red on unfurling. Furthermore, it was anticipated that the progeny would inherit a flowering period midway between precocious-flowering species and the early April flowering of *M. acuminata* (late May to July in cultivation).

The Asiatic species used as pollen parents were *Magnolia liliiflora* and *M. denudata.* The progeny of *M. acuminata* with *M. liliiflora* was named *M. ×brooklynensis* in 1971 and is referred to under its own name. The other breeding programme occurring at the same time used *M. denudata* as the pollen parent. It yielded excellent results, with flowers being of a good yellow colour, size, quality, and quantity. Furthermore, the flowers of these hybrids appeared significantly later than those of the precocious-flowered parent, flowering generally before the leaves started to unfurl. Brooklyn Botanic Garden led the way in 1956 when Eva

Previous pages: A private garden in southern England owned by John Gallagher uses *Magnolia ×soulangeana* and the de Vos and Kosar hybrids to provide a riot of colour in spring. Photo by John Gallagher.

Maria Sperber made an inspired choice and achieved the first yellow-flowered precocious hybrid, 'Elizabeth'.

'**Elizabeth**' (*Magnolia acuminata*× *M. denudata*) is a small to medium-sized multistemmed tree with creamy yellow flowers that are seen over four to six weeks during late April and May in the south of England. This colouration is more intense when seen under stronger light levels such as in South Korea and New Zealand. The specimen at Wisley is a broad-spreading vigorous small to medium-sized tree about 7.6 m (25 ft.) tall and currently growing 45–60 cm (1½–2 ft.) per year. The six to nine tepals, which on the first day of opening are midway between the parents in shape—fuller than *M. acuminata* yet lacking the rounded poise of *M. denudata*—open fully after a few days to 20 cm (8 in.), revealing red stamens. The first flowers are a more "intense" colour, which gradually fades as the flowering season progresses but is quite noticeable when the flowers are seen with the young unfurling leaves that open a dull reddish colour and quickly turn to a dark green upper surface. 'Elizabeth' was named in 1978 in honour of Elizabeth van Brunt, a patron of the Brooklyn Botanic Garden.

Lola Koerting made further crosses in the 1960s (code numbers 11/60 and 11/64). In 1998, Brooklyn named 11/60 'Lois' after Lois Carswell, a past chairman of the Board of Trustees. The nine tepals are 8 cm (3 in.) long and, on opening, are a clear primrose yellow and have the poise of the Asiatic "grandparent." Maurice Foster, who grows a specimen in Kent, tells me that it flowers precociously over four to five weeks from mid-April and that, unlike 'Elizabeth', it does not fade as the season progresses. Foster considers it the best yellow yet. The still unnamed 11/64 is a

Magnolia 'Elizabeth'. When grown in the British Isles, this clone exhibits flowers whose colour is best described as creamy-yellow. In the Chollipo Arboretum, South Korea, where light levels and temperature are generally better at flowering time, the intensity of the yellow colour is noticeably improved, as seen in this photograph. The Chollipo Arboretum contains one of the most comprehensive collections of magnolias in the world. Photo by Jim Gardiner.

peach-coloured hybrid of *Magnolia acuminata* crossed with a *M. denudata* × *M. ×soulangeana* 'Brozzoni' hybrid.

August Kehr has hybridised 'Elizabeth' with *Magnolia ×soulangeana* 'Lennei' to produce **'Gold Cup'** and with *M. ×brooklynensis* 'Woodsman' to produce **'Hot Flash'**. The tetraploid 'Gold Cup' is distinct amongst the yellows and has good cup-shaped flowers that are 15 cm (6 in.) wide. Ultimately it becomes a broadly upright small tree to 6 m (20 ft.). 'Hot Flash' has narrow 12.5 cm (5 in.) deep yellow flowers with a rose flushed base to each tepal. It has an upright habit ultimately developing into a small to medium-sized tree to more than 9 m (30 ft.) tall.

Other than the individuals associated with Brooklyn Botanic Garden, Phil Savage of Bloomfield Hills, Michigan, has contributed to *Magnolia acuminata* being popularised as a seed parent. Savage has hybridised magnolias since the early 1960s and has been active in the Magnolia Society, holding all positions of note. He has been extremely conscious of the lack of hardiness in the flamboyant Asiatic species and has tried to combat this, often very successfully, when linking them with the hardy *M. acuminata*. The first hybrid I grew from Savage was 'Gold Star', and I have corresponded with him since its introduction into the British Isles in 1990. His all-round understanding of the genus, its history of cultivation in the United States, and his knowledge of everyone associated with its cultivation in the United States is particularly inspiring.

Magnolia 'Gold Star'. This Phil Savage hybrid with yellow *stellata*-like flowers and an upright habit eventually grows to a small tree. Photo by Jim Gardiner.

'Gold Star' (*Magnolia acuminata* subsp. *subcordata* 'Miss Honeybee' × *M. stellata* 'Rubra') is an upright-growing small to medium-sized tree. It takes on the habit of its seed parent, yet maintains the side branch network of an open-growing *M. stellata*. It grows quickly, 45–60 cm (1½–2 ft.) per year on young plants. The leaves are elliptic to ovate in shape, bronze red as they unfurl, turning green (paler beneath) as they mature. The creamy yellow starlike flowers opening to 10 cm (4 in.) wide appear in late March and April before the foliage. They have 14 strap-shaped tepals, thus creating a yellow *stellata*. This clone was raised by Phil

Savage of Bloomfield Hills, Michigan, and inevitably will be very hardy, including the flowers, which are frost tolerant.

'**Butterflies**' (*Magnolia acuminata* 'Fertile Myrtle' × *M. denudata*) is a fast-growing small to medium-sized tree with an upright habit. The deep yellow precocious flowers have 10–14 tepals and are midway in shape and poise between the parents. Like the flowers of 'Elizabeth', they have prominent red stamens. This clone was raised by Phil Savage using 'Fertile Myrtle', a free-fruiting clone, with a good form of *M. denudata* obtained from Ken Sawada of Semmes, Alabama.

'**Flamingo**' (*Magnolia acuminata* 'Fertile Myrtle' × *M. sprengeri* var. *sprengeri* 'Diva') is an upright-growing medium-sized tree with rose-pink "flamingo" flowers. It comes into flower well before the foliage; however, the last flowers tend to "fade" as the leaves unfurl. The flowers have an upright tulip shape with the outer tepals reflexed to the horizontal. Tepals are 10.0–12.5 cm (4–5 in.) long. This clone flowered for the first time after 14 years from seed. It is an extremely hardy plant, being unscathed after temperatures as low as −34°C (−29°F), or U.S. hardiness zone 5. It was raised by Phil Savage of Bloomfield Hills, Michigan.

'**Peachy**' (*Magnolia acuminata* 'Fertile Myrtle' × *M. sprengeri* var. *sprengeri* 'Diva') is a fast-growing medium-sized tree, initially upright in habit but spreading with age. The fragrant orange-pink flowers, creamy white on the inside, are quite large, initially tulip shaped but having nine rather floppy tepals that open to 20 cm (8 in.) wide as the first leaves are starting to unfurl in late April or early May. The three outer tepals are a distinctive peach colour. This clone is hardy to U.S. hardiness zone 5. It was raised by Phil Savage of Bloomfield Hills and was registered by Dick Figlar in 1994.

'**Sundance**' (*Magnolia acuminata* × *M. denudata*) is a fast-growing small to medium-sized tree with precocious barium yellow flowers 20 cm (8 in.) wide during late April to early May. Professor Joe McDaniel gave August Kehr seed from this cross, which flowered four years later. '**Sun Ray**', a colchicine-doubled form of 'Sundance', has 10 sets of chromosomes. Its flowers are larger and a deeper yellow than those of 'Sundance' and appear later. '**Golden Sun**' (*M. acuminata* × *M. denudata*) is a strong-growing small to medium-sized tree with yellow flowers similar to those of 'Sundance', though the outer tepals have a definite green colouration. The six tepals reflex to a saucer shape and are 17.5 cm (7 in.) wide. The tree blooms as the leaves open in early to mid-May in Ohio.

It was raised by David Leach of North Madison, Ohio. **'Ivory Chalice'** (*M. acuminata* × *M. denudata*), another hybrid from David Leach, produces 15 cm (6 in.) creamy white to yellowish green flowers over a long period from mid-April onwards. It is also extremely hardy, to –30°C (–22°F).

Magnolia acuminata subsp. *subcordata* has been crossed with *M. denudata* and other species to produce interesting yellow-flowered hybrids.

'Golden Endeavour' and 'Sleeping Beauty' (both *Magnolia acuminata* subsp. *subcordata* 'Miss Honeybee' × 'Sundance') are tetraploid hybrids of 'Sundance.' **'Golden Endeavour'** has heavy textured yellow flowers with a green flush at the base, about 10 cm (4 in.) in diameter, which are produced in tremendous numbers. It is a small round-headed tree to 6 m (20 ft**.**). **'Sleeping Beauty'** (R17-12) is unique for remaining fully dormant for three to four weeks after all other magnolias have flowered and leafed out. It ultimately becomes an upright-growing small tree. Although it may have use as a seed parent, it has no ornamental value.

'Golden Goblet' (*Magnolia acuminata* subsp. *subcordata* 'Miss Honeybee' × *M. denudata*), a cross by David Leach, has the makings of a small to medium-sized pyramidal tree. The tulip-shaped deep yellow flowers to 16 cm (6½ in.) wide are seen during late April.

'Goldfinch' (*M. acuminata* subsp. *subcordata* 'Miss Honeybee' × *M. denudata* 'Sawada's Cream') is an upright-growing small tree with precocious pale yellow flowers seen during late March to mid-April. Its leaves unfurl just as the last flowers are seen. This clone was raised by Phil Savage of Bloomfield Hills, Michigan, and registered in 1989.

'Yellow Lantern' (*Magnolia acuminata* subsp. *subcordata* 'Trade Form' × *M.* ×*soulangeana* 'Alexandrina') is a fastigiate small tree with precocious tall tulip-shaped pale lemon flowers and abundant fruits. The habit suggests it has potential as a street tree. This clone was raised by Phil Savage of Bloomfield Hills, Michigan, and registered in 1985.

Blumhardt Hybrids

Oswald Blumhardt of Whangarei, North Island, New Zealand, has been interested in growing magnolias, michelias, and other members of the Magnoliaceae in his nursery since the 1970s and has been responsible for introducing several fine hybrids.

'**First Flush**' (*Magnolia×soulangeana*'Amabilis' × *M. campbellii*) is an early flowering small tree, with white tepals that are flushed with pink on the lower half of the outside.

'**Star Wars**' (*Magnolia liliiflora× M. campbellii*) is indeed a star performer, flowering for six to eight weeks from mid-March onwards. The 27.5 cm (11 in.) long flowers have 12 rich pink tepals, paler on the upper surface, and very freely borne. The pyramidal outline of the medium-sized tree too is quite distinct, especially when seen in full flower. Blumhardt wrote of this clone in the journal of the Magnolia Society (18/2, 1982):

> At four years, several purplish ones flowered plus one with bright pink blossoms showing only the slightest trace of mauve. It is also the most vigorous plant in the batch, with a

Magnolia 'Star Wars'. More vigorous than its sister seedling 'Early Rose', 'Star Wars' was named for its tepals that point in all directions and for its flowers that are borne freely. It was raised in New Zealand by Oswald Blumhardt in the 1970s. Photo by Dr. Helmut Orth.

Magnolia 'Early Rose'. This sister seedling to 'Star Wars' was raised in New Zealand by Oswald Blumhardt in the 1970s. Photo by Jim Gardiner.

strong central trunk and wide-spreading branches. The flowers are fairly large and the outer tepals are rolled into tubes or spikes sticking out all around the buds and the opening blooms. As they are borne freely and point in all directions, I call the plant 'Star Wars.'

'Red Lion' and **'Early Rose'** are sisters of 'Star Wars' with the flowers of 'Early Rose' slightly smaller and paler.

Magnolia × brooklynensis

This name is given to the *Magnolia acuminata* × *M. liliiflora* cross originally carried out at the Brooklyn Botanic Garden and later repeated by Professor Joe McDaniel and August Kehr. The seedlings of this cross varied in leaf shape, size, and texture, and in flower size and colour. Backcrosses increased the percentage of *M. acuminata* while searching for better yellow flower colours, potentially at the expense of flowers and foliage opening simultaneously.

'Eva Maria' is a multistemmed large shrub or small tree growing about 45–60 cm (1½–2 ft.) a year. The oval leaves have an acuminate apex and a silvery, silky pubescence on the underside. The colour of the tulip-shaped flowers when originally seen was quite unique, being magenta-rose with shades of yellow and green running through the six erect tepals that are up to 10 cm (4 in.) long. In the southern part of the British Isles this clone flowers towards the end of May or early June, while in New York it can flower up to two weeks earlier in early May. This seedling, the first to flower, was named after Eva Maria Sperber and registered in 1968.

'Yellow Bird' (*Magnolia × brooklynensis* 'Eva Maria' × *M. acuminata*) is a small to medium-sized upright-growing pyramidal-shaped tree. The daffodil-yellow flowers have six erect tepals 7.5–10.0 cm (3–4 in.) long. The first cup-shaped flowers show colour just as the young leaves start to unfurl. In the south of England the flowering period begins in mid-May and lasts for three weeks. This clone was raised by Doris Stone at the Brooklyn Botanic Garden in 1967 and registered in 1981.

'Hattie Carthan' (*Magnolia × brooklynensis* 'Eva Maria' × *M. brooklynensis* No. 209) is a second-generation hybrid of *M. × brooklynensis*. It is a large pyramidal-shaped shrub or small tree with greenish yellow flowers and a hint of magenta-rose arising from the base of the tepals. The flowers appear in mid-May, and the tepals are 10–12 cm (4–5 in.) long. Raised in 1968, this clone was named in 1984 in honour of Hattie Carthan, founder of Magnolia Tree Earth Center in Brooklyn and supporter of Brooklyn Botanic Garden.

'**Woodsman**' flowered in 1972 with slightly larger and darker flowers than those of 'Eva Maria'. Professor Joe McDaniel recreated the *Magnolia* ×*brooklynensis* hybrid cross using *M. acuminata* 'Klassen', a large-flowered tree, with *M. liliiflora* 'O'Neill', a compact-growing form with very dark purple flowers. '**Golden Girl**', a hybrid of August Kehr, is similar in most respects to *Magnolia* ×*brooklynensis* 'Woodsman', except the flower colour is a light yellow with only a hint of purple. It is a full sister seedling to 'Woodsman'.

'**Daybreak**' (*Magnolia* ×*brooklynensis* 'Woodsman' × *M.* 'Tina Durio') is potentially a small to medium-sized upright-growing tree. The fragrant flowers have eight rose-pink 12.5 cm (5 in.) tepals that splay out to 23–25 cm (9–10 in.) and appear from an early age. This clone is extremely promising for its habit, rate of growth, and floriferousness. The original tree, now 12 m (40 ft.) tall and only 2.5 m (8 ft.) wide, was raised by August Kehr, who rates it as one of his best hybrids. It was registered in 1991.

Magnolia ×*brooklynensis* 'Hattie Carthan'. This second-generation hybrid was named for Hattie Carthan, who had strong links with the Brooklyn Botanic Garden. Photo by John Gallagher.

'**Gold Crown**' (*Magnolia* ×*brooklynensis* 'Woodsman' × *M.* 'Sundance') is potentially a small to medium-sized tree, upright in habit, with 8–9 golden yellow tepals that open cup-shaped to approximately 20–25 cm (8–10 in.) wide. The foliage is *acuminata*-like to 20 cm (8 in.) long by 15 cm (6 in.) wide with a distinctive wavy margin. This clone was raised from seed by August Kehr in 1984 and flowered seven years later. The flowers are said to be deeper than those of 'Sundance' or 'Elizabeth'.

'**Solar Flair**' (R15-18), '**Stellar Acclaim**' (R15-23), '**Sunburst**' (R16-22), and '**Tranquillity**' (R15-20) are hybrids of *Magnolia* ×*brooklynensis* 'Woodsman' × *M.* 'Gold Star'. They have deep yellow flowers, apart from 'Tranquillity', which has pale yellow flowers with a rose blush at the base. According to August Kehr, who raised these clones, 'Sunburst' is a very floriferous tree that he regards as excellent. The deep canary-yellow flowers have narrow 12.5 cm (5 in.) tepals that open just as the foliage starts to open, so that the tree appears to be covered with candle flames. This magnolia, which ultimately becomes a small tree to 9 m (30 ft.), has a fairly fast growth rate and an upright habit.

'**Ultimate Yellow**' (*Magnolia* ×*brooklynensis* × *M. acuminata*) is potentially a small to medium-sized tree with six yellow tepals that open cup-shaped to 15 cm (6 in.) wide. It was raised by Professor Joe McDaniel and selected by Harry Heineman of Scituate, Massachusetts, in 1991.

Magnolia campbellii Hybrids

I do not doubt that *Magnolia campbellii* has produced and will continue to produce magnificent, fast-blooming hybrids of great quality to adorn our gardens now and in the future. Various breeders around the world have used this aristocrat to great effect for its flower colour and poise and for its habit.

Magnolia campbellii, *M. campbellii* var. *alba*, *M. campbellii* subsp. *mollicomata*, and *M. campbellii* subsp. *mollicomata* 'Lanarth' have all been hybridised either deliberately or, more often than not, by accident in several famous Cornish gardens where splendid specimens are growing and flowering alongside one another.

'**Buzzard**' and '**Hawk**' are seedlings named by Nigel Holman of Chyverton, Cornwall. They were originally given to him from Caerhays Castle and are hybrids of either *Magnolia campbellii* or *M. campbellii* subsp. *mollicomata*. 'Hawk' produces abundant rose-purple flowers during March, which according to Nigel Holman, have the flower colour quality not far removed from 'Lanarth'. 'Buzzard' is similar but not so highly regarded. It got its name when Nigel Holman drew a sketch of its overwintering flower buds for a friend who promptly replied, "It looks as if one of your buzzards had sat on it."

'Philip Tregunna' (*Magnolia sargentiana* var. *robusta* × *M. campbellii*) resulted from seed collected of *M. sargentiana* var. *robusta* growing in Caerhays Castle, Cornwall, in 1960. The 11–12 broad purplish pink tepals open to reveal a paler purplish pink on the upper surface. The flowers are 19 cm (7½ in.) in diameter and are seen during March in the southwest of England. The plant is named after the head gardener of Caerhays Castle.

'Princess Margaret' (*Magnolia campbellii* var. *alba* × *M. sargentiana* var. *robusta*) arose as a seedling of *M. campbellii* var. *alba* sent to the Crown Estate

Magnolia 'Princess Margaret'. Sir Eric Savill was so impressed with the quality and beauty of this seedling of *M. campbellii* var. *alba* that he named it after Her Royal Highness. The sister of Queen Elizabeth II, Princess Margaret takes a keen and knowledgeable interest in plants and gardens. Photo by John Gallagher.

Commissioners at Windsor in the late 1950s. It quickly grows into a small to medium-sized tree that produces cup-and-saucer shaped deep pink flowers fading to cream on the inside of the tepals. The 11 tepals are 27.5–30.0 cm (11–12 in.) in diameter on opening and are seen during mid to late March or early April. When this magnolia was first shown at the Royal Horticultural Society's show in Vincent Square on 17 April 1973, it was labelled as 'Windsor Belle' but because of the huge interest generated by the quality of the bloom, it was decided to rename it 'Princess Margaret'. The flowers of 'Princess Margaret' are slightly deeper coloured with tepals less rounded when compared with those of 'Michael Rosse'.

'**Michael Rosse**' and '**Moresk**' both have a similar origin and parentage to 'Princess Margaret'. 'Michael Rosse' was received as a young seedling of *Magnolia campbellii* var. *alba* from Hillier Nurseries of Winchester, which in turn received seed from Caerhays Castle. It was purchased by the Countess of Rosse and planted at Nymans Gardens in Sussex. The flowers of 'Michael Rosse' are rich pink in colour with a *campbellii* shape. The outer tepals reflex, however, giving the flower a slightly floppy appearance. 'Moresk' takes the locality name of Treseder's nursery in Truro, Cornwall, where it was growing. It is very similar to 'Michael Rosse' and flowers in March or early April.

'**Sir Harold Hillier**' (*Magnolia denudata* × *M. campbellii* var. *alba*) is a small tree that exhibits white goblets of a quite exceptional quality: the flowers are larger than those of the parent, about 25–30 cm (10–12 in.) in diameter. It was grown and named by Nigel Holman at Chyverton.

'**Caerhays Surprise**' (*Magnolia campbellii* subsp. *mollicomata* × *M. liliiflora* 'Nigra') is a small tree resulting from a deliberate cross made by Philip Tregunna, head gardener of Caerhays Castle, in 1959. The plant flowered for the first time in 1967. The 9–12 narrow tepals are soft lilac pink in colour and deeper to red-purple on the underside., They flower on the end of slender arching shoots, almost nodding and looking outwards from an early age. The flowers are about 20–25 cm (8–10 in.) in diameter, and the last one is seen with the unfurling foliage. The flowering season is long, from the end of March until May. With the introduction of *M. liliiflora* into the breeding line, the plant is tolerant of hotter summers than *M. campbellii* subsp. *mollicomata*, thereby widening the planting appeal of this underrated hybrid.

'**Hot Lips**' (*Magnolia campbellii* subsp. *mollicomata* × *M. sprengeri* var.

sprengeri 'Diva') produces pale pink flowers that deepen to an intense maroon base to the outside of the eight tepals, while the inside surfaces are white with a hint of pink. Although sparsely produced, the flowers are seen during later March or early April and measure 20 cm (8 in.) wide. The obovate-elliptic leaves are 23 cm (9 in.) long and wide. This clone was named and registered by Philippe de Spoelberch of Herkenrode, Belgium, in 1994, who considered the name to reflect the "rich voluptuous base of the tepals." He purchased this plant from Dick van Gelderen of Firma C. Esveld in Boskoop, Netherlands, in 1986 as *M. campbellii* subsp. *mollicomata*. Its hybrid origin quickly became apparent when the plant proved quite hardy in Belgium (U.S. hardiness zones 6–7) whereas *M. campbellii* subsp. *mollicomata* is not.

'**Treve Holman**' and '**Mossman's Giant**' are both crosses of *Magnolia campbellii* subsp. *mollicomata* with *M. sargentiana* var. *robusta*. 'Treve Holman' was purchased as a seedling by Treseder's nursery of Truro, and sold to Nigel Holman of Chyverton, Cornwall, in 1964. It grows quickly into an upright-growing medium-sized tree with strong horizontal branches. The 30 cm (12 in.) cup-and-saucer shaped rose-pink flowers (pale pink on the upper) are seen during late March or April in the south of England. The plant is named after Nigel Holman's father, who was responsible for much of the early planting at Chyverton. 'Mossman's Giant', a medium-sized tree, bears enormous 35 cm (13½ in.) cup-and-saucer shaped flowers during March and early April. The pale rose-violet tepals quickly flop over, revealing the creamy white upper surface. Despite their size, they are not profusely seen on the plant. This plant was a chance seedling growing at the Iufer Nursery in Salem, Oregon, and purchased by Frank Mossman of Vancouver about 1963.

'**Eleanor May**' (*Magnolia campbellii* subsp. *mollicomata* 'Lanarth' × *M.* ×*soulangeana*) is a vigorous upright-growing hybrid

Magnolia 'Treve Holman'. One of Cornwall's great gardening enthusiasts, Nigel Holman, purchased a seedling from Treseder's nursery of Truro as he was intrigued by its purported parentage, said to be *M. campbellii* subsp. *mollicomata* × *M.* ×*soulangeana*. When the seedling flowered for the first time, Holman "shed tears of excitement" because of the beauty of the flower. He named it after his father, who built up the plant collection at Chyverton over a 30-year period. Photo by Jim Gardiner.

that flowers in five to seven years. The deep red-purple buds open to a clear red-purple bowl that fades to a silvery purple.

'**Elizabeth Holman**' (*Magnolia campbellii* subsp. *mollicomata* 'Lanarth' × *M. sargentiana* var. *robusta*) was given to Treve Holman of Chyverton by Michael Williams of Lanarth, Cornwall, in 1954 and shown by Nigel Holman in 1988 at the Royal Horticultural Society's February show at Vincent Square. The 11 tepals are a strong reddish purple with a white flush pink on the reverse, and measure about 20 cm (8 in.) in diameter. Holman considers this plant as good as, if not better than, 'Lanarth' in colour and poise.

Magnolia ×*veitchii* is also a hybrid of *M. campbellii* and is referred to under its own name.

Magnolia cylindrica Hybrids

Hybrids of *Magnolia cylindrica* are relatively few. These are highlighted below.

'**Albatross**' (*Magnolia cylindrica* × *M.* ×*veitchii* 'Peter Veitch') is probably the best-known hybrid of *M. cylindrica*. A small to medium-sized tree, it was one of three seedlings raised at the Cornish garden of Trewithen by the head gardener, Michael Taylor, in 1970. In 1974, Peter Borlase, formerly the head gardener at Lanhydrock in Cornwall, was given one of these seedlings by Alison Johnstone, owner of Trewithen. It flowered for the first time in 1981 and was named in 1985, reflecting the size and poise of the large white flowers that appear to "float" on its branches. It is developing into a small to medium-sized tree, being broadly upright in habit with young plants growing up to 64 cm (24 in.) per year. The green leaves are obovate to elliptic, 17.5–20.0 cm (7–8 in.) long by 7.5–10.0 cm (3–4 in.) wide, green above, greyish green and puberulent beneath. The large white flowers, with a hint of pink at the base, are made up of 9–12 broad tepals, each up to 7.5 cm (3 in.) wide and 12.5 cm (5 in.) long, which on opening are cup-shaped, ultimately splaying open to 25–30 cm (10–12 in.) wide and are seen during late March and early April, depending on the season.

'**Fireglow**' (*Magnolia cylindrica* × *M. denudata* 'Sawada's Pink') is a hardy upright-growing, spruce-shaped small tree raised by Phil Savage of Bloomfield Hills, Michigan. The cup-shaped flowers have six tepals 10.0–12.5 cm (4–5 in.) long. They are light pink with a beautiful rich red-magenta flash to the base of each tepal leaching over the lower third. A thin magenta stripe is also present, running the length of each tepal. In the 1970s Phil Savage reversed the cross by hand pollinating *M. denudata* with Krossa's *M. cylindrica*. Vigorous and intermediate seedlings resulted. In habit they are upright and will eventually form a small to medium-sized tree. One seedling selected by Savage has been given the cultivar name '**Lu Shan**'.

'**Leda**' (*Magnolia cylindrica* × *M.* ×*veitchii* or *M. campbellii* var. *alba*) was raised in 1972–73 by Dick van Gelderen of Boskoop in the Netherlands. Mr. van Gelderen was given a seed cone of *M. cylindrica* (the Hillier cultivar now known as *M.* 'Pegasus') by Nigel Holman, who was growing it in his garden at Chyverton, Cornwall. Two seeds germinated, one of which was given to fellow Boskoop nurseryman, Rein Bulk of Bulkhard Nurseries. That seed grew into a small upright-growing tree that flowered at 12 years. Large, very hairy buds burst

Magnolia 'Leda'. The name means "the swan" and was given by Dick van Gelderen of Boskoop when he first saw the flowers in the nursery of Mark and Rein Bulk of Boskoop. This small tree is proving hardy for Vicomte Philippe de Spoelberch, who grows it in his arboretum at Herkenrode, Belgium. Photo by Vicomte Philippe de Spoelberch.

open in late March, revealing a beautiful pure white cup-and-saucer shaped flower to 20 cm (8 in.) wide. The nine pointed tepals are thick-textured. When Rein Bulk and his son Mark first saw the plant in flower, they thought it was a hybrid, possibly with *M. campbellii* var. *alba*. Philippe de Spoelberch of Herkenrode in Belgium also grows 'Leda'. This first-class plant was initially sold to him as *M. cylindrica* in 1984. When it flowered, however, he too thought it was a hybrid, possibly with *M. campbellii* var. *alba*, and it was registered as 'White Lips'. The plant has proved quite hardy, surviving the bad winters of 1985, 1986, and 1987. Its parentage is questioned as de Spoelberch cannot grow 'Albatross' (*M. cylindrica* × *M.* ×*veitchii*) whereas 'Leda' appears much hardier.

Magnolia 'Ann Rosse'. Like so many chance seedlings in British gardens, this one has proved to be a great success for the Countess of Rosse, after whom it was named, at her famous garden of Nymans, in Sussex. Photo by Jim Gardiner.

In the late 1980s *Magnolia cylindrica* (now 'Pegasus') was used as the seed parent by Peter Dummer, propagator at Hillier Nurseries of Winchester, who pollinated it with *M. campbellii* 'Darjeeling'. About a dozen seedlings resulted, which are now in various gardens in the south of England. All are vigorous upright-growing multistemmed potentially medium-sized trees. The tree at the Hillier Gardens and Arboretum has flowered, but none of the three planted at Wisley have. According to Allen Coombes, botanist at the Hillier Arboretum, it flowered in early April with goblet-shaped pink flowers, which were not exceptional. Given the parents of this pedigree, other seedlings may prove otherwise.

Magnolia denudata Hybrids

The best-known hybrid of *Magnolia denudata* is *M.* ×*soulangeana*, which is referred to under its own name. Several other quality hybrids exist.

'Ann Rosse' (*Magnolia denudata* × *M. sar-*

gentiana var. *robusta*) resulted from seed of a plant of *M. denudata* growing at Nymans Gardens, Haywards Heath in Sussex. Sown in the early 1960s, this seed grew into an upright-growing small to medium-sized tree, indicating that it was a hybrid between the two parents which were growing in close proximity. It flowered for the first time after seven years. The tulip-shaped flowers have nine pointed tepals 12.5 cm (5 in.) long, which open progressively over four weeks starting towards the end of March. The outer tepals are rich pink in colour, deepening to a reddish purple; they reflex horizontally, then droop, revealing a pinkish white inner surface. This hybrid was named in honour of the Countess of Rosse.

'Cecil Nice' (*Magnolia denudata* × *M. sargentiana* var. *robusta*), another hybrid from Nymans Gardens, was named after the head gardener at Nymans. The nine broad rounded tepals are a soft pink and almost a warm white within, with just the base of the inner three tepals maintaining a hint of pink. The outer six tepals reflex to an open cup shape.

'Emma Cook' (*Magnolia denudata* × *M. stellata* 'Waterlily') is a reverse cross of 'Pristine' raised by Frank Galyon of Knoxville, Tennessee. It develops into a medium-sized twiggy shrub. The 9–11 tepals are a pale lavender-pink on the outside and pinkish white within; they splay out to 15 cm (6 in.) wide. The flowers are scented and are seen in late March or early April.

'Marj Gossler' (*Magnolia denudata* × *M. sargentiana* var. *robusta*) is an erect fast-growing medium-sized tree with fragrant white flowers with a deep reddish purple base to them. The broad 7–8 tepals splay over to a cup shape, 25–30 cm (10–12 in.) wide, and are nodding. The flowers are seen during mid to late March. This hybrid was raised by Phil Savage of Bloomfield Hills, Michigan, and named after Marj Gossler of Gossler Farms Nursery, Oregon, who sent pollen of *M. sargentiana* var. *robusta* to Savage.

'Pristine' (*Magnolia stellata* 'Waterlily' × *M. denudata*) was raised by Professor Joe

Magnolia 'Pristine'. Professor Joe McDaniel raised this pretty pure white hybrid that is less vigorous than its pollen parent, *M. denudata*, and thus can be used in smaller gardens. The flowers are similar in shape to those of the pollen parent. Photo by Jim Gardiner.

McDaniel. The pure white flowers are held similarly in bud to those of *M. denudata*—erect on side branches. They splay out on or after the second day to 12.5–15.0 cm (5–6 in.) wide, revealing the 9–15 tepals that are smaller and more petite than *M. denudata.* The flowers appear during late March or early April. In habit, this hybrid develops into a broad-spreading medium-sized shrub. It grows about 30 cm (1 ft.) a year.

'Snow White' (*Magnolia denudata* × *M. salicifolia*), also known as 'Wada's Snow White', was introduced into the British Isles by Sir Peter Smithers from the nursery firm of Wada in Japan. It grows into a free-flowering small bushy tree with pure white flowers that open at the end of April or early May. The flowers are intermediate between the two parents, with eight or nine narrow tepals more than 8 cm (3 in.) long. These tepals "sit up" like those of *M. denudata.*

de Vos and Kosar Hybrids

In April 1965, eight cultivars of *Magnolia* were formally named by the U.S. National Arboretum in Washington, D.C. They resulted from a breeding programme carried out 10 years before, initially by Francis de Vos, arboretum geneticist, and continued by William Kosar, arboretum horticulturist. Pollen from *Magnolia stellata* 'Rosea' was transferred to *M. liliiflora* 'Nigra' to produce six of the eight hybrids; 'Rosea' pollen with *M. liliiflora* 'Reflorescens' and *M. stellata* 'Waterlily' pollen with 'Reflorescens' produced the remaining two. *Magnolia liliiflora* 'Nigra' and 'Reflorescens' were selected for their hardiness and late-blooming characteristics, while *M. stellata* 'Rosea' and 'Waterlily' were selected for their habit, prolific flowering, fragrance, and mildew resistance.

All eight resultant hybrids are multistemmed, rounded or conical in habit, and erect in growth habit to about 4.6 m (15 ft.) tall, depending on the cultivar. The leaves vary between ovate to elliptic in shape, averaging 15 cm (6 in.) long by 7.5 cm (3 in.) wide. In eastern North America the flower buds show colour and open just before the leaves appear in late March or April, and continue on leafy shoots into late May or early June in the British Isles; they are generally not worried by late spring frosts. The fragrant flowers are held upright and are either cup-shaped or saucer-shaped; they vary in colour from pale pink through to purple. In North America all eight cultivars flower about three weeks earlier, seem more vigorous, and have a more intense flower colour than plants grown in the British Isles. This better performance is probably due to the more favourable summer temperatures and light conditions to which the North American plants are exposed. In plants grown both in the British Isles and North America, the flower colour and number of tepals appear to vary from year to year, which may be due to environmental conditions. All eight hybrids prefer an open, sunny site and a moisture-retentive acid soil.

The de Vos and Kosar hybrids are affectionately known as the "Eight Little Girls"—named after secretaries who worked at the arboretum or after wives and daughters of staff. The hybrids are listed here in order of flowering. The time of flowering and colour of flowers refers to plants in eastern North America.

'**Ann**' (*Magnolia liliiflora* 'Nigra' × *M. stellata* 'Rosea') is an erect-growing plant that begins to flower during early to mid-April. The erect flowers up to 10 cm (4 in.) wide are red-purple in bud, paling to rich pink-red on opening, paler on the inside of the eight tepals. The sickle-shaped buds bear the *M. liliiflora* trademark.

'**Betty**' (*Magnolia liliiflora* 'Nigra' × *M. stellata* 'Rosea') produces flowers in mid to late April that are large, opening flat, up to 20 cm (8 in.) wide, and have 12–19 tepals; they are red-purple on the outside and white on the inside. In North America this cultivar is the most treelike in habit, while in the British Isles it is shrubby.

'**Judy**' (*Magnolia liliiflora* 'Nigra' × *M. stellata* 'Rosea') has candlelike flowers that open during late April; they are small, up to 7.5 cm (3 in.) wide. The 10 tepals are red-purple on the outside and creamy white on the inside. This slow-growing plant has a fastigiate habit.

'**Randy**' (*Magnolia liliiflora* 'Nigra' × *M. stellata* 'Rosea'), a very floriferous hybrid, flowers during mid to late April. The blooms are up to 12.5 cm (5 in.) wide. The buds, initially held erect, then sickle-shaped, are red-purple externally, paling to a rich pink and white inside; 9 to 11 tepals splay out on opening. 'Randy' is an erect grower with an almost columnar habit.

'**Ricki**' (*Magnolia liliiflora* 'Nigra' × *M. stellata* 'Rosea') produces red-purple flowers that open during late April and are up to 15 cm (6 in.) wide; the 15 tepals are often twisted. It is a vigorous grower with an erect habit.

'**Susan**' (*Magnolia liliiflora* 'Nigra' × *M. stellata* 'Rosea') is a compact grower

Magnolia 'Ann'. An early bloomer, 'Ann' has small, erectly held, scented flowers with an almost columnar habit to the plant. It was named by the U.S. National Arboretum, where de Vos and Kosar worked, and affectionately known as one of the "Eight Little Girls." Photo by John Gallagher.

Magnolia 'Betty'. The flowers are similar in shape to those of 'Randy', opening wide with "twisted" tepals, but are larger to 17.5–20.0 cm (7–8 in.) wide. The plant has a treelike habit in the United States, but is shrubby and compact in the British Isles. Photo by Jim Gardiner.

Magnolia 'Randy'. This plant is extremely floriferous and has a columnar habit. The flowers flare in a similar manner to those of 'Betty' but are smaller in size. Photo by John Gallagher.

Magnolia 'Susan'. Among the de Vos and Kosar hybrids, 'Susan' has the darkest flowers, with red tepals that are sickle-shaped in bud and typical of *M. liliiflora*. The flowers are also sweetly scented. Photo by John Gallagher.

with fragrant flowers in late April. The six red-purple tepals are slightly paler on the inwardly rolled upper tepals. The buds are sickle-shaped.

'Jane' (*Magnolia liliiflora* 'Reflorescens' × *M. stellata* 'Waterlily') is distinguished by its beautifully shaped, very fragrant flowers, red-purple on the outside and white on the inside, which open in early May. The 8–10 tepals measure 10 cm (4 in.) wide. 'Jane' is a strong, vigorous grower with an upright habit.

'Pinkie' (*Magnolia liliiflora* 'Reflorescens' × *M. stellata* 'Rosea') has a compact, rounded habit. It is the latest of these hybrids to flower—from late April to mid-May—and has the palest flowers. The flowers are white inside and pale red-purple outside, up to 18 cm (7 in.) wide, and have 12 tepals.

Magnolia 'Pinkie'. One of the last of the de Vos and Kosar hybrids to bloom, 'Pinkie' flowers over the longest period and is the most distinctive of the group. It has pale pink flowers with broad, thick tepals. Photo by John Gallagher.

Freeman Hybrids

Oliver Freeman of the U.S. National Arboretum, Washington, D.C., pollinated *Magnolia virginiana* with *M. grandiflora* during 1930 from trees growing in the Washington area. Two years later several young plants were lined out in nursery rows; they started to flower some six years after being sown. Despite resembling *M. grandiflora*, the seedlings were quite variable in leaf shape and size of flower, but primarily in their habit.

Two plants were selected and named: '**Freeman**' and '**Maryland**'. Both flower from an early age, inheriting this attribute from *Magnolia virginiana*. They take after *M. grandiflora* in their adaptability to various sites and soils, although they prefer a hot, sunny site in a moisture-retentive soil. Both remained unscathed when temperatures have dropped to −14°C (7°F), equivalent to U.S. hardiness zone 7, in the southeast of England. 'Maryland' develops into a multistemmed wide-spreading large shrub in the British Isles or a small tree in North America. The leaves are similar to those of *M. grandiflora*; they are evergreen, oblong-lanceolate, to 22 cm (8½ in.) long by 9 cm (3½ in.) wide, with undulating mar-

Magnolia 'Maryland'. One of the two named hybrids of *M. grandiflora* with *M. virginiana* raised by the U.S. National Arboretum, Washington, D.C., this cross has a spreading habit, while the other hybrid, 'Freeman', is an upright grower with small flowers. Both flower from an early age. Photo by Jim Gardiner.

Magnolia 'Porcelain Dove'. This beautifully fragrant hybrid was raised by Todd Gresham. Its name combines the porcelain-white appearance of the flower with the name of Gresham's home, Hill of Doves, in Santa Cruz, California. Photo by Dr. Helmut Orth.

gins. The lemon-scented flowers are much larger than those of 'Freeman', open more widely to a distinctive cup shape, and are seen during July and August in the British Isles (May and June in North America, with a second flush in August). 'Maryland' was named by Frederick Meyer of the U.S. National Arboretum, in 1971. 'Freeman' has an upright-growing, almost columnar habit with tulip-shaped white flowers that rarely open to a cup shape to 12.5 cm (5 in.) wide, as they do in warmer growing conditions. It was named by William Kosar of the U.S. National Arboretum, in 1962.

Magnolia globosa Hybrids

Two hybrids of *Magnolia globosa* are described here.

'Porcelain Dove' (*Magnolia globosa* × *M. virginiana*) is a small to medium-sized multistemmed evergreen tree with large porcelain-white fragrant flowers. The semi-evergreen leaves point towards *M. virginiana* var. *australis* as the pollen parent. This clone was selected and named by Tom and Bill Dodd of Semmes, Alabama, in 1986. The Dodds received plants from Todd Gresham's home at the Hill of Doves in Santa Cruz, California, in 1965.

'Summer Solstice' (*Magnolia globosa* × *M. obovata*) is a chance seedling that grows into a small tree with scented deep pink globular flowers which are creamy white inside. The flowers are 10 cm (4 in.) in diameter, have 12 tepals, and are seen during June. The broadly ovate to obovate leaves are glaucous green beneath and quite hairy. Maurice Foster of Sevenoaks, Kent, obtained a plant being sold as *M. globosa* from the plant centre at the Savill and Valley Gardens, Berkshire. Noticing differences, Maurice grew it and has been rewarded by this hybrid, which is more vigorous and hardier than its seed parent. It was pollinated by the-pink flowered form of *M. obovata*. Several sister seedlings to 'Summer Solstice' are being grown in the Valley Gardens, Windsor.

Magnolia × gotoburgensis

Magnolia × gotoburgensis (*Magnolia obovata × M. wilsonii*) was created by Tor Nitzelius, former dendrologist at the Göteborg (Gothenburg) Botanic Garden, who transferred pollen from a wild collected plant of *M. obovata* collected in central Hokkaido, Japan, onto a plant of *M. wilsonii*. Germination took place the following spring, with three seedlings being planted, two in favoured locations in Sweden—one in the garden of Nitzelius on the west coast of Sweden, the other by the sea of Kattegatt—and the third at Chollipo Arboretum in South Korea. The plants vary in growth between a large multistemmed shrub and an upright small tree. The obovate leaves are up to 30 cm (12 in.) long, pale green above, whitish green beneath with scented upward-facing saucer-shaped white flowers up to 17 cm (6½ in.) wide. The flowers have 10 tepals surrounding crimson filaments and, like the pollen parent, are upward facing during June. This hybrid has inherited hardiness from its pollen parent as the seed parent subsequently died during a severe winter. The shrubby clone, growing in the garden of Tor Nitzelius, flowered 17 years after germination and has been named '**Fragrance**'.

Gresham Hybrids

During the mid-1950s, the late Todd Gresham of Santa Cruz, California, a founding member of the Magnolia Society, embarked on a massive *Magnolia* hybridisation programme, the rewards of which are still being reaped some 40 years later wherever magnolias are grown. The marriage of royal Asiatic trees with commonly grown cultivars of *M. × soulangeana* has proved the intrinsic value of this mating. It is worthwhile recording Gresham's philosophy as he saw it in "Deciduous Magnolias of Californian Origin" (1964):

> It is not too great a stretch of the imagination to envisage magnolias of the future, and their spectacular appeal for the modern gardener. They will bloom quickly from seed or graft; under Californian conditions maiden blooms from seed may be expected in four to five years; blossoms will be larger, to 12 and 14 in. [30–35 cm], of heavy substance, wide variation in form, and increased tepals; pure colour, tints and shades of warm pink, pink-salmon, rose, true reds, red-violet, blue-violet, yellow-apricot, orange and scarlet; novelty combinations of colour and colour pattern; trees will be arborescent, vigorous in growth, and better branching habit; foliage ornamental, showing plum red and foxy red spring colouring with less tendency to chlorosis; stature dwarf or treelike to suit any conceivable garden situation.

Gresham saw certain qualities in the parents he selected. *Magnolia* ×*veitchii* is a vigorous tree and was selected for having much of the flower colour quality of *M. campbellii* yet being hardier and later flowering than its parent. In fact, Gresham used a second-generation *M.* ×*veitchii* 'Rubra'. Another parent, *Magnolia liliiflora*, is a very floriferous shrub that flowers over a comparatively long period from April through to June. It is quite variable in colour from a pink to a deep purple, and some clones are even scented, similar to a tea rose. The third parent, *M.* ×*soulangeana* 'Lennei Alba', is among the best cultivars of *M.* ×*soulangeana* with large ivory white goblet-shaped flowers.

More than 100 seedlings were originally raised by Gresham, with 24 plants from each cross planted out. Seven years after germination, flowering started in earnest with about 12 crosses being named by Gresham from the 1955 sowings. Six cultivars resulting from the cross of *Magnolia liliiflora* 'Nigra' with *M.* ×*veitchii* were named in 1961. A check of the parental influences involved shows that *M. campbellii* contributed the 12 tepals, of which 8 reflex at maturity and 4 remain upright. *Magnolia* ×*veitchii* has contributed the high-standing bud, and *M. liliiflora* the depth of colour often found in the tepals. 'Heaven Scent' (heavily flushed dark pink or rose-purple tepals), 'Peppermint Stick' (white flowers heavily flushed with dark pink), 'Dark Raiments' (red-violet flowers), and 'Raspberry Ice' (large lavender-pink flowers) are beautiful and notable examples of Gresham's hybrids, which he christened his "Svelte Brunettes" and his "Buxom Nordic Blondes" for their distinct floristic characters.

The Svelte Brunettes (when using *Magnolia liliiflora*) are strong upright-growing small to medium-sized trees. They flower reliably towards the end of the *M. ×soulangeana* season, which generally is during the second half of April or early May. More recently their appearance has been not so easy to predict with peak flowering up to a month earlier. In California where they were first raised, they flower from late February onwards. In the cooler climate of the British Isles their flowers are a pale to rich pink with 12 tepals. In warmer climes such as California, flower colour is often much darker, being a violet or wine-red.

The Buxom Nordic Blondes (when using *Magnolia* ×soulangeana 'Lennei Alba') too develop into small to medium-sized trees. The habit even from young plants is more broad-spreading and generally multistemmed. The flowers differ from those of the Svelte Brunettes; they are milk white, but flushed with a delicate shade of pink at the base of the nine tepals. Ten cultivars have been named; 'Sayonara' (globular white flowers with pink flush), 'Sulphur Cockatoo' (large, fragrant, white flowers), and 'Rouged Alabaster' (white flowers flushed with a rich purple-pink) are three examples. Both the Blondes and the Brunettes start flowering generally between three and five years from propagation.

In the 1960s Gresham was most productive, producing over 15,000 hybrids using a cocktail of species and hybrids including *Magnolia sargentiana* var. *robusta*, *M. sprengeri* var. *sprengeri* 'Diva', and other *M. ×soulangeana* cultivars. In 1966 he selected the Tom Dodd Nurseries at Semmes, Alabama, and the Gloster Arboretum (Frank and Sara Gladney) in Mississippi as two sites where

Magnolia Gresham Hybrid. JG 26 is an unnamed Gresham hybrid selected by John Giordano, an amateur grower of magnolias, who assisted Frank and Sara Gladney of the Gloster Arboretum in the task of identifying plants of merit. Photo by Jim Gardiner.

these hybrids should be grown on and evaluated for their ornamental potential. This arrangement combined the values of linking to a commercial nursery with financial security. Sixteen hundred hybrids were sent to the Gloster Arboretum, representing the earlier crosses which Gresham had registered, together with others for evaluation as and when they flowered. The Gladneys were able to call on expert advice from Professor Joe McDaniel, Ken Durio (Louisiana Nursery of Opelousas), John Giordano of Eight Mile, Alabama, and the late Dr. John Allen Smith (Magnolia Nursery, Chunchula, Alabama), for this purpose.

Further shipments in 1966 (10,000 plants), 1968 (1900), and 1969 (2000) were sent to Tom Dodd Nurseries, where they were lined out. Ultimately the seedlings became tall and straggly from a lack of thinning and transplanting. Many of these plants resulted from Gresham's later work when he used new species and cultivars that he had only recently obtained. As is true for many hybridisation programmes, in this one also the hybridiser failed to see the conclusions of his work. Todd Gresham died in 1969 shortly after the final shipment of plants had been made to Tom Dodd Nurseries.

It is inevitable that with so many hybrids of similar parentage a number will warrant no further attention. A number, however, have provided the *Magnolia* grower with improvements over *M.* ×*soulangeana* and all that it offers. The first-generation Greshams (the Svelte Brunettes and the Buxom Nordic Blondes) have now established themselves worldwide. Several second-generation Greshams can be seen in specialist collections and will become better known outside the United States once garden visitors see their appeal. Without exception, all the Greshams flower prolifically from an early age, many with very large flamboyant flowers. They are vigorous, forming multistemmed or single-stemmed small to medium-sized trees. They generally flower during late March, April, and into early May, depending on the location in Europe; in the West Coast and southern United States they flower earlier, but generally towards the end of the *M.* ×*soulangeana* flowering period. They appear to be quite hardy, to U.S. hardiness zone 6, and grow well both in full sun and dappled shade. It is inappropriate to list every cultivar; however, a wide range of what is currently available is listed below.

'Candy Cane' (JG 28 unknown parentage) has nine white tepals 7.5 cm (3 in.) long. A rose-pink stripe runs along the length of the tepals. This clone was selected by John Giordano and named by the late Dr. John Allen Smith of Magnolia Nursery, Chunchula, Alabama.

'**Darrell Dean**' (*Magnolia ×soulangeana* 'Rustica Rubra' × *M. ×veitchii*) has very large deep pink-red goblet-shaped flowers with 9–12 tepals. The flowers, up to 30 cm (12 in.) wide, face outwards instead of up. This clone was selected by Ken Durio of Louisiana Nurseries, Opelousas, and named in honour of his late son, Darrell Dean Durio.

'**David Clulow**' (LA20 of unknown parentage but probably *Magnolia ×soulangeana* 'Lennei Alba' × *M. ×veitchii* 'Rubra') has very large white cup-and-saucer shaped flowers with a hint of pink at the base of the tepals. This clone was selected by Ken Durio of Louisiana Nurseries, Opelousas, and named by David Clulow, formerly of Bletchingly, Surrey.

'**Deep Purple Dream**' (an open-pollinated *Magnolia ×soulangeana* 'Lennei') has large deep purple-red goblet-shaped flowers. The late Dr. John Allen Smith of Magnolia Nursery, Chunchula, Alabama, considered them among the dark-

Magnolia 'David Clulow'. This Gresham hybrid was selected by Ken Durio and named by David Clulow in 1991. Clulow, an enthusiastic amateur grower of orchids and magnolias, travelled the world in search of new hybrids for his collection. He grew this plant at his home in Bletchingly, Surrey, prior to moving to Venezuela. Photo by John Gallagher.

Magnolia 'Darrell Dean'. This Gresham hybrid was selected by Ken Durio of Louisiana Nurseries, Opelousas, and named after his son, Darrell Dean Durio. Photo by Jim Gardiner.

est coloured flowers. On the inside, the flowers are creamy pink in colour. This clone, which originally grew at the Tom Dodd Nursery, Semmes, Alabama, was selected by David Ellis of Magnolia Nursery, Chunchula, Alabama, who saw it at the Gloster Arboretum in Mississippi.

'Elisa Odenwald' (*Magnolia* ×*soulangeana* 'Lennei Alba' × *M.* ×*veitchii*) has large creamy white cup-shaped flowers with a hint of purple-pink at the base. Inside the flowers are pure white. This upright multistemmed small to medium-sized tree flowers towards the end of the flowering season. It was named and selected by Ken Durio of Louisiana Nurseries, Opelousas, in 1984.

'14 Karat' (*Magnolia denudata* × *M.* ×*veitchii*) has beautiful cup-shaped porcelain-white flowers with soft pink on the basal third of each tepal. It was selected by the late Dr. John Allen Smith.

'Frank Gladney' (*Magnolia* unnamed Gresham hybrid × *M. campbellii*) has deep pink cup-and-saucer shaped flowers up to 30 cm (12 in.) wide with 12 tepals that are white on the inside. It has an upright-growing habit and blooms

Magnolia '14 Karat'. This Gresham hybrid was selected by the late Dr. John Allen Smith of Magnolia Nursery and Display Gardens, Chunchula, Alabama. A former president of the Magnolia Society, John, with his wife, Fran, grew an extensive collection of magnolias from which their nursery evolved. Photo by John Gallagher.

towards the end of the flowering season. This clone was named and selected by Ken Durio of Louisiana Nurseries, Opelousas.

'**Full Eclipse**' (unknown parentage JG 25) has deep pink to red tulip-shaped flowers that contrast with the pure white inside of the nine pointed 12.5 cm (5 in.) long tepals. This strong grower with an upright columnar habit was selected by the late Dr. John Allen Smith of Magnolia Nursery, Chunchula, Alabama.

'**Heaven Scent**' (*Magnolia liliiflora* 'Nigra' × *M. ×veitchii*) has tulip-shaped, heavily flushed dark pink or rose-purple flowers that ultimately splay open maintaining upright-pointed tepals surrounded by horizontal tepals. One of the early Gresham introductions, this clone flowers prolifically in April.

'**Joe McDaniel**' (*Magnolia×soulangeana* 'Rustica Rubra' × *M. ×veitchii*) produces magnificent goblet-

Magnolia 'Full Eclipse'. This Gresham hybrid is grown for its tulip-shaped bicoloured flowers and its upright, almost columnar habit. It was named by the late Dr. John Allen Smith of Magnolia Nursery and Display Gardens, Chunchula, Alabama, from a plant raised by John Giordano (JG 25) of Eight Mile, Alabama. Photo by Jim Gardiner.

Magnolia 'Heaven Scent'. An original Gresham hybrid and the one most frequently grown in gardens in the British Isles, 'Heaven Scent' is known for its reliable flowering qualities and habit. It develops into a small upright-growing tree. Photo by Dr. Helmut Orth.

shaped rich red-purple flowers. It is among the darkest of the Gresham hybrids. The outer broad rounded tepals splay open revealing a white inside which contrasts dramatically with the outer colour. This clone was named by Ken Durio of Louisiana Nurseries, Opelousas, in honour of Professor Joe McDaniel, former president of the Magnolia Society and among its most influential figures. McDaniel was often seen in his home town of Urbana with a ladder on the roof of his car to obtain propagation material from selected magnolias.

'**Jon Jon**' (unknown parentage JG 3), a very late profusely flowering cultivar with nine broad white tepals with a rich red-pink base, was selected and named by David Ellis of Magnolia Nursery, Chunchula, Alabama.

'**Kim Kunso**' (*Magnolia* ×*soulangeana* 'Lennei' × *M.* ×*veitchii* 'Peter Veitch'), an upright multistemmed grower, has large cup-shaped magenta-red flowers up to 25 cm (10 in.) wide. The inside is a glistening white with the magenta bleeding through from the outside to the base of each tepal. Ferris Miller (Min Pyong-gal), seeing this unnamed Gresham growing at Louisiana Nursery, named it after a member of his staff.

'**Manchu Fan**' (*Magnolia* ×*soulangeana* 'Lennei Alba' × *M.* ×*veitchii*) has tulip-shaped white flowers with a hint of pink at the base of the tepals seen midway through the flowering season on upright small trees. The flowers are smaller than many, but the effect is not lessened due to their profusion. This clone is one of the original Greshams.

'**Mary Nell**' (*Magnolia* ×*soulangeana* 'Lennei Alba' × *M.* ×*veitchii* 'Peter Veitch') has large white open cup-shaped flowers 25 cm (10 in.) wide. The nine fleshy tepals are stained on the outside with a rich red-purple at their bases, which is continued with a fine line through to each tip. The inside of the tepals is white. This clone develops into a bushy multistemmed small tree. It was named by Ken Durio of Louisiana Nurseries, Opelousas, in honour of Mary Nell McDaniel whose husband, Joe, was an admirer of this plant.

'**Peppermint Stick**' (*Magnolia liliiflora* 'Nigra' × *M.* ×*veitchii*) produces white flowers with a pink flush. The inner pointed tepals are held erect, while the outer are reflexed almost to the horizontal and are rolled inwards. The flowers are seen in profusion on small upright-growing trees.

'**Peter Smithers**' (*Magnolia* ×*soulangeana* 'Rustica Rubra' × *M.* ×*veitchii*) produces large pink flowers with white on the inner surface of the 12.5 cm (5 in.) tepals. This fast-growing multistemmed or single-stemmed small to medium-

Magnolia 'Joe McDaniel'. Huge goblets of intense rich pink to red-purple flowers are seen on this, the darkest of the Gresham hybrids. It was named by Ken Durio of Louisiana Nurseries, Opelousas, in honour of Joe McDaniel, professor of ornamental horticulture at the University of Illinois, and former president of the Magnolia Society. Professor McDaniel had an intense knowledge of magnolias, particularly the American species, and could take people to individual specimens of note in the Urbana (Illinois) area. Photo by Dr. Helmut Orth.

Magnolia 'Peppermint Stick'. One of the original Gresham hybrids, 'Peppermint Stick' has white flowers suffused with pink. The tepals are inward rolled and pointed. Photo by Jim Gardiner.

sized tree was named by Ken Durio of Louisiana Nurseries, Opelousas, in honour of Sir Peter Smithers of Vico Morcote in Switzerland.

'Pink Goblet' (Unknown parentage G66-12) has large rich pink goblet-shaped flowers seen in profusion during the early part of the season. The nine rounded tepals up to 12.5 cm (5 in.) long are a uniform pink on the outside and white on the inside. This vigorous grower develops into a multistemmed small tree and was selected and named by David Ellis of Magnolia Nursery, Chunchula, Alabama.

'Raspberry Ice' (*Magnolia liliiflora* 'Nigra' × *M.* ×*veitchii*) produces rich lavender-pink flowers with 12 tepals fading to white at their tips. The outer tepals reflex to the horizontal position revealing the white inside. This clone flowers midseason and develops into a multistemmed large shrub or small tree. It is one of the original Gresham hybrids named in 1962.

'Rouged Alabaster' (*Magnolia* ×*soulangeana* 'Lennei Alba' × *M.* ×*veitchii*), an early flowering cultivar, has 30 cm (12 in.) wide flowers that are arranged symmetrically in three groups of three tepals. The inner tepals are a rose-pink, while

Magnolia 'Spring Rite'. One of the original Gresham hybrids, 'Spring Rite' has beautiful silvery pink cup-shaped flowers. It was named in 1962. Photo by Jim Gardiner.

the outer, prior to reflexing, are a pleasant "rouged" rose-pink at the base. The inside is white. This clone is one of the original Gresham hybrids named in 1962.

'**Royal Crown**' (*Magnolia liliiflora* 'Nigra' × *M. ×veitchii*) has rich reddish pink flowers with 12 narrow pointed tepals 12.5–15.0 cm (5–6 in.) long and a marbled white on the inside. The outer tepals are rolled inwards, an inheritance from *M. liliiflora*, which gives the effect of a crown's upstanding points. This clone is one of the original Gresham hybrids named in 1962. It is a tall vigorous grower.

'**Sayonara**' (*Magnolia ×soulangeana* 'Lennei Alba' × *M. ×veitchii*) has large goblet-shaped creamy white flowers flushed with a rich purple-pink at the base. Each flower has 12 tepals up to 12.5 cm (5 in.) long. This strong, vigorous grower is usually multistemmed, and it flowers early to midseason.

'**Spring Rite**' (*Magnolia ×soulangeana* 'Lennei Alba' × *M. ×veitchii*) produces large open cup-shaped silvery pinkish white flowers with a hint of rose-pink at the base of the nine tepals. The flowers are 25–30 cm (10–12 in.) wide, and the tree is small and broad-spreading. This clone is one of the original Greshams named in 1962. It was introduced into the trade by Gossler Farms Nursery, Springfield, Oregon, in 1991.

'**Sweet Sixteen**' (JG 16 *Magnolia ×soulangeana* 'Lennei Alba' × *M. ×veitchii*) produces 12.5 cm (5 in.) long soft pink candlelike buds that open out to a pure white cup-shaped flower, with only a hint of pink staining at the base of the tepals. The flowers are seen profusely on the broad-spreading multistemmed small tree. Ken Durio of Louisiana Nurseries, Opelousas, named and introduced this cultivar in 1984.

'**Tina Durio**' (*Magnolia ×soulangeana* 'Lennei Alba' × *M. ×veitchii*) has huge white cup-and-saucer shaped pure white flowers,

Magnolia 'Tina Durio'. This magnificent white-flowered Gresham hybrid was named in 1984 by Ken Durio of Louisiana Nurseries, Opelousas, after his daughter. It is seen here growing to perfection at the Chollipo Arboretum in South Korea. The arboretum has one of the largest collections of named Gresham hybrids. Photo by Jim Gardiner.

with a hint of pink at the base of the 12 tepals, measuring up to 30 cm (12 in.) wide. This hybrid was named in 1984 for the daughter of Ken Durio of Louisiana Nurseries, Opelousas.

'Todd Gresham' (*Magnolia* ×*veitchii* × *M.* ×*soulangeana* 'Rustica Rubra') has pinkish violet, flat, cup-shaped 25 cm (10 in.) flowers revealing white on the inner surface of the nine tepals and a reddish boss. It is one of the few Gresham hybrids that produces a plentiful crop of bright red seed cones each year. Introduced by Ken Durio of Louisiana Nurseries, Opelousas, it was named in honour of the originator of this vibrant group of hybrids.

Magnolia 'Todd Gresham'. This large-flowered Gresham hybrid has cup-shaped rich pink flowers that are produced in quantity each year. It is a quality plant named by Ken Durio of Louisiana Nurseries, Opelousas, after the original hybridiser. Todd Gresham was a visionary when it came to *Magnolia* hybridisation, combining the attributes of *M.* ×*veitchii* with either *M. liliiflora* (giving his Svelte Brunettes) or *M.* ×*soulangeana* 'Lennei Alba' (his Buxom Nordic Blondes). Huge numbers of seedlings have been produced over the years using this formula. Initially, however, only 100 plants were raised with 12 crosses being named from the 1995 sowing. Photo by John Gallagher.

Jury Hybrids

Mark and Abbie Jury of North Taranaki, New Zealand, are using *Magnolia camp-bellii* subsp. *mollicomata* 'Lanarth' either as a direct parent or as 'Mark Jury' (*M. sargentiana* var. *robusta* × *M. campbellii* subsp. *mollicomata* 'Lanarth') to produce an exciting range of hybrids. Mark's father, Felix, started raising magnolias during the early 1960s after establishing himself as a camellia breeder of international standing. Ten years earlier, he imported *M. campbellii* subsp. *mollicomata* 'Lanarth' from Hillier Nurseries. When it flowered, it produced a large soft pink flower and was thought to be a hybrid between 'Lanarth' and *M. sargentiana* var. *robusta*. Jury decided to call it 'Mark Jury' after his son. The new hybrid turned out to be a stroke of luck as it proved to be a wonderful pollen parent, producing spectacular hybrids when crossed with *M.* ×*soulangeana* 'Lennei' and 'Lennei Alba'. **'Mark Jury'** has 25.0–27.5 cm (10–11 in.) wide rich pink flowers with the upper surface being a cream with a hint of lavender in the colour of the tepals during March and early April. In habit it grows into a small to medium-sized narrow pyramidal tree.

'Iolanthe' (*Magnolia* ×*soulangeana* 'Lennei' × *M.* 'Mark Jury') was the first of Jury's hybrids to be released in the early 1970s. It develops into a broad-spreading small tree with the original plant 8 m (26 ft.) tall and wide after 30 years. It produces an abundance of large, soft pink bowl-shaped blooms, paler inside, within five years from propagation. The flowers are of a heavy texture and face outwards. It is among the most easily recognised magnolias in bud with masses of huge hairy perules pointing outwards at various angles during January and February, bursting into flower during mild periods in mid-March, even on young plants.

'Atlas', a sister of 'Iolanthe', has huge flowers at least 30 cm (12 in.) wide even

Magnolia 'Atlas'. This sister of 'Iolanthe' has possibly the largest blooms of any magnolia, up to 35 cm (13½ in.) wide. These are seen during the end of March or early April even on plants that are under five years old. 'Atlas' is more vigorous than 'Iolanthe', producing strong upright shoots about 60 cm (2 ft.) long. Photo by Jim Gardiner.

on young plants. The flowers appear two to three weeks after those of 'Iolanthe'. They are a beautiful soft pink in colour and unlike 'Iolanthe' are held upright on branches. It will ultimately make a small to medium-sized tree which when young will grow between 60 cm (2 ft.) and 90 cm (3 ft.) per year. It really needs a wind-protected site to grow, as winds have a shredding effect on those huge flowers.

'Athene', 'Lotus', and 'Milky Way' (all *Magnolia* ×*soulangeana* 'Lennei Alba' × *M.* 'Mark Jury') are three further crosses. Strong-growing small potentially medium-sized trees, they generally flower at the same time as 'Atlas'. 'Athene' is pink at the base and white within, while 'Milky Way' is whiter but retains a hint of pink at the base of the tepals. 'Lotus' is well named for the shape of its creamy white flowers, but is not as floriferous as its sisters.

Another breeding line followed by Jury crossed *Magnolia campbellii* subsp. *mollicomata* 'Lanarth' with *M. liliiflora*. **'Apollo'** is an exceptionally heavy flowering hybrid. The star-shaped flowers are deep violet in colour with a paler upper surface to the tepals. The later flowers, seen with the unfurling foliage, are deep rose-pink in colour. This hybrid flowers during late March and April (July–August in New Zealand) and grows into a small round-headed tree.

Magnolia 'Milky Way'. The cup-and-saucer shaped white blooms crowd the branches during April and, when seen from below, have a soft pink flush at the base of the tepals. Photo by Jim Gardiner.

'Vulcan' is a full sister of 'Apollo' with deep port-wine red 20 cm (8 in.) cup and saucer flowers on an upright-growing, potentially small tree. The flower colour has yet to be consistent on plants in the British Isles, giving rise to speculation over juvenile and adult flowers. Having seen the plant flowering to potential in the garden of Otto Eisenhut, Ticino, Switzerland, I can vouch that it is well worth waiting for!

'Black Tulip' and **'Felix Jury'** are the next generation of Jury hybrids. 'Black Tulip', a cross between 'Vulcan' as seed parent and possibly 'Iolanthe' as pollen parent, has gob-

Magnolia 'Apollo'. The influence of *M. campbellii* subsp. *mollicomata* 'Lanarth' is evident in this clone. The tepals are a beautiful rose-pink in colour on the outside, turning, when they open during warm weather, to an intense pinkish purple. Photo by John Gallagher.

Magnolia 'Felix Jury'. This cultivar (front right) was named for the breeder of the current range of Jury hybrids and father of Mark. The next generation of *Magnolia* hybrids (back row) is being raised by Mark and Abbie Jury. Photo by Abbie Jury.

let-shaped flowers that are a beautiful port-wine red colour, but more intense than the seed parent. 'Felix Jury', a cross between 'Vulcan' as seed parent and an unnamed pendulous sister seedling of 'Iolanthe', has bicoloured white and port-wine red flowers shaped like water lilies.

Magnolia ×*kewensis*

Magnolia ×***kewensis* 'Kewensis'** (*M. kobus* × *M. salicifolia*) is a broad-spreading, small to medium-sized tree that first arose as a chance seedling at the Royal Botanic Gardens, Kew, in 1938. Discovered by Charles F. Coates, propagator in charge of the arboretum's nursery, it was described and named in 1952, when it was considered intermediate in both floral and foliage characters between two Japanese species, *M. salicifolia* and *M. kobus*. The broad-leafed clone of *M. salicifolia* is generally acknowledged to belong here. Being a grex, the original plant and propagules from it should be known as *M.* ×*kewensis* 'Kewensis'. It grows vigorously, upright initially but spreading to form a broad-spreading tree. The green leaves are oblong-lanceolate to elliptic in shape, 12.5 cm (5 in.) long by 6 cm (2¼ in.) wide, and closely resemble those of *M. kobus*. The young stems when rubbed do, however, have a lemon-verbena scent. The fragrant, pure white flowers open during late March through late April on leafless stems. The six inner tepals are held horizontally and, when fully out, the flowers are slightly nodding. The three outer tepals are small and calyxlike. All nine tepals are about 10.0–12.5 cm (4–5 in.) wide and are borne unfailingly and abundantly. Plants flower well from an early age. *Magnolia* ×*kewensis* 'Kewensis' grows best in a sunny site in a moisture-retentive, preferably acid soil. It is hardy to U.S. hardiness zone 5.

Magnolia ×*kewensis* **'Iufer',** an American form introduced by the Iufer (pronounced "ee-you-fer") Nursery, Salem, Oregon, and registered in 1986, grows into a narrow pyramidal-shaped small to medium-sized tree that grows 30 cm (12 in.) a year when young. It has large pure white flowers with red tips to the stamens and is highly regarded in the northwestern United States.

Magnolia ×*kewensis* **'Nippon'** was raised as a seedling of *M. kobus* by Captain Collingwood Ingram in the 1950s but is now regarded as a cultivar of *M.* ×*kewensis*. It produces large cup-shaped white flowers, similar in size to those of *M. denudata*, during late March and early April.

Magnolia ×kewensis 'Wada's Memory'. This hybrid is stunning in flower and habit. It was named by Brian Mulligan, former director of the Washington Park Arboretum, after Koichiro Wada, who had sent him seed from which this cultivar was selected. The plant photographed is on the grounds of the Henry Francis du Pont Museum in Delaware. Photo by Vicomte Philippe de Spoelberch.

Magnolia ×*kewensis* 'Wada's Memory', a small tree with a compact upright habit, was named by the University of Washington Arboretum, Seattle, when it was selected from a batch of seedlings received in March 1940 from Japan. The director of the arboretum, Brian Mulligan, wrote:

> *Magnolia* ×*kewensis* 'Wada's Memory' was one out of a number of plants of this species purchased from the nursery of K. Wada, Numazu-shi, Japan. Undoubtedly they were all seedlings, since most of the progeny have very ordinary flowers, typical of *M. kobus*. This one, however, which by chance was placed in a very prominent position in the arboretum, has flowers about twice the size of the normal type [15–17 cm or 6–7 in. wide] when expanded, but the segments soon reflexing or drooping.

The plant was named in honour of Koichiro Wada while he was still alive. It is a free-growing, single-stemmed or multistemmed small tree that retains a compact conical habit. A magnificent tree at Winterthur, now on the grounds of the Henry Francis du Pont Museum in Delaware, is more than 12 m (40 ft.) tall by 5.5 m (18 ft.) wide after 40 years. As they unfurl, the leaves are a distinctive mahogany red. They mature green and are elliptic in shape and 12.5 cm (5 in.) long by 5.75 cm (2¼ in.) wide. The fragrant flowers are borne on leafless stems between late March and late April in such profusion that they present the viewer with a glistening white pyramid of flower. The six tepals are at first held horizontally, but within a day of opening they increase in size and droop as if the flower was past its best. This effect is quite startling, when on a sunny cloudless day a gentle breeze causes the tepals to dance like butterflies hovering over a flower prior to collecting nectar. The value of 'Wada's Memory' as a garden plant is increased because it flowers from an early age. It should be planted in a sunny yet sheltered site with moisture-retentive soil that can be either side of the neutral line. This magnolia is hardy to U.S. hardiness zone 5.

Magnolia kobus Hybrids

Along with the hybrids listed here, *Magnolia kobus* is also parent of *M.* ×*kewensis* and *M.* ×*loebneri*, both of which are referred to under their own names.

'Eskimo' (*Magnolia kobus* 'Norman Gould' × *M.* ×*soulangeana* 'Lennei') was crossed by August Kehr of Hendersonville, North Carolina. The white cup-

Magnolia 'Pickard's Stardust'. This hybrid of *M. kobus*, raised by Amos Pickard, is rarely seen outside specialist collections, yet deserves wider attention. Photo by Jim Gardiner.

shaped flowers with a subtle hint of lilac are 12.5–15.0 cm (5–6 in.) wide. They are of particular interest for their frost hardiness, as the open flowers have withstood at least six degrees of frost. Another, unnamed, clone has up to 15 strap-shaped, slightly crinkled tepals with star-shaped flowers.

'Pickard's Stardust' was raised as a seedling of *M. kobus* by Amos Pickard of Canterbury, Kent, who is better known for his *M. ×soulangeana* 'Picture' hybrids. 'Pickard's Stardust' flowers later than other *M. kobus* hybrids—during the second half of March and throughout early April, successively over several weeks. The flowers have six pointed tepals with a flush of pink at the base and three reflexed tepals. This cultivar grows into a multistemmed medium-sized shrub with ascending branches and abundant flowers. It is an underrated hybrid that deserves wider attention.

Magnolia liliiflora Hybrids

Magnolia liliiflora is an extremely important and influential parent in *Magnolia* breeding programmes. Its freedom of flowering, variable flower colour and form, time of flowering, hardiness, and ability to link with various pollen or seed parents have provided the hybridiser with a wealth of opportunity. Mark and Abbie Jury and Oswald Blumhardt of New Zealand, William Kosar of the U.S. National Arboretum, Eva Maria Sperber of Brooklyn Botanic Garden, Todd Gresham, and of course Etienne Soulange-Bodin, among others, have used this species successfully in creating magnolias that have considerably widened their appeal to gardeners who otherwise would not consider planting a magnolia in their gardens.

Magnolia liliiflora has been hybridised with *M. acuminata, M. campbellii, M. campbellii* subsp. *mollicomata, M. denudata, M. sprengeri* var. *sprengeri* 'Diva', and *M. stellata*.

'George Henry Kern' (*Magnolia liliiflora* 'Nigra' × *M. stellata* 'Rosea') is a medium-sized deciduous shrub that was raised in 1935 by Carl E. Kern of Wyoming Nurseries, Cincinnati, Ohio, and named after the owner, who was killed on active service with the United States naval reserve in 1945. It was originally thought to be a hybrid between *Magnolia×soulangeana* and *M. stellata,* and is often listed under the de Vos and Kosar hybrids. In growth it resembles *M. stellata.* 'George Henry Kern' increases by up to 30 cm (12 in.) per year, but it is distinct in its flower colour and its time of flowering. The flowers are composed of between 8 and 10 strap-shaped, thick-textured tepals and are rose-pink in bud opening to a light pink. The flowering period is exceptional, starting on leafless shoots in mid to late April and continuing into the summer months, when the plant is in full leaf. In North America the colour seems intensified, being a deep reddish purple in bud, opening to a rose-pink on the outer surface and a pale pink on the inner surface. 'George Henry Kern' prefers a sunny situation in a moisture-retentive, acid soil and is hardy to U.S. hardiness zone 5.

'Lileny' (*Magnolia liliiflora*× *M.* ×*soulangeana* 'Lennei') was raised by Amos Pickard of Canterbury, Kent. The pink-flowered hybrid is a compact grower

Magnolia 'George Henry Kern'. Thought at one time to be a hybrid of *M.* ×*soulangeana*, but now considered to have the same parentage as the de Vos and Kosar hybrids, this slow-growing shrub is ideal for the small garden, not only for its compact size, but also for its flowering qualities. The flowers are soft pink in colour and are seen over a six- to eight-week period from early April in the south of England. Photo by Jim Gardiner.

reminiscent of 'George Henry Kern'. It flowers in early April and has beautiful clear pink candles, highlighting *M. liliiflora* as one of its parents.

'Marillyn' (*Magnolia liliiflora* 'Nigra' × *M. kobus*), a medium-sized to large multistemmed shrub, has slightly fragrant tulip-shaped 12.5 cm (5 in.) flowers during late March and April, opening over four weeks. The six tepals are a rich red-purple on the outside, paler within, with prominent veins running along their length. The elliptic leaves are 15.0–17.5 cm (6–7 in.) long and, on unfurling, have a distinctive copper-green colour. This floriferous plant has proved extremely hardy, to U.S. hardiness zone 4. It was raised at the Brooklyn Botanic Garden by Eva Maria Sperber in 1954 and named after a friend and benefactor of the garden.

'Orchid' (*Magnolia stellata* × *M. liliiflora*) is a medium-sized deciduous shrub resembling *M. liliiflora* in growth, leaf, and flower. The flower tends to be larger than normal, with each of the six tepals 15.0–17.5 cm (6–7 in.) long and uniform reddish purple in colour. Flowering occurs in late April and May and sometimes into June and again sporadically in August. 'Orchid' is considered more cold hardy than either of its parents. It is a chance seedling found at Hillenmayer Nursery, Lexington, Kentucky, in 1961.

'Galaxy' and **'Spectrum'** (*Magnolia liliiflora* 'Nigra' × *M. sprengeri* var. *sprengeri* 'Diva') are small to medium-sized trees that initially have an upright habit; however, both develop a broadly pyramidal outline after 15–20 years. Both magnolias were raised by William Kosar at the U.S. National Arboretum in 1963. 'Galaxy' retains a single leader dominance, while 'Spectrum' is less so. When young they increase by 38–50 cm (15–20 in.) per year, slowing to 30–38 cm (12–15 in.). The leaves are elliptic in shape and 18 cm (7 in.) long. 'Galaxy', the first selection to be named, has 11 or 12 tepals, deep reddish purple in bud, opening to a rich pink-purple on the outside, lighter

Magnolia 'Lileny'. This hybrid from Amos Pickard of Canterbury, Kent, who is better known for his hybrids of *M.* ×*soulangeana* 'Picture', is a slower growing shrub suitable for the small garden. It is of similar parentage to the "Eight Little Girls." Photo by Jim Gardiner.

on the inside and up to 12.5 cm (5 in.) long. 'Spectrum' flowers are larger than those of 'Galaxy' and in bud are more curved. The outer tepals are 14 cm (5½ in) long. Sometimes 'Spectrum' is seen with fewer tepals than 'Galaxy', varying between 8 and 12 in number. The flower colour is a brighter red-purple, opening to a rich pinkish red on the outside and paler within. 'Galaxy' flowered in 1971 and 'Spectrum' in 1973. 'Galaxy' is more cold hardy, to U.S. hardiness zones 4–5, while 'Spectrum' is hardy to U.S. hardiness zones 6–7 and performs more effectively in warmer climates.

Magnolia 'Galaxy'. An excellent small tree for the smaller garden, 'Galaxy' has an upright habit, which enables it to grow in comparatively confined spaces, and prodigious flowering, seen for six weeks from early to mid-April onwards. It was raised in the early 1960s at the U.S. National Arboretum by William Kosar. Photo by Jim Gardiner.

Magnolia ×*loebneri*

The early work of hybridising *Magnolia kobus* with *M. stellata* was carried out by Max Loebner, the garden inspector at the Botanic Gardens in Bonn, but formerly at Dresden in Germany prior to 1914. Loebner's magnolia flowered for the first time in 1917, with 12 tepals compared with 8 or 9 of *M. kobus* and approximately 18 of *M. stellata*. Five plants were sold by Loebner to Wilhelm Kordes, who owned a nursery at Sparrieshoop in Germany. Similar deliberate hybridisation programmes have taken place in North America, notably at the Arnold Arboretum and the University of Illinois, with fragrant, very floriferous cultivars resulting. Chance hybrids have also appeared in established European gardens, such as Nymans Gardens in England and the Villa Taranto in Italy, with particularly fine cultivars being produced.

A diversity of habits has resulted, ranging between single-stemmed ultimately broad-crowned trees to 9 m (30 ft.) and multistemmed large shrubs. Growth rates vary too, but may be 50 cm (20 in.) a year on established plants. The leaves are similar in size to those of *Magnolia stellata*, 12.5 cm (5 in.) long by 5 cm (2 in.) wide, elliptic to oblong, and a slightly lighter green beneath. The flowers are seen most abundantly from an early age, with hardly a bare branch to be seen on mature plants. They vary in size, from 11.5 cm (4½ in.) to 15 cm (6 in.) wide; in colour, from pure white to a lilac-purple; and in number of tepals, from 8 to 30. In the British Isles these flowers are seen at their best between the second half of March and the second half of April. They stand up well to late frosts. For example, during late April 1997 frosts in the southeast of England measured between –2° and –3°C (26°–28°F). Although these temperatures are not exceptional, they severely damaged the many magnolias that had put on several inches of growth resulting from mild growing conditions. In amongst this "blackness" shone *M. ×loebneri, M. kobus,* and *M. stellata,* all of which had not been affected. In North America the flowers generally open slightly earlier, though plants in the southern United States have been known to open as early as January.

All forms of *Magnolia ×loebneri* are remarkably tolerant of a wide range of soil types, from acid to alkaline and from a light sand to a moisture-retentive (but not waterlogged) clay. They flower in dappled shade but are best in full sun. They are surprisingly wind resistant and quite hardy (to U.S. hardiness zone 5).

Where deliberate crosses have been made, seedlings of intermediate height and flower type have resulted, particularly where *Magnolia stellata* was the seed parent. In experiments by Professor Joe McDaniel in the late 1960s, seedlings from selfed *M. stellata* were reasonably uniform in leaf shape and vigour.

'**Ballerina**' was raised by Professor Joe McDaniel at the University of Illinois during the 1960s and registered in 1969. McDaniel is unclear whether this is a second-generation clone of *Magnolia ×loebneri* 'Spring Snow' or a backcross to *M. stellata* 'Waterlily'. It develops into a small tree, increasing by about 30–38 cm (12–15 in.) a year. It is more compact than 'Merrill', and it is among the last of the group to flower. The fragrant flowers are white with a pale pink flush towards the base of the tepals, of which there may be as many as 30. '**Encore**' and '**Powder Puff**' (*M. ×loebneri* 'Ballerina' seedlings) were named by August Kehr of Hendersonville, North Carolina. They will ultimately grow into medium-sized to large bushy shrubs. The white flowers have 18–25 tepals. The flower buds of 'Encore' appear in groups of up to four on the tips as well as along the stem, thus giving an "encore" as the flowering period is extended, with flowers opening in succession. 'Powder Puff', on the other hand, holds its tepals at all angles including upright, thus giving a powder-puff or brush appearance.

'**Donna**', an upright-growing large, densely branched shrub, has large pure white fragrant flowers to 15.0–17.5 cm (6–7 in.) wide. Appearing in early April, they have 12–13 broad tepals that reflex backwards. This extremely beautiful, very hardy selection was selected by Harry Heineman of Scituate, Massachusetts, and named after his wife.

'**Leonard Messel**', probably the least vigorous clone, develops a more crowded branch framework than the others. The full, soft pink flowers, 12.5 cm (5 in.) wide and composed of up to 12 strap-shaped tepals, appear in April and are quite frost resistant. This clone was raised by James Comber, the head gardener to the Countess of Rosse at Nymans Garden, near Haywards Heath in Sussex in the 1950s, and registered in 1955. Plants of 'Leonard Messel' have flowered at the Royal Horticultural Society's Garden at Wisley during March. A single plant there varied in flower colour during different years, from a very pale pink to a very rich pink (see accompanying photos). The average daytime temperature prior to and during flowering varied by 3.5°C (7°F), with the pale pink flower colour averaging 11°C (51°F) while the rich pink flower colour averaged 14.6°C (58°F). Similarly the nighttime temperature was lower for the paler colour—2°C (36°F)—and higher for the rich pink colour—5°C (41°F). In addition, temperatures below 0°C (32°F) were recorded the year the pale colour was in flower.

'**Merrill**', probably the most vigorous clone, develops into a broad-spreading tree which in North America exceeds 9 m (30 ft.) tall and wide. Plants at the Hillier Gardens and Arboretum are about 6 m (20 ft.) tall after 20 years. Pure white flowers, 10–15 cm (4–6 in.) wide, with up to 15 broad tepals, are seen in profusion during late March and April. This clone was raised at the Arnold Arboretum in 1939 and flowered first in 1944. It was subsequently named in 1952 after Elmer Merrill, director of the Arnold Arboretum.

'**Neil McEacharn**' was raised in the gar-

Magnolia ×*loebneri* 'Donna'. One of the most beautiful and large flowered of the recent *M.* ×*loebneri* introductions, 'Donna' was named by Harry Heineman of Scituate, Massachusetts, after his wife. Photo by Jim Gardiner.

Magnolia ×*loebneri* 'Leonard Messel' (right, below, and opposite, top). Probably among the most popular shrubs for the smaller garden, 'Leonard Messel' is extremely floriferous with the flowers quite frost resistant. What is interesting is that all three pictures were taken of the same plant but during different years. The paler flowers reflect the lower day and night temperatures, while the richer pink flowers saw higher temperatures by some 3°C (5° or 6°F). Photos by Jim Gardiner.

Magnolia ×loebneri 'Merrill'. One of the most vigorous clones of *M. ×loebneri*, 'Merrill' grows into a small to medium-sized tree with a profusion of pure white flowers. It was named after Elmer Merrill, former director of the Arnold Arboretum, Massachusetts, and registered by Karl Sax, professor of botany, in 1952. Photo by Jim Gardiner.

dens at Windsor Great Park from seed of *Magnolia stellata* 'Rosea' sent from the garden of Captain Neil McEacharn at Villa Taranto on Lake Maggiore, Italy. It is a vigorous broad-spreading large shrub that bears white multi-tepalled flowers to 10 cm (4 in.) wide.

'Raspberry Fun' is a densely branched large shrub with clusters of pink flowers during late March and April. The 16 tepals are very similar in size to those of 'Leonard Messel' and are a lighter pink on the inside, dark pink on the outer, with a deep strip running the length of the tepals. 'Raspberry Fun' has more tepals than 'Leonard Messel' (16 against 12), and these are generally seen in clusters of two to three flowers, whereas 'Leonard Messel' is rarely seen in this way. This clone was named and selected by Ferris Miller (Min Pyong-gal) at Chollipo Arboretum, South Korea, in 1987 from open-pollinated seed of 'Leonard Messel'.

'Snowdrift' is a branched medium-sized to large shrub with pure white flowers. The 12 tepals open horizontally. This clone is among the original seedlings sent to Hillier Nurseries of Winchester, Hampshire, by German nurseryman Wilhelm Kordes.

'Spring Snow' is a round-headed small tree with fragrant large pure white flowers. The 15 tepals, each about 7.5 cm (3 in.) long, reflex beyond the horizontal with age. The flowers appear in late March for about one month; however, in Semmes, Alabama, they are seen as early as January. This clone was selected by Professor Joe McDaniel of Urbana, Illinois, and registered in 1970. McDaniel named it for the first flowers, which open during the last spring snow but are seldom damaged by it.

'Wildcat' is a seedling selected by Larry Langford of Gibson, Tennessee, from a batch of seed of *Magnolia kobus* var. *borealis* sent by William Skidl of Wisconsin. When the soft pink blooms open, they resemble pompom chrysanthemums and have 52 tepals measuring 10–12.5 cm (4–5 in.) across. The plant flowers at the same time as other cultivars of *M.* ×*loebneri* and over a six-week period.

Magnolia macrophylla Hybrids

Magnolia macrophylla is the parent of two hybrids named for Swedish supporters of the Magnolia Society.

'Birgitta Flinck' and **'Karl Flinck'** were raised by Phil Savage of Bloomfield

Hills, Michigan. He pollinated a northern clone of *M. macrophylla* with *M. virginiana*, also from a northern provenance. The flowers are intermediate between the two parents, with 'Birgitta Flinck' having pure white flowers while 'Karl Flinck' has purple spotted flowers. These clones were named after Karl Flinck and his wife, Birgitta, who have been long-time supporters of the Magnolia Society and keen and knowledgeable growers both in their native Sweden and Switzerland.

Magnolia obovata Hybrids

Magnolia obovata is the parent of two hybrids described here. It is also a parent of *M. ×wieseneri,* which is referred to under its own name.

'Nimbus' (*Magnolia virginiana × M. obovata*) is an upright-growing small to medium-sized tree that can be grown as a single-stemmed or multistemmed specimen. It is "partially" evergreen, with elliptic leaves to 30 cm (12 in.) long, glossy green above, and glaucous white beneath. The very fragrant white cup-shaped flowers have 11 tepals (3 green and calyxlike) to 10 cm (4 in.) long and are seen in May or June depending on location. The plant is hardy to −23°C (−9°F). It was raised by William Kosar of the U.S. National Arboretum in 1956 and first flowered in 1964.

'Silver Parasol' (*Magnolia obovata × M. tripetala*) is a medium-sized pyramidal tree with parasol-like whorls of leaves at the end of each stem. Measuring up to 40 cm (16 in.) long by 20 cm (8 in.) wide, the leaves are quite attractive for their silvery underside, especially when seen "dancing" in a light breeze. The clear ivory-white fragrant flowers inherited from the seed parent measure up to 25 cm (10 in.) wide and have nine inner tepals and three reddish green outer tepals. This hybrid was introduced by the Arnold Arboretum, Jamaica Plain, Massachusetts, and registered in 1981.

Magnolia 'Nimbus'. Selected as the best seedling in 1974, this hybrid was introduced into the trade by the U.S. National Arboretum in 1980. It was named for its flowers, which float like the white nimbus clouds during high summer. Photo by Vicomte Philippe de Spoelberch.

Magnolia ×*proctoriana*

This small pyramidal tree arose as a selected seedling from a batch of *Magnolia salicifolia* seed sent to the Arnold Arboretum in 1928 by T. R. Proctor, who had opened a private arboretum at Topsfield, Massachusetts. It was described and named in 1939 when it was considered to be intermediate between two Japanese species, *M. salicifolia* and *M. stellata*.

Mikinori Ogisu of Tokyo and Seiju Yamaguchi of Mizunami City tell me of a hilly area not too far from Mizunami City, Gifu, and above 500 m (1600 ft.) where *Magnolia* ×*proctoriana* is found in the wild. *Magnolia stellata* can be found both as a shrub and a small tree, while higher up the hillside and flowering later can be found *M. salicifolia*. In between are plants of *M.* ×*proctoriana*. During one or two seasons in the past, *M. stellata* must have flowered late, with a few blooms overlapping with those of *M. salicifolia* or vice versa, but in either case *M. salicifolia* is almost certainly the pollen parent. The wood of *M.* ×*proctoriana* is similar to that of *M. salicifolia* and is scented when crushed, while the perules of *M.* ×*proctoriana* are intermediate between the two parents and have a scattering of hairs.

In habit, this hybrid grows into a broad-spreading large shrub or small tree with slender, ascending shoots. It grows 38–60 cm (15–24 in.) per year. The leaves are similar to those of *Magnolia salicifolia*: oblong lanceolate in shape, 12.5 cm (5 in.) long by 4.5 cm (1¾ in.) wide, and a paler green beneath. As the leaves unfurl they are a coppery green colour, which disappears as they expand to their full size. The leaves when crushed are scented but not nearly to the same degree as those of *M. salicifolia*. The abundant flowers open during mid to late April on leafless stems. They are white with a hint of pink at the base of the tepals, which are generally six in number but vary up to twelve. The slightly fragrant blooms open horizontally to 10 cm (4 in.) wide and tend to nod once they are fully open.

Closely related to this hybrid is *Magnolia* ×*proctoriana* 'Slavins Snowy', which was raised at Highland Park, Rochester, New York. The latter develops into a small tree of an upright ultimately spreading habit that flowers profusely at the same time as *M.* ×*proctoriana*, but has fragrant, slightly larger flowers to 15 cm (6 in.) wide, with a distinctive pink blotch at the base of each of the six to nine tepals.

Stephen Spongberg considers *Magnolia* ×*proctoriana* to be a variant of *M. salicifolia*, and therefore subsumes *M.* ×*proctoriana* under *M. salicifolia*. All the examples I have seen of *M.* ×*proctoriana*, however, show a distinctive habit not normally encountered in *M. salicifolia*.

A rich, acidic, moisture-retentive soil in full sun ideally suits this plant, but it will flower well in semi-shade in gardens in southern England. Allow plenty of space for this broad-spreading tree to flourish. It is hardy to U.S. hardiness zone 5.

Magnolia sargentiana var. *robusta* Hybrids

Magnolia sargentiana var. *robusta* is the parent of several fine floriferous hybrids listed below. It also has hybridised either intentionally or spontaneously in gardens with several other species, primarily *M. campbellii*, to produce many hybrids of excellence.

'Caerhays Belle' (*Magnolia sargentiana* var. *robusta* × *M. sprengeri* var. *sprengeri* 'Diva') is a small to medium-sized tree that produces large rich salmon-pink cup-shaped flowers to 30 cm (12 in.) wide in great profusion in March. The 12 heavily textured broad tepals are spoon-shaped, the tips of the inner ones are curved upwards, thus highlighting the deeper colour of the outside of the tepal. This was a deliberate cross carried out by Charles Michael, the head gardener of Caerhays Castle in Cornwall in 1951. It flowered for the first time in 1965; however, young grafted plants produce flowers in fewer than five years. This cultivar fruits freely, producing decorative pink-coloured seed cones up to 20 cm (8 in.) long.

'Susanna van Veen' is thought to be of similar parentage to 'Caerhays Belle', but it

Magnolia 'Caerhays Belle'. Charles Michael, former head gardener at Caerhays Castle in Cornwall, appreciated the value of having so many aristocrats to enable him to carry out deliberate crosses. Linking the qualities of *M. sargentiana* var. *robusta* with the goddess magnolia, *M. sprengeri* var. *sprengeri* 'Diva', was undoubtedly a winning formula. The flowers of 'Caerhays Belle' are rich, blowsy salmon-pink in colour and sideways swept rather than held in the classical upright position. Photo by John Gallagher.

Magnolia 'Susanna van Veen'. The sumptuous flowers suggest a similar parentage to 'Caerhays Belle', but the tepals are more loosely held and slightly darker in colour. Photo by Dr. Helmut Orth.

is darker in colour, being a rose-pink, darker on the outside, and with a rather floppy habit. The winter flower buds are an attraction in their own right, having very "furry" perules.

'**Sweetheart**', a 'Caerhays Belle' seedling raised by Peter Cave of Hamilton, New Zealand, is a small to medium-sized tree that is more upright in habit than its parent. The 12 broad tepals are a deep rich pink on the outside and a pale pink on the inside. They are seen in profusion during July and August in New Zealand (March in the British Isles).

Magnolia sieboldii Hybrids

Magnolia sieboldii is the parent of the two hybrids described below.

'**Aashild Kalleberg**' (*Magnolia sieboldii* × *M. obovata*) resulted from *M. sieboldii* seed being sown in the Göteborg (Gothenburg) Botanic Garden in 1987. Following germination in 1988, it first flowered in 1995. In habit it is similar to *M. obovata* being a single-stemmed medium-sized potentially large tree with leaves measuring 43 cm (17 in.) tall by 17.5 cm (7 in.) wide. The flowers have three outer tepals and eight to nine inner, which are pure white. They are cup-shaped on the first day, opening to a saucer shape 15 cm (6 in.) wide on the second. So far it has shown itself to be floriferous and very hardy in Sweden.

'**Charles Coates**' (*Magnolia sieboldii* × *M. tripetala*) is a multistemmed large shrub or small tree that arose as a chance seedling in the Azalea Garden of the Royal Botanic Gardens, Kew, around 1946. Charles F. Coates, the propagator in charge of the arboretum nursery, identified it as a distinct, self-sown seedling, and it was named in his honour by Sydney Pearce of the Royal Botanic Gardens, Kew. The main stems are strongly ascendant, while the lateral branches give a broad-spreading effect increasing by 45–60 cm (1½–2 ft.) when young and vigorous, slowing to 30–38 cm (12–15 in.). The leaves resemble those of *M. tripe-*

tala, even to the extent of congregating on the ends of the shoots. The papery green leaves are broadly elliptic in shape, 27 cm (10½ in.) long by 14.5 cm (6 in.) wide, and are a glaucous green on the underside with distinctive hairs along the midrib. The fragrant flowers resemble those of *M. sieboldii* but instead of nodding they are held erect; they are saucer shaped, to 18 cm (7 in.) wide. The eight tepals are creamy white in colour and generally have a crumpled appearance with three smaller reflexed tepals; they have a most distinctive red ring of stamens that can be seen clearly during mid-May and early June. This hybrid prefers an acidic moisture-retentive soil and a sheltered site in dappled shade. In the southeast of England young leaves have a tendency to scorch if they are

Magnolia 'Charles Coates'. A chance hybrid between an American and Asiatic species combining the best qualities of both parents, this plant was found by Charles Coates at the Royal Botanic Gardens, Kew. The scented flowers are sparsely seen during early summer on a broad-spreading large shrub or small tree. Photo by Jim Gardiner.

exposed to strong direct sunlight, but this may not be the case in areas where light intensity or temperature is not so great, or where atmospheric humidity levels are greater. The plant is quite hardy, to U.S. hardiness zone 6.

Magnolia ×*soulangeana*

This multistemmed large shrub or broad-spreading small tree is probably the best known and most widely planted of all magnolias; it is the archetypal magnolia. Driving into most towns and cities, especially in southern England during late March and early April, you are instantly aware of this tree's presence. White, pink, and reddish purple blooms are seen in profusion on every major road or tucked under the lee of boundary walls.

The story of *Magnolia* ×*soulangeana* can be traced back to the early nineteenth century. Europe was just recovering from the Napoleonic wars, where vast armies had criss-crossed the continent. Etienne Soulange-Bodin, a cavalry officer in Napoleon's army, had seen great botanical collections of the day at Schonbrunn (Vienna), Stuttgart, and Moscow during the campaigns and had

Magnolia ×*soulangeana*. The most widely planted magnolia throughout the British Isles is probably *M.* ×*soulangeana*. From the centre of cities to country gardens, it makes a broad-spreading large shrub or small tree similar to this plant at The Winnings, Colwell, near Great Malvern, Hereford and Worcester. Photo by Jim Gardiner.

been saddened with what he saw, suggesting that it would have been "better for both parties to have stayed at home and planted their cabbages." On his return from the war, Soulange-Bodin founded the Royal Institute of Horticulture at Fromont, near Paris, and became its first director. It was here in 1820 that he pollinated *M. denudata* with *M. liliiflora*. The resulting hybrid flowered for the first time in 1827 and "was remarkable for its treelike habit . . . and above all for its wide-spreading brilliant flowers, in which the purest white is tinged with a purplish hue."

With the upturn of economic fortunes in the British Isles during the 1820s, new plants were introduced by the (Royal) Horticultural Society and nursery firms, including Soulange-Bodin's first batch of *Magnolia* ×*soulangeana*. J. C. Loudon in the *Gardener's Magazine* of 1834, reported that the hybrid had "produced throughout April this year the most beautiful effect in the Vauxhall nursery belonging to Messrs. Chandler & Sons where it is trained against a wall exposed to the west." Thus our love affair with *M.* ×*soulangeana* began.

Clones of *Magnolia* ×*soulangeana* have been raised by numerous hybridisers in Europe (including the British Isles), Japan, and North America. It is probable earlier hybrids existed in Japan prior to 1830, as it was likely both plants were growing in proximity to one another in temple gardens or nurseries. Since that time, however, both second- and third-generation hybrids have been raised, providing a complexity of colour forms from milky white through various shades of pink to an intense reddish purple, while some are bicoloured. Shape varies from a tulip shape, cup and saucer shape to a goblet, while size of bloom and time of flowering too are quite variable, depending on the clone and season. In the south of England the last week of March to the end of April or early May is generally the peak flowering period, while in California flowering starts in mid-February. Even young plants of two or three years of age produce flowers in quantity. The flowers are made up of nine tepals and are generally of a firm constitution and fairly weather resistant, though not frost tolerant.

Their leaves are quite variable, being broadly elliptic to obovate in shape, up to 20 cm (8 in.) long by 11.5 cm (4½ in.) wide. In colour they are dark glossy green above, paler beneath, with fine hairs along the mid-rib and main veins. In habit the plants are all broad-spreading multistemmed shrubs, which in time attain plants of treelike proportions and are generally freestanding. Their shape and size can be controlled by pruning which is done either immediately after

Magnolia ×soulangeana 'Etienne Soulange-Bodin'. The numerous clones of *M. ×soulangeana* vary in flower colour from white to an intense purple, shape of flower from tulip, cup and saucer to goblets, and bloom for six to eight weeks. The most commonly seen clone is 'Etienne Soulange-Bodin', seen here at The Winnings near Great Malvern, Hereford and Worcester. It is warm pink in colour with a cup-and-saucer shaped flower. Photo by Jim Gardiner.

flowering or during late summer. Growth is affected by clonal differences that are reflected in the vigour of the plant. For instance 'Lilliputian' and 'Sweet Simplicity' are the least vigorous, while 'Rustica Rubra', 'Brozzoni', and 'Picture' are three of the more vigorous.

Magnolia × *soulangeana* has the reputation of being the easiest magnolia to cultivate. It grows successfully in most soil types, apart from the thinnest of dry chalky soils. It is among the most wind-tolerant of magnolias and is quite hardy while dormant in the British climate. The time of year when magnolias are most vulnerable is during spring, when severe frosts occur on two or three mornings following a long period of mild weather that has brought the plant into active vegetative growth. All the young growth will be killed and if strong sunlight hits the plant early in the morning, the action of rapid freezing and thawing will kill even mature plants—generally those that are in a poor condition. This is what happened during the spring of 1995, when air frosts of at least −3°C (26°F) on three successive nights in mid-April caused all new growth to be killed. Within six weeks, however, most plants had re-established new vigorous growth. Regrowth depends on the vigour of the plant and on the soil moisture content. Provided the soil is wet a magnolia will grow comparatively freely. If the soil is dry after a dry winter, then a tree's ability to regrow will be reduced. Dependent on cultivar, *Magnolia* × *soulangeana* is regarded as between the maximum and minimum ranges of U.S. hardiness zone 5.

More than 100 published names of *Magnolia* × *soulangeana* are recorded. Many have stood the test of time, having been raised in the nineteenth century, while others are more recent. The most commonly seen clone is *M.* × *soulangeana*. Thought to be the "type," it should perhaps be called by the cultivar name 'Etienne Soulange-Bodin'. The cup-and-saucer shaped flowers are a beautiful warm pink in bud, opening to white inside with flushed pink on the outside deepening to a purplish pink at the base. It flowers mid-season during the second half of April. There are several large specimens at Wisley, notably on Seven Acres and Battleston Hill.

'Alba Superba', among the earliest clones to flower, has pure white tepals with basal blotches of pink-purple. The flowers are shaped like a cup and saucer. This clone was raised in Belgium during the mid-nineteenth century. It is among the most frequently seen clones on Battleston Hill at Wisley Garden, Surrey.

'**Alexandrina**', originally introduced by Cels of Montrouge, Paris, in 1831, appears to have been mixed over the years, and the name covers an assortment of clones. The French clone, which has nine tepals, flowers over a long period starting a week after the flowering peak of the *M. ×soulangeana* group. The flower is fragrant, tulip-shaped, 10 cm (4 in.) long, white flushed with purple on the outside, and white inside. Another erect form recognised under this name produces pure white flowers that are slightly larger, up to 11.5 cm (4½ in.) long. These two are considered to be probably the hardiest of the clones.

'**Brozzoni**' is a second-generation seedling raised in the garden of Camillo Brozzoni at Brescia, Italy, in 1873. The narrow-shaped, almost candlelike flowers, although ultimately cup and saucer shaped, are some of the last to come into flower and are generally seen over a long period of time in the second half of April. The colour of the flowers is pure white with a hint of pink at the inner

Magnolia ×soulangeana 'Alba Superba'. One of the first *M. ×soulangeana* clones to flower, 'Alba Superba' is frequently planted. It was first made available through the Van Geert Nursery of Ghent in Belgium. Photo by Jim Gardiner.

base of the whorl of tepals, each of which is 14 cm (5½ in.) long. 'Brozzoni' is among the best cultivars.

'Burgundy', a floriferous, early flowering hybrid, was raised by W. B. Clarke of San Jose in the 1930s and named in 1943. It was introduced into the British Isles in the 1960s. The flowers are rose-pink in colour and open to 20 cm (8 in.) wide. In North America, where light conditions differ from the British Isles, the flowers are a deep purple-red that better justifies the cultivar name.

'Coates' is among the more recent American introductions from the Leonard Coates Nursery, San Jose, California, with a beautiful cup-and-saucer shaped reddish pink outer, white to pink inner flower. It arose as a seedling of *Magnolia ×soulangeana* 'Rustica Rubra' and is a softer paler colour. It was introduced into the trade by Gossler Farms Nursery of Springfield, Oregon, in 1973.

'Dark Splendor' is an upright-growing, floriferous American hybrid with wine-red flowers. It is the result of a backcross by Otto Spring of Okmulgee, Oklahoma, in the 1960s, of *Magnolia ×soulangeana* 'Rustica Rubra' with *M. liliiflora* 'Nigra'.

Magnolia ×soulangeana 'Brozzoni'. One of the best *M. ×soulangeana* clones in cultivation, 'Brozzoni' is also the last to bloom and produces some of the largest flowers. It was raised in Camillo Brozzoni's garden in Brescia, Italy, in 1873 and distributed by André Leroy of Angers, France. Photo by John Gallagher.

'Grace McDade', an American cultivar introduced by Clint McDade of Semmes, Alabama, is said to have the largest flowers of all the *M. × soulangeana* cultivars: 30–35 cm (12–13½ in.) wide. The flowers are white with a pink-purple flush.

'Just Jean' is a floriferous hybrid that resulted as a chance seedling found by John Gallagher in Dorset, England, during the 1970s. It has a compact habit and distinctive, large, obovate foliage. In mid-April it produces clear pink, goblet-shaped flowers flushed deep pink at the base.

'Lennei', an important clone that should not be overlooked, was raised in the province of Lombardy, northern Italy, during the middle of the nineteenth century, by Giuseppe Manetti, who named it after Peter Joseph Lenne (1787–1866), a German botanist. It was introduced into the trade by A. Topf, a nurseryman of Erfurt, Prussia. The tulip-shaped flowers, rose-purple on the outer, white within, are late flowering. 'Lennei' is fast growing and free flowering and has been used by the Jurys in their *Magnolia* breeding programmes.

'Lennei Alba' has pure ivory white flowers

Magnolia ×soulangeana 'Lennei'. Raised by Giuseppe Manetti in the 1850s, this important clone was reportedly sold to Alfred Topf of Erfurt, Prussia, for 10,000 francs. It was named after Peter Lenne, the superintendent of the Prussian Royal Gardens. Photo by John Hillier.

Magnolia ×soulangeana 'Lennei Alba'. With good floristic qualities, 'Lennei Alba' has been recognised as an excellent parent. Todd Gresham and Felix Jury have used it to produce hybrids of excellence. Photo by Jim Gardiner.

that are not strictly goblet-shaped but rather an inverted flask shape! It is a third-generation 'Lennei' seedling raised by Froebel of Zurich, Switzerland, in 1905 and introduced into the trade by W. Keessen of Aalsmeer, Netherlands in 1930–31. This broader-spreading plant was used by Gresham to produce his Buxom Nordic Blondes (see under Gresham hybrids in chapter 7). Several clones probably masquerade under this name with smaller and creamy coloured flowers.

'**Lilliputiana**', the smallest of the *Magnolia* ×*soulangeana* clones, has white flowers tinged with pink. It was introduced by Semmes Nursery of Alabama.

'**Norbertii**' has goblet-shaped, slightly scented flowers that are white flushed with pink. It flowers at the same time as 'Alexandrina', in early April, and its

Magnolia ×*soulangeana* 'Picture'. Often known as 'Wada's Picture', this clone has some of the largest flowers of the *M.* ×*soulangeana* clones. More than one clone has been given this name. The one shown here, at the National Trust property at Trelissick, differs from the 'Picture' at Hillier Nurseries in having a cleaner white to the upper tepals and a more concentrated staining, though the central line still reaches the tip of the tepals. Photo by Jim Gardiner.

tepals are about 10 cm (4 in.) long. It was introduced by Cels of Montrouge, Paris.

'**Picture**' or 'Wada's Picture' is a Japanese clone introduced by Wada's Nursery of Yokohama in the 1930s. It has one of the largest flowers with tepals 15.0–17.5 cm (6–7 in.) long and typically cup and saucer shaped. In colour they are white or sometimes a pale pinkish white on the inside with a heavy red-purple staining on the outside. Two clones of 'Picture' are in cultivation in the British Isles. Both have very large flowers, one with a more clearly defined colour separation with far more white in the flower. Open-pollinated seedlings of 'Picture' have been named.

During the late 1960s, Amos Pickard of Canterbury, Kent, raised several open-pollinated seedlings of *Magnolia* ×*soulangeana* 'Picture'. All these seedlings grew into multistemmed upright-growing large shrubs or small to medium-sized trees and flower prolifically where spring temperatures are high during late March or early April and where light levels are good. Most have six tepals of good substance and three more that are sepal-like in appearance. These plants are surprisingly cold tolerant when dormant and are grown in collections in Poland, Germany, and Sweden. Sir Peter Smithers at Vico Morcote in Switzerland has had considerable success with them. The following are worthy of cultivation. '**Pickard's Garnet**' has goblet-shaped wine-red flowers. Its colour is highly regarded by Otto Eisenhut of Ticino, Switzerland. '**Pickard's Opal**', also with goblet-shaped flowers, is white with a hint of purple at the base of the inside and outside each tepal. '**Pickard's Ruby**' has goblet-shaped purple-red flowers, whose tepals exhibit an almost picotee effect. '**Pickard's Schmetterling**' is an extremely elegant looking flower with 15 cm (6 in.) long narrow tepals, creamy white and deeply stained with reddish purple on the outside. It was named by Mrs. Pickard. '**Pickard's Snow Queen**' has large vase-shaped pure white flowers with no hint of pink or purple at the base

Magnolia ×*soulangeana* 'Pickard's Schmetterling'. One of Pickard's hybrids, 'Pickard's Schmetterling' has very large, narrowly upright flowers. Photo by Jim Gardiner.

of the tepals. **'Pickard's Sundew'** or 'Sundew' produces goblet-shaped pink flowers contrasting with creamy white on the inside which, Sir Peter Smithers indicates, is enhanced by "the hint of an orange undertone." He regards 'Sundew' among his best magnolias.

'Rustica Rubra' is a Dutch clone raised at the end of the nineteenth century in Boskoop. The reddish purple flowers, pink-white within, are the classic goblet shape and appear in mid-season (the middle of April).

'San Jose' was introduced by W. B. Clarke Nursery, of San Jose, California. This large, goblet-shaped deep pink-flowered form with white on the inside was raised in the 1930s and is the form known in the British Isles. It is among the later

Magnolia ×*soulangeana* 'Pickard's Garnet'. Probably the darkest of Pickard's hybrids, 'Pickard's Garnet' has flowers that are a deep wine-red colour. Photo by Sir Peter Smithers.

clones to flower. Phil J. Savage of Bloomfield Hills, Michigan, refers to a plant cultivated in North America under the same name but with a different description: "The entire bloom is a pure marble white, except for a striking 'thumb print' of dark pink, almost red at the very base of each tepal." Both cultivars have probably been mixed since they were raised in the 1930s, so it is impossible now to know which is the "correct" description.

'Triumphans' is a goblet-shaped rose-red flower with a pinkish white interior. The flowers are seen during mid-April.

'Verbanica', a clone of French origin, was raised by Leroy of Angers in 1873. The cup-shaped flowers are an attractive rich clean pink fading to white at the

Magnolia ×*soulangeana* 'Rustica Rubra'. Raised from seed of *M.* ×*soulangeana* 'Lennei' and selected by a Boskoop nurseryman, 'Rustica Rubra' differs from 'Lennei' in that its purple goblet-shaped flowers are darker in colour and bloom marginally earlier. Photo by John Gallagher.

Magnolia ×*soulangeana* 'Verbanica'. Within the shelter of the Alpes Maritime, the water meadows of the Villa Noailles, near Grasse, were planted by Vicomte de Noailles in the early 1950s with *M.* ×*soulangeana* clones including 'Verbanica.' The large shrubs make a splendid display during March. Photo by Jim Gardiner.

tips of the tepals. 'Verbanica' is probably among the last clones of *Magnolia ×soulangeana* to flower in mid-April or May in the British Isles, but generally a month earlier in the Mediterranean. When cultivated well, it produces an attractive display of well-spaced clean pink flowers, but when it is starved or badly sited or where temperatures are lower the flowers are smaller and more crowded and have a distinctive "dirty pink" colour.

'White Giant', another Wada's Nursery selection, has huge milky-white flowers (sometimes with a hint of pink) which are goblet shaped and splay open on the second day, very much like those of *Magnolia grandiflora*.

Magnolia ×soulangeana 'Triumphans'. This early nineteenth century clone has small pinkish red flowers seen in abundance towards the end of the *M. ×soulangeana* flowering period. Photo by Jim Gardiner.

Magnolia sprengeri Hybrids

Magnolia sprengeri has been hybridised with several species and has produced some superb hybrids. *Magnolia* 'Galaxy' and *M*. 'Spectrum' (with *M. liliiflora*) and *M*. 'Caerhays Belle' (with *M. sargentiana* var. *robusta*) are established hybrids that have proved their value around the world and are discussed elsewhere. *Magnolia sprengeri* var. *sprengeri* 'Diva' has been crossed with *M*. ×*soulangeana* by Frank Galyon of Knoxville, Tennessee, and by Phil Savage of Bloomfield Hills, Michigan.

'Big Dude' (*Magnolia* ×*soulangeana* 'Picture' × *M. sprengeri* var. *sprengeri* 'Diva') is a multistemmed large shrub or small tree with fragrant large cup-shaped reddish purple flowers and white fading to rose-pink on the inside of the 9–12 tepals. As the flowers enlarge, they nod over to the horizontal and become rather floppy. This clone is highly regarded by Phil Savage for its hardiness: it flowered after a winter where temperatures fell to –34°C (–29°F). It was registered by Savage in 1989.

Magnolia 'Big Dude'. Phil Savage of Bloomfield Hills, Michigan, raised this flamboyant hybrid and named it as a Detroit citizen would describe a large and formidable friend. It is the hardiest and best of 48 seedlings to bloom from this cross. Photo by Phil Savage.

'J. C. Williams' (*Magnolia sargentiana* var. *robusta* × *M. sprengeri* var. *sprengeri* 'Diva') was raised by Philip Tregunna, the head gardener at Caerhays Castle, Cornwall, between 1956 and 1996. This plant has an aristocratic parentage: the seed parent is E. H. Wilson's original *M. sargentiana* var. *robusta* and the pollen parent is the original 'Diva' purchased from Veitch's Coombe Wood Nursery sale in 1913. The flower colour is very similar to that of *M. campbellii* subsp. *mollicomata* 'Lanarth'. The plant was named by F. Julian Williams after his grandfather, who was responsible for planting Caerhays Castle gardens.

'Paul Cook' (*Magnolia* ×*soulangeana* 'Lennei' seedling × *M. sprengeri* var. *sprengeri* 'Diva') is a fast-growing small to medium-sized tree with large 20–25 cm (8–10 in.) lavender-pink rather floppy flowers, with white on the inside of the 6–9 tepals. It was registered by Frank Galyon of Knoxville, Tennessee, in 1975.

'Thomas Messel' (*Magnolia sprengeri* var. *elongata* × ?*M. campbellii*) is a small tree. Its 10–12 white tepals have a staining of rich pink at the base on their outside. The outer tepals reflex leaving the inner four upright, which in time reflex, giving the flower a rather floppy appearance. This clone originated as a seedling raised in the 1960s from a plant of *M. sprengeri* var. *elongata* growing at Nymans Gardens in Sussex. The seedling grew near to *M. campbellii*, and its leaf shape suggests that *M. campbellii* is the pollen parent.

Magnolia ×*thompsoniana*

This wide-spreading large shrub is a hybrid between two North American magnolias, *Magnolia virginiana* and *M. tripetala*. It first arose in the nursery of Archibald Thompson at Mile End, London, in 1808, which makes it the first magnolia hybrid to have arisen in the Western world, predating *M.* ×*soulangeana* by about 12 years. One theory is that a seedling was selected from a batch of imported seed sown by Thompson. Another, which considers that *M. tripetala* had been cultivated in the London area for about 50 years, is that seed from a plant of *M. virginiana* grown by Thompson was sown, germinated, and selected on site. J. C. Loudon in *Arboretum et Fruticetum Britannicum* (1844) wrote that "it was noticed in a pot of seedlings by Mr. Thompson in his nursery at Mile End and by him kept distinct and propagated under the above name." Loudon also mentioned a hybrid that originated in Belgium and was imported by Mr. Knight of the Exotic Nursery, Kings Road, Chelsea. Evidence supports both theories, but when the plant was first featured in *Curtis's Botanical Magazine* of 1820, it was not considered a hybrid. Rather, it was considered a large-leaved form of the American sweet bay, *M. virginiana.* It was not until 1876 that the Dutch botanist C. de Vos confirmed its current status, which has more recently been supported by Professor Joe McDaniel. In the 1960s, McDaniel carried out deliberate cross-pollinations between the two suspected parents and produced plants that conformed almost exactly to the 1820 description in *Curtis's Botanical Magazine.*

Magnolia ×*thompsoniana* grows into a rather ungainly shrub to 6 m (20 ft.) tall with a spread of 4.5 m (15 ft.) in the southeast of England, though larger in milder habitats and in the southern United States. The leaves are very variable in size, but up to 23 cm (9 in.) long by 10 cm (4 in.) wide. Generally elliptic in shape, often with undulating margins, they are glossy green in colour above and a glaucous to silvery green beneath, with fine hairs coating the entire un-

Magnolia ×*thompsoniana.* First grown in Archibald Thompson's Mile End nursery in London in 1808, *M.* ×*thompsoniana* is rather ungainly in its habit, but has deliciously scented flowers over a long period during the summer months. Photo by Jim Gardiner.

dersurface. In most parts of the British Isles, this shrub is deciduous, losing its leaves late in November or December. In mild localities or in the southern United States it is semi-evergreen. In the British Isles the flowers are creamy white to primrose-yellow; they are borne sporadically, on leafy shoots, from May but primarily in July and August. They are quite fragrant (a quality inherited from *M. virginiana*), vase-shaped, and 12.5–15.0 cm (5–6 in.) wide with 12 tepals, each up to 10 cm (4 in.) long.

Professor Joe McDaniel's selection that confirmed the original cross has been named 'Urbana' and was registered in 1969. The fragrant flowers have prominent, reflexed outer tepals more reminiscent of *Magnolia tripetala* than *M. virginiana*, but they have the initial goblet shape of *M. virginiana* and flower during June and July.

Magnolia ×*thompsoniana* deserves to be more widely distributed because of the attractiveness of its foliage and of its flowers, which are seen from an early age and over a long period. It needs a hot, sunny, yet sheltered site and space to spread. It is quite hardy, to U.S. hardiness zone 6; however, exposure to −31°C (26°F) in the United States has been recorded. Young plants 90 cm (3 ft.) high and one year from planting survived temperatures of −12°C (10°F) in southern England without damage, which is a fair indicator of their hardiness rating.

Magnolia ×*veitchii*

This name is given to the *Magnolia denudata* × *M. campbellii* cross, the first recorded hybrid of *M. campbellii*. This fast-growing tree was first raised in Exeter at the Royal Nurseries of Peter C. M. Veitch in 1907. Veitch's objective was to raise a hybrid that was "as beautiful as its parents, more hardy, and that would flower in a reasonable time."

According to the late W. T. Andrews, Veitch's nursery manager, pollen was taken from *Magnolia denudata* and other magnolias, including *M.* ×*soulangeana* and *M. stellata,* and transferred to a free-flowering specimen of *M. campbellii* that was growing at the New North Road nursery site. (J. G. Millais in 1927 and J. E. Dandy in 1950 reported the cross as being the other way round.) Six seedlings resulted, only two of which were retained—'Peter Veitch', with pink flowers, and 'Isca' (the Roman name for Exeter), with white flowers, pale pink in bud. Both grow into medium-to-large trees.

'Peter Veitch' is more vigorous and upright than 'Isca', which has a distinctly broader-spreading habit, and is clearly the poorer of the two. Young trees of 'Peter Veitch' can increase in growth by more than 90 cm (3 ft.) per year, less so with 'Isca'. Both have a reputation for casting limbs during high winds, particularly 'Peter Veitch' because it is a heavy-limbed tree, often multistemmed, with congested branches. A tree growing at Caerhays Castle in Cornwall was found to be more than 29 m (95 ft.) tall when measured in 1984, making it the tallest tree magnolia in the British Isles. (It was planted in 1921.) With the violent storms of 1987 and 1990, when hurricane force winds lashed the southern British Isles, many champion trees were lost with the tallest magnolia now thought to be *Magnolia acuminata* and *M. obovata* growing in Margam Park, South Wales, and Westonbirt Arboretum, Gloucestershire.

The green leaves of 'Peter Veitch' are obovate or oblong in shape, to 30 cm (12 in.) long by 18 cm (7 in.) wide, with a distinctive point at the apex. When they first unfurl they have a purplish tinge, especially on the underside, which quickly disappears as the leaf increases in size. The fine grey down is found on the underside along the midrib and partially along the main veins. 'Peter Veitch' is the cultivar normally encountered. Its pink chalice-shaped flowers have nine tepals up to 12.5 cm (5 in.) long and are seen on leafless branches in mid-April. It is a most prolific-flowering tree and reliably so.

Magnolia ×veitchii 'Peter Veitch'. The blooms of this vigorous clone are soft pink, fading on the inside. Photo by Jim Gardiner.

'Isca' has pure-white flowers that are smaller and less prolifically produced than those of 'Peter Veitch'. 'Isca' is said to open a week before 'Peter Veitch' in Devon and Cornwall, but specimens in the Hillier Gardens and Arboretum open more or less on the same day.

Both 'Peter Veitch' and 'Isca' take from 7 to 10 years before they start to flower reliably. The flowers of *Magnolia ×veitchii* are erect and chalice-shaped and lack the "saucer" shape seen in *M. campbellii*. A sunny yet sheltered site is needed for these vigorous growers, which require moisture-retentive soil, preferably on the acid side of neutral. They are regarded as hardy to U.S. hardiness zone 7.

'**Rubra**' was raised by W. B. Clarke, nurseryman of San Jose, California. It is similar in all respects to 'Peter Veitch' except for the flower, which is a wine-red colour when in bud. Another quality is that it flowers from an early age. In Clarke's *Garden Aristocrats* catalogue of 1945, the plant is described thus:

> Remarkably vigorous growth bearing enormous flowers which are soft shell pink without the slightest suggestion of purple. As to hardiness, it has flowered and fruited in Seattle, which reminds us that the red fruit, up to 30 cm (1 ft.) long, is highly effective in autumn.

Magnolia ×veitchii 'Isca'. Raised at Veitch's Royal Nurseries in Exeter in 1907, this hybrid flowered for the first time 10 years later. Two clones were selected, 'Peter Veitch' with pink flowers, and 'Isca' with white flowers and a noticeably weaker constitution. Photo by Jim Gardiner.

'Rubra' is hardy to U.S. hardiness zone 6 and has been used by hybridisers as a parent of the Gresham hybrids.

Magnolia ×*veitchii* has been used by hybridisers as a parent of the Gresham hybrids (see separate entry for these) and of several other hybrids.

'**Columbus**' (*Magnolia denudata* × *M.* ×*veitchii* 'Peter Veitch') was one of three propagules sent by the U.S. National Arboretum to the Crown Estate Commissioners at Windsor in 1975. John Bond, formerly keeper of the gardens, considered the large cup-shaped white flowers sufficiently distinct and, with the arboretum's permission,

Magnolia ×*veitchii* 'Rubra'. This second-generation clone was raised by W. B. Clarke of San Jose, California, and used by Todd Gresham as a parent of the Gresham hybrids. Photo by Jim Gardiner.

named this tree in 1992 to commemorate its Atlantic crossing and to mark the 500th anniversary of Columbus's voyage. The original cross was made by William F. Kosar in 1960. Frank S. Santamour Jr. selected the clone in 1973 and distributed rooted cuttings in 1975 to American nurseries and arboreta as well as European gardens of which Windsor was one.

'**Curly Head**' (*Magnolia acuminata* 'Fertile Myrtle' × *M.* ×*veitchii* 'Peter Veitch') is a Phil Savage hybrid that grows into a tall, straight-stemmed medium-sized tree. The pastel pink and yellow or white flowers open at the same time as the unfurling leaves. Not only does the introduction of *M. acuminata* improve the hardiness rating of *M.* ×*veitchii* hybrids, but it also improves their durability as *M.* ×*veitchii* is reputedly rather brittle. This hybrid was originally named 'Editor Hopkins' in honour of Harold C. Hopkins, former editor of the Magnolia Society's newsletter.

'**Helen Fogg**' (*Magnolia denudata* 'Sawada's Pink' × *M.* ×*veitchii* 'Peter Veitch') is a Phil Savage hybrid that grows into a vigorous symmetrical medium-sized tree. The flowers are white, cup-shaped, with a distinct pinkish hue to the lower half of the tepals. This plant is much hardier than *M.* ×*veitchii*. It was named in 1989 after the wife of John M. Fogg, a founding member of the Magnolia Society.

Magnolia ×*wieseneri*

Magnolia ×*wieseneri*, a deliciously scented, multistemmed, large shrub or broad-spreading small tree, is a hybrid between two Japanese species, *M. obovata*, which has a wide distribution from Hokkaido in the north to the Ryukyu Islands in the south, and the Japanese form of *M. sieboldii* subsp. *japonica* from Honshu, Shikoku, and Kyushu. It is unlikely this hybrid occurred naturally in the wild. *Magnolia* species generally protect themselves against natural hybridisation by occupying different habitats and by flowering at slightly different periods. In the artificial surroundings of a garden landscape, however, these natural defences are broken down. It is probable that this hybrid occurred spontaneously or by design in Japanese gardens during the nineteenth century or before. The Japanese know the plant as Gyo Kusui and Ukesaki Oyamarenage, meaning "upward-facing *Magnolia sieboldii*."

This magnolia first appeared in Europe on the Japanese Court stand at the Paris Exposition of 1889. Many admired it, including W. J. Bean who acquired a specimen for the Royal Botanic Gardens, Kew. Some two years later Joseph Hooker (later Sir Joseph), director of Kew, described it and named it *Magnolia* ×*watsonii* after W. Watson, an assistant curator at Kew. Unknown to Hooker, another plant had been purchased by a Mr. Wiesener, a local landowner, who had bought a plant labelled *M. parviflora* (*M. sieboldii*) from Mr. Tokada, a Japanese horticulturist exhibiting at the Trocadero in Paris at the same time as the Paris exhibition. This hybrid was named by Elie A. Carrière when he described it in 1890, some six months before Hooker. Under the rules of the International Code of Botanical Nomenclature, the earlier name takes priority.

Magnolia ×*wieseneri*. This deliciously sweetly scented magnolia fills warm summer evenings with a rich fragrance virtually unequalled. It was named after a Mr. Wiesener, who purchased a plant from a Japanese horticulturist exhibiting at the Trocadero in Paris during 1889. Photo by Jim Gardiner.

Neil Treseder in *Magnolias* (1978) pointed out minor botanical differences such as stamen colour and shape of the flower bud among different plants in cultivation, which indicates *Magnolia* ×*wieseneri* should be regarded as a grex name. The habit and botanical characteristics of *M. ×wieseneri* are midway between its two parents; it is a multi-stemmed large shrub or small bushy tree to 6 m (20 ft.) tall. It is a strong, upright grower when established, increasing by up to 60 cm (2 ft.) a year, but when initially planted into a garden situation it is often slow to establish and to grow. The obovate leaves are quite leathery in texture, approximately 20 cm (8 in.) long by 10.5 cm (4 in.) wide. They are green above and a glaucous green beneath.

The plant is mainly grown for the scent of its flowers, which has been variously described as ethereal, medicinal, spicy, aromatic, and like pineapples. On the first day of opening the upward-facing flowers are cup-shaped, 10.0–12.5 cm (4–5 in.) wide, with up to nine ivory-white tepals. On opening, the central boss of deep red stamens is revealed, creating an eye-catching combination of colour. The globular shape is maintained for a few days (depending on the levels of insect pollinators present), then the flower splays out to 15–20 cm (6–8 in.) wide and loses some of its appeal. The plant starts to flower from a fairly early age, with the flowers appearing rather sporadically from late May or early June and lasting for about a month.

When this plant was first introduced into cultivation, it reportedly was slow and difficult to grow, but presumably because only poorly grafted specimens were then available. With modern propagation techniques it is not uncommon for a plant to attain a height of 1.5 m (5 ft.) in 15 months after budding. It is quite hardy in the British Isles and in the United States is hardy to U.S. hardiness zone 5. It is not widely distributed even in specialist collections, a fact that needs to be remedied. I have seen it growing on well-drained, sandy soil where regular top dressings are carried out, and on a heavy, loamy (but not waterlogged) clay. On both of these soils it was giving a good account of itself.

'William Watson' resulted as a chance seedling in the garden of Sir Peter Smithers at Vico Morcote in Switzerland. *Magnolia ×wieseneri* produced a seed cone that probably resulted from this hybrid being pollinated by a *M. obovata* flowering at the same time. 'William Watson' grows into an upright, medium-sized, potentially large tree. The beautiful cup-shaped white flowers are seen in June. They are slightly larger in size and, importantly, similar in scent to *M. ×wieseneri* and were seen only six years after germination of the seed. This tree was named after William Watson, former assistant curator of the Royal Botanic Gardens, Kew, after whom *M. ×wieseneri* was originally named.

Recommended Magnolias

Magnolias with Yellow Flowers

M. acuminata 'Seiju'

M. acuminata subsp. *subcordata* 'Mr. Yellowjacket'

M. 'Butterflies'

M. 'Elizabeth'

M. 'Gold Crown'

M. 'Gold Cup'

M. 'Gold Star'

M. 'Goldfinch'

M. 'Sundance'

M. 'Yellow Bird'

Magnolias with White Flowers

M. 'Albatross'

M. 'David Clulow'

M. grandiflora 'Goliath'

M. ×kewensis 'Wada's Memory'

M. 'Leda'

M. 'Pegasus'

M. 'Sir Harold Hillier'

M. ×soulangeana 'Brozzoni'

M. stellata 'Centennial'

M. ×veitchii 'Columbus'

Magnolias with Pink Flowers

M. 'Atlas'

M. 'Caerhays' Belle'

M. campbellii (Raffillii Group) 'Charles Raffill'

M. dawsoniana 'Clarke'

M. 'Daybreak'

M. ×loebneri 'Leonard Messel'

M. ×soulangeana 'Lennei'

M. sprengeri 'Copeland Court'

M. 'Star Wars'

M. stellata 'Jane Platt'

Magnolias with Purple/Red/Magenta Flowers

M. campbellii 'Darjeeling'

M. campbellii subsp. *mollicomata* 'Lanarth'

M. 'Joe McDaniel'

M. liliiflora 'O'Neill'

M. liliiflora 'Nigra'

M. sargentiana var. *robusta* 'Blood Moon'

M. ×soulangeana 'Pickard's Garnet'

M. ×soulangeana 'Rustica Rubra'

M. sprengeri 'Marwood Spring'

M. 'Susan'

M. 'Vulcan'

Magnolias with Scented Flowers

M. 'Charles Coates'

M. grandiflora

M. macrophylla

M. 'Nimbus'

M. 'Porcelain Dove'

M. obovata

M. sieboldii

M. virginiana

Magnolias with Scented Flowers, cont.

M. ×wieseneri

M. ×wieseneri 'William Watson'

M. wilsonii

M. wilsonii 'Highdownensis'

Magnolias for Autumn Foliage

M. acuminata 'Busey'

M. fraseri

M. kobus

M. ×loebneri

M. obovata

M. officinalis var. *biloba*

M. salicifolia

Magnolias with Good Foliage Qualities

M. delavayi

M. grandiflora

M. macrophylla

M. macrophylla subsp. *ashei*

M. macrophylla subsp. *dealbata*

M. nitida

M. obovata

M. officinalis

M. officinalis var. *biloba*

M. rostrata

M. salicifolia (scented)

M. 'Silver Parasol'

M. tripetala

Magnolias for Alkaline Soils

M. acuminata

M. acuminata subsp. *subcordata*

M. delavayi

M. denudata

M. fraseri

M. grandiflora

M. kobus

M. ×loebneri

M. obovata

M. ×soulangeana

M. ×veitchii

Magnolias for Small Gardens

M. 'Ann'

M. 'George Henry Kern'

M. grandiflora 'Bracken's Brown Beauty'

M. grandiflora 'Little Gem'

M. liliiflora 'Nigra'

M. liliiflora 'O'Neill'

M. ×loebneri 'Leonard Messel'

M. 'Marillyn'

M. 'Orchid'

M. 'Pinkie'

M. 'Pristine'

M. sieboldii

M. stellata 'Centennial'

M. stellata 'Jane Platt'

M. stellata 'Waterlily'

M. 'Susan'

Magnolias for Medium-sized Gardens

M. 'Albatross'

M. 'Athene'

M. 'Atlas'

M. 'Caerhays Surprise'

M. 'David Clulow'

M. 'Elizabeth'

M. 'Galaxy'

M. 'Heaven Scent'

M. ×kewensis 'Wada's Memory'

M. ×loebneri 'Merrill'

M. ×loebneri 'Spring Snow'

M. 'Milky Way'

M. 'Peppermint Stick'

M. 'Royal Crown'

M. 'Sayonara'

M. ×soulangeana 'Brozzoni'

M. ×soulangeana 'Lennei Alba'

M. ×soulangeana 'Pickard's Schmetterling'

M. ×*soulangeana* 'Picture'

M. ×*soulangeana* 'San Jose'

M. 'Tina Durio'

M. wilsonii 'Highdownensis'

Magnolias for Large Gardens

M. acuminata 'Golden Glow'

M. campbellii (Raffillii Group) 'Charles Raffill'

M. campbellii (Raffillii Group) 'Kew's Surprise'

M. campbellii subsp. *mollicomata* 'Lanarth'

M. campbellii subsp. *mollicomata* 'Peter Borlase'

M. grandiflora 'Gallissonniere'

M. grandiflora 'Goliath'

M. grandiflora 'Samuel Sommer'

M. macrophylla 'Whopper'

M. 'Moresk'

M. obovata

M. 'Princess Margaret'

M. sprengeri 'Copeland Court'

M. sprengeri var. *sprengeri* 'Diva'

M. 'Star Wars'

M. ×*veitchii* 'Columbus'

M. ×*veitchii* 'Peter Veitch'

Magnolias with a Fastigiate Habit

M. 'Ann'

M. 'Daybreak'

M. 'Galaxy'

M. 'Gold Star'

M. grandiflora 'Bracken's Brown Beauty'

M. grandiflora 'Gallissonniere'

M. grandiflora 'Russet'

M. 'Jane'

M. ×*kewensis* 'Wada's Memory'

M. 'Marj Gossler'

M. 'Peachy'

M. sprengeri var. *elongata*

M. 'Yellow Lantern'

Magnolias with a Broad/Rounded Habit (trees and shrubs)

M. 'Athene' (T)

M. 'Atlas' (T)

M. campbellii (T)

M. campbellii (Raffillii Group) 'Charles Raffill' (T)

M. campbellii subsp. *mollicomata* (T)

M. delavayi (S)

M. 'George Henry Kern' (S)

M. grandiflora 'Goliath' (T)

M. grandiflora 'Samuel Sommer' (T)

M. grandiflora 'St. Mary' (T)

M. 'Iolanthe' (T)

M. kobus 'Norman Gould' (T)

M. liliiflora 'Nigra' (S)

M. liliiflora 'O'Neill' (S)

M. ×*loebneri* 'Leonard Messel' (S)

M. ×*loebneri* 'Merrill' (T)

M. ×*loebneri* 'Raspberry Fun' (S)

M. macrophylla (T)

M. obovata (T)

M. 'Pegasus' (S)

M. 'Pinkie' (S)

M. sargentiana var. *robusta* (T)

M. sieboldii subsp. *sinensis* (S)

M. ×*soulangeana* (S)

M. sprengeri 'Burncoose' (T)

M. sprengeri 'Copeland Court' (T)

M. sprengeri var. *sprengeri* 'Diva' (T)

M. stellata 'Centennial' (S)

M. stellata 'Jane Platt' (S)

M. stellata 'Royal Star' (S)

M. 'Susan' (S)

M. ×*thompsoniana* (S)

M. wilsonii (S)

Award-winning Magnolias

It is easy enough to evaluate the quality of a magnolia's flower (and, often, leaf) by looking at a flower (or foliage) vase on display at one of the Royal Horticultural Society's shows held in London at Vincent Square or Chelsea. But to judge the plant's other qualities and attributes (or lack of them) is more difficult and for these there is no more reliable guide than the awards given by the Royal Horticultural Society. All awards for magnolias are made by the Council of the Royal Horticultural Society on the recommendation of Floral Committee B. Three awards are given for exhibition—First Class Certificate, Award of Merit, and Preliminary Commendation—and one for garden decoration—Award of Garden Merit.

The Award of Garden Merit (AGM), reinstituted in 1992, recognises plants of outstanding excellence for garden decoration or use, whether grown in the open or under glass. Any plant that has received this award will have fulfilled all the following criteria:

- It should be excellent for ordinary garden decoration or use.
- It should be of good constitution.
- It should be available in the horticultural trade.
- It should not be particularly susceptible to any pest or disease.
- It should not require highly specialised care, other than providing the appropriate conditions for the type of plant concerned.
- It should not be subject to an unreasonable degree of reversion in its vegetative or floral characteristics.

Uniquely among the society's awards the AGM is subject to periodic review. Plants that no longer measure up to the stringent standards or that have dropped out of circulation will be removed, thus keeping the award relevant and up to date.

The First Class Certificate (FCC), instituted in 1859, is given on the recommendation of the committees to plants of outstanding excellence for exhibition.

The Award of Merit (AM), instituted in 1888, is given on the recommendation of the committees to a new plant of promise for exhibition.

The Certificate of Preliminary Commendation (PC), instituted in 1931, is given on the recommendation of the committees to a new plant of promise for exhibition.

Finally, the Certificate of Cultural Commendation (CC), instituted in 1872, is given on the recommendation of the committees to growers whose exhibits show evidence of great cultural skill.

M. acuminata 'Koban Dori', PC (Clulow 1992)

M. 'Albatross', FCC (Foster 1996)

M. 'Ann', AGM (1993)

M. 'Ann Rosse', AM (Nymans 1973)

M. 'Betty', AGM (1993)

M. 'Caerhays Surprise', AM (F. J. Williams 1973)

M. campbellii, FCC (Gumbleton, R. Veitch 1903)

M. campbellii var. *alba*, FCC (C. Williams 1951)

M. campbellii var. *alba* 'Nancy Hardy', AM (AE Hardy 1984)

M. campbellii 'Betty Jessel', AM (Jessel 1972)

M. campbellii subsp. *mollicomata*, FCC (Aberconway 1939)

M. campbellii subsp. *mollicomata* 'Lanarth', FCC (M. P. Williams 1947)

M. campbellii subsp. *mollicomata* 'Mary Williams', AM (C. Williams 1954)

M. campbellii 'Queen Caroline', AM (Kew 1977)

M. campbellii (Raffillii Group) 'Charles Raffill', PC (Windsor 1959), AM (Windsor 1963), FCC (Windsor 1966), AGM (1993)

M. campbellii (Raffillii Group) 'Kew's Surprise', FCC (F. J. Williams 1967)

M. 'Charles Coates', PC (Kew 1962), AM (Windsor 1973)

M. 'David Clulow', PC (Clulow 1991)

M. dawsoniana, AM (M. P. Williams 1939)

M. dawsoniana 'Chyverton', AM (N. T. Holman 1974)

M. delavayi, FCC (J. Veitch 1913)

M. denudata, AGM (1993), FCC (1968)

M. denudata 'Purple Eye', AM (Stephenson Clarke 1926)

M. 'Elizabeth', AGM (1993)

M. 'Elizabeth Holman', FCC (N. T. Holman 1995)

M. 'Eric Savill', AM (Windsor 1986)

M. fraseri, AM (Stephenson Clarke 1948)

M. 'Galaxy', AGM (1993)

M. globosa, AM (Stair 1931)

M. grandiflora 'Exmouth', AGM (1993)

M. grandiflora 'Goliath', AM (Preston 1931), FCC (Roberts 1951), AGM (1993)

M. 'Heaven Scent', AGM (1993)

M. 'Iolanthe', AGM (1993)

M. 'Jane', AGM (1993)

M. 'Judy', AGM (1993)

M. ×*kewensis* 'Kewensis', AM (Kew 1952)

M. ×*kewensis* 'Wada's Memory', FCC (Windsor 1986), AGM (1993)

M. kobus, AGM (1993)

M. kobus (as *M. kobus* var. *borealis*), AM (Price 1948), AM (Aberconway 1942)

M. kobus 'Norman Gould', FCC (Wisley 1967)

M. liliiflora 'Nigra', AM (Cuthbert 1907), AGM (1993), FCC (Martyn Simmons 1981)

M. ×*loebneri* 'Leonard Messel', PC (Nymans 1954), AM (Nymans 1955), FCC (Nymans 1969), AGM (1993)

M. ×*loebneri* 'Merrill', FCC (Smart 1979), AGM (1993)

M. ×*loebneri* 'Neil McEacharn', PC (Windsor 1966), AM (Windsor 1967)

M. macrophylla, FCC (J. Veitch 1900)

M. 'Maryland', AGM (1993)

M. 'Michael Rosse', AM (Nymans 1968)

M. 'Nippon', AM (Collingwood Ingram 1969)

M. nitida, AM (F. J. Williams 1966)

M. obovata, FCC (J. Veitch 1893), AGM (1993)

M. obovata 'Pink Form' (as *M. officinalis* 'Pink Form'), AM (Windsor 1971)

M. officinalis var. *biloba*, AGM (1993)

M. 'Osaka', AM (Gauntlett 1902)

M. 'Pegasus', AM (Windsor 1963), AGM (1993)

M. 'Peppermint Stick', AGM (1993)

M. 'Phillip Tregunna', FCC (J. Williams 1992)

M. 'Pinkie', AGM (1993)

M. 'Princess Margaret', FCC (Windsor 1973)

M. ×*proctoriana*, AGM (1993)

M. 'Randy', AGM (1993)

M. 'Ricki', AGM (1993)

M. rostrata, AM (Hillier 1974)

M. salicifolia, AM (Rothschild 1927), AGM (1993), FCC (Windsor 1962)

M. sargentiana, FCC (Messel 1935)

M. sargentiana var. *robusta*, FCC (Aberconway 1947)

M. 'Sayonara', AM (J. Gallagher 1990), AGM (1993)

M. sieboldii, FCC (J. Veitch 1894), AGM (1993)

M. sieboldii subsp. *sinensis*, AM (Bodnant 1927), FCC (R. Veitch 1931), AGM (1993)

M. 'Snow White', AM (Clulow 1991)

M. ×*soulangeana* 'Alba Superba', AGM (1969)

M. ×*soulangeana* 'Alexandrina', AGM (1993)

M. ×*soulangeana* 'Brozzoni', FCC (Rothschild 1929), AGM (1993)

M. ×*soulangeana* 'Etienne Soulange-Bodin', AGM (1993)

M. ×*soulangeana* 'Lennei', FCC (Paul 1863), AGM (1993)

M. ×*soulangeana* 'Lennei Alba', AGM (1993)

M. ×*soulangeana* 'Norbertii', AM (Pilkington 1960)

M. ×*soulangeana* 'Picture', AM (Russell 1969)

M. ×*soulangeana* 'Rustica Rubra', AM (Pilkington 1960), AGM (1993)

M. ×*soulangeana* 'San Jose', AM (Windsor 1986)

M. sprengeri, AM (Aberconway 1942, 1947)

M. sprengeri 'Claret Cup', AM (Aberconway 1963)

M. sprengeri var. *elongata*, AM (Aberconway 1955)

M. sprengeri 'Marwood Spring', FCC (Smart 1995)

M. sprengeri var. *sprengeri* 'Diva', CC (Upcher 1964)

M. sprengeri 'Wakehurst', AM (Price 1948)

M. 'Star Wars', AM (Clulow 1991)

M. stellata, FCC (J. Veitch 1878), AGM (1993)

M. stellata 'Jane Platt', AM (Clulow 1993)

M. stellata 'Rosea', AM (J. Veitch 1893)

M. stellata 'Rubra', AM (Notcutts 1948)

M. stellata 'Water Lily', AGM (1993)

M. 'Summer Solstice', AM (Foster 1994)

M. 'Susan', AGM

M. 'Sweetheart', AM (Foster 1997)

M. 'Thomas Messel', AM (Nymans 1979)

M. ×*thompsoniana*, AM (Thomas 1958)

M. ×*veitchii* 'Peter Veitch', FCC (R. Veitch 1921)

M. 'Wada's Snow White', AM (Clulow 1991)

M. ×*wieseneri*, AM (Martyn Simmons 1917), FCC (Camden 1975)

M. wilsonii, AM (Clarke 1930), AGM (1993)

M. wilsonii (as *M.* ×*highdownensis*), AM (Loder 1932), AM (Stern 1937), PC (Windsor 1965), FCC (Simmons 1971)

Champion Magnolias

Within the British Isles we are fortunate to have more than 300 tree collections of national importance. In addition, significant specimen trees are found singly and in small groups in innumerable parks and gardens. The Tree Register of the British Isles (T.R.O.B.I.) was founded in 1988 by the late Alan Mitchell, an internationally acclaimed dendrologist, and Victoria Schilling. The work of this charitable trust continues through a network of enthusiasts working on tree measurements that are collected and added to the tree register.

Measurements of notable trees in the United States can be found in Arthur Lee Jacobson's excellent book *North American Landscape Trees*. Listed below are notable examples of *Magnolia* and where they are found. The references either relate to the city or the garden where these plants are grown. The value of such a list lies in the fact that measurements often survive after the actual specimens have been lost.

NAME	HEIGHT	DATE OF MEASUREMENT (date planted)	LOCATION
M. acuminata	38 m (125 ft.)	1946	Great Smoky Mountains National Park, Tennessee
M. acuminata	36.5 m (120 ft.)	1980	Warren County, Pennsylvania
M. acuminata	27 m (88 ft.)	1985	Margam Park, South Wales
M. acuminata	27 m (88 ft.)	1984	Leonardslee, Sussex
M. acuminata	20 m (65 ft.)	1998	RHS Wisley, Surrey
M. acuminata subsp. *subcordata*	31 m (102 ft.)	1993 (1800)	Longwood Gardens, Pennsylvania
M. acuminata subsp. *subcordata*	19 m (62 ft.)	1995	Dyffryn Gardens, South Wales
M. 'Buzzard'	15 m (50 ft.)	1991	Chyverton, Cornwall
M. campbellii	11 m (36 ft.)	1988	Overbecks, Devon
M. campbellii	27 m (88 ft.)	1989	Leonardslee, Sussex
M. campbellii	24 m (80 ft.)	1991	Trebah, Cornwall
M. campbellii	19.5 m (64 ft.)	1994 (1978)	Seattle, Washington
M. campbellii var. *alba*	20 m (65 ft.)	1995 (1925)	Borde Hill, Sussex
M. campbellii 'Darjeeling'	14 m (46 ft.)	1993	Savill Gardens, Berkshire
M. campbellii subsp. *mollicomata*	21 m (70 ft.)	1995	Trewithen, Cornwall
M. campbellii Raffillii Group	19 m (62 ft.)	1991	Anthony House, Cornwall
M. campbellii Raffillii Group	19.5 m (64 ft.)	1998	RHS Wisley, Surrey

NAME	HEIGHT	DATE OF MEASUREMENT (date planted)	LOCATION
M. campbellii (Raffillii Group) 'Sidbury'	17 m (56 ft.)	1994	Sidbury Manor, Devon
M. cylindrica	15 m (50 ft.)	1992	Bloomfield Hills, Michigan
M. dawsoniana	16 m (52 ft.)	1987 (1946)	Birr Castle, County Offaly, Ireland
M. dawsoniana	23 m (75 ft.)	1994 (1951)	Seattle, Washington
M. dawsoniana 'Valley Splendour'	19 m (62 ft.)	1993	Valley Gardens, Windsor, Berkshire
M. delavayi	18 m (60 ft.)	1993	Caerhays Castle, Cornwall
M. delavayi	13 m (43 ft.)	1993 (1959)	Berkeley, California
M. denudata	13 m (43 ft.)	1980	Old Greenwich, Connecticut
M. denudata	16 m (52 ft.)	1995	Endsleigh, Devon
M. 'Elizabeth'	9 m (30 ft.)	1998 (1981)	RHS Wisley, Surrey
M. 'Eric Savill'	10 m (33 ft.)	1993	Savill Gardens, Berkshire
M. fraseri	33 m (110 ft.)	1993	Great Smoky Mountains National Park, Tennessee
M. fraseri	16 m (52 ft.)	1996	Leonardslee, Sussex
M. 'Galaxy'	11 m (36 ft.)	1998 (1985)	Oldfield, Dorset
M. globosa	6 m (20 ft.)	1991	Chyverton, Cornwall
M. grandiflora	43 m (140 ft.)	1985	Tangipahoa Parish, Louisiana
M. grandiflora	10 m (33 ft.)	1989	Nonsuch Park, Ewell, Surrey
M. grandiflora 'Exmouth'	12 m (40 ft.)	1995	Homewood School, Kent
M. ×*kewensis* 'Kewensis'	18 m (60 ft.)	1996	Grayswood Hill, Surrey
M. ×*kewensis* 'Wada's Memory'	13 m (43 ft.)	1996	Winterthur, Delaware
M. kobus	20 m (65 ft.)	1984	Borde Hill, Sussex
M. kobus	18 m (60 ft.)	1988	Westonbirt Arboretum, Gloucestershire
M. kobus 'Norman Gould'	10.5 m (35 ft.)	1998	RHS Wisley, Surrey
M. ×*loebneri* 'Leonard Messel'	10 m (33 ft.)	1993	Hillier Arboretum, Hampshire
M. ×*loebneri* 'Merrill'	9 m (30 ft.)	1992	Aurora, Oregon
M. macrophylla	19 m (62 ft.)	1994	Killerton, Devon
M. macrophylla	32 m (105 ft.)	1989	Daniel Boone National Forest, Kentucky
M. macrophylla	12 m (40 ft.)	1984	Savill Gardens, Berkshire
M. macrophylla subsp. *ashei*	16 m (52 ft.)	1993	Henry Foundation, Gladwyne, Pennsylvania
M. 'Michael Rosse'	12 m (40 ft.)	1996	Nymans Gardens, Sussex
M. nitida	9 m (30 ft.)	1984	Caerhays Castle, Cornwall
M. obovata	26 m (85 ft.)	1988	Westonbirt Arboretum, Gloucestershire
M. obovata	18 m (60 ft.)	1998	RHS Wisley, Surrey
M. obovata	12 m (40 ft.)	1987	Belvoir Castle, Leicestershire
M. officinalis	17 m (56 ft.)	1985	Birr Castle, County Offaly, Ireland
M. officinalis var. *biloba*	12 m (40 ft.)	1994 (1959)	San Francisco, California
M. 'Pegasus'	9 m (30 ft.)	1998	Hillier Arboretum, Hampshire
M. salicifolia	17 m (56 ft.)	1990	Savill Gardens, Berkshire
M. salicifolia	15 m (50 ft.)	1993 (1949)	Seattle, Washington
M. salicifolia	13 m (43 ft.)	1987	Plas Newydd, Isle of Anglesey
M. sargentiana	18.5 m (61 ft.)	1975	Caerhays, Cornwall
M. sargentiana	15 m (50 ft.)	1996	Nymans Gardens, Sussex

NAME	HEIGHT	DATE OF MEASUREMENT (date planted)	LOCATION
M. sargentiana var. *robusta*	18 m (60 ft.)	1995	Borde Hill, Sussex
M. sargentiana var. *robusta*	21 m (70 ft.)	1994 (1953)	Seattle, Washington
M. sieboldii	12 m (40 ft.)	1990	Bodnant, North Wales
M. 'Silver Parasol'	15 m (50 ft.)	1981	Arnold Arboretum, Massachusetts
M. ×*soulangeana*	11 m (36 ft.)	1995	Sevenoaks, Kent
M. ×*soulangeana*	9 m (30 ft.)	1980	Philadelphia Zoo, Pennsylvania
M. sprengeri var. *elongata*	16 m (52 ft.)	1984	Bodnant, North Wales
M. sprengeri var. *sprengeri* 'Diva'	18.5 m (61 ft.)	1995	Trewithen, Cornwall
M. sprengeri 'Westonbirt'	24.5 m (80 ft.)	1999 (1959)	Westonbirt, Gloucestershire
M. tripetala	10 m (33 ft.)	1995	Benenden, Kent
M. tripetala	19 m (62 ft.)	1989 (1940)	Seattle, Washington
M. tripetala	9 m (30 ft.)	1986 (1924)	Royal Botanic Gardens, Kew
M. ×*veitchii*	24 m (80 ft.)	1995	Lanhydrock, Cornwall
M. ×*veitchii* 'Peter Veitch'	18 m (60 ft.)	1993	Savill Gardens, Berkshire
M. ×*veitchii* 'Peter Veitch'	29 m (95 ft.)	1984 (1921)	Caerhays Castle, Cornwall
M. virginiana	28 m (91 ft.)	1971	Leon County, Florida
M. virginiana	12 m (40 ft.)	1982	Knap Hill, Surrey
M. ×*wieseneri*	8 m (26 ft.)	1996	Nymans Gardens, Sussex
M. ×*wieseneri*	7 m (23 ft.)	1993	Seattle, Washington State
M. wilsonii	8 m (26 ft.)	1991	Howick Hall, Northumberland
M. wilsonii 'Highdownensis'	10 m (33 ft.)	1998	RHS Wisley, Surrey

Where to See Magnolias

Listed below is a selection of gardens around the world where good collections of magnolias can be found. It will be worthwhile contacting garden owners before you visit to ensure that it is convenient to do so.

BELGIUM

Arboretum Bokrijk, Limburg, B3600 Gent

Herkenrode, B-3150 Wespelaar (Vicomte Philippe de Spoelberch)

Hemelrijk, 93, B-2910 Essen (Mme. de Belder)

Kalmthout Arboretum, Heuvel 2, Kalmthout, B2920 (R. de Belder)

BRITISH ISLES

ENGLAND

Berkshire

The Savill and Valley Gardens, Windsor Great Park (Crown Estate Commissioners)

Whiteknights (University of Reading), Reading

Cambridgeshire

University Botanic Garden, Cambridge

Cheshire

Ness Botanic Gardens, Neston, South Wirral (University of Liverpool)

Cornwall

Anthony House, Torpoint (National Trust)

Burncoose Gardens, Gwennap, Redruth (F. J. Williams C.B.E.)

Caerhays Castle, Gorran, St. Austell (F. J. Williams)

Chyverton, Zelah, Truro (Nigel Holman)

Glendurgan, Mawnan Smith, Falmouth (National Trust)

Lanhydrock, Bodmin (National Trust)

Penwarne, Mawnan Smith, Falmouth (Dr. and Mrs. H. Beister)

Tregrehan, Par. (Tom Hudson)

Trelissick, Feock, Truro (National Trust)

Trengwainton, Madron, Penzance (National Trust)

Trewithen, Grampound Road, Truro (A. M. J. Galsworthy)

Cumbria

Holker Hall, Cark-in-Cartmel, Grange over Sands (The Lord Cavendish of Furness)

Muncaster Castle, Ravenglass (Mrs. P. R. Gordon-Duff-Pennington)

Devon

Dartington Hall Gardens, Totnes (Dartington Hall Trust)

Exeter University Gardens (The University of Exeter)

The Garden House, Buckland Monacho-
rum, Yelverton (The Fortescue Garden
Trust)

Killerton Gardens, Broadclyst, Exeter
(National Trust)

Knightshayes Garden, Tiverton (National
Trust)

Marwood Hill Gardens, Barnstaple (Dr. J.
A. Smart)

Overbecks, Sharpitor, Salcombe (National Trust)

RHS Garden Rosemoor, Great Torrington
(Royal Horticultural Society)

Dorset

Abbotsbury Gardens, Weymouth (Ilch-
ester Estates)

Gloucestershire

The Batsford Arboretum, Moreton in
Marsh (The Batsford Foundation)

Westonbirt Arboretum, Tetbury (Forest
Enterprise)

Hampshire

Exbury Gardens, Southampton (Edmond
de Rothschild)

The Hillier Gardens and Arboretum,
Romsey (Hampshire County Council)

Spinners, Boldre, Lymington (Diana and
Peter Chappell)

Hereford and Worcester

Hergest Croft Gardens, Kington (W. L.
Banks)

Northumberland

Howick Hall Gardens, Alnwick (Howick
Trustees)

Oxfordshire

Nuneham Courtenay Arboretum (University of Oxford)

Surrey

The Royal Botanic Gardens, Kew, Richmond (Kew Trustees)

RHS Garden Wisley, Woking (Royal Horticultural Society)

Sussex

Borde Hill Gardens, Haywards Heath
(Borde Hill Garden)

The High Beeches Handcross (High
Beeches Gardens Conservation Trust)

Leonardslee Gardens, Lower Beeding,
Horsham (R. R. Loder)

Nymans Gardens, Handcross (National
Trust)

Wakehurst Place, Ardingly (Royal Botanic
Gardens, Kew)

Wiltshire

Broadleas, Devizes (Broadleas Gardens
Charitable Trust)

Yorkshire

Castle Howard, York (Castle Howard Estates)

Wentworth Castle Gardens, Northern
College, Barnsley (Barnsley M.D.C.)

SCOTLAND

Dumfries and Galloway

Logan Botanic Gardens, Stranraer (Royal
Botanic Garden, Edinburgh)

Edinburgh

The Royal Botanic Garden, Edinburgh
(Scottish Office Board of Trustees)

Strathclyde

Ardanaiseig Gardens by Taynuilt (Robert
Francis)

Arduaine Gardens, Loch Melford, Oban
(National Trust for Scotland)

Brodick Castle Gardens, The Isle of Arran
(National Trust for Scotland)

Strathclyde, continued
Culzean Castle, Maybole
Glenarn, Rhu, Helensburgh (Mr. & Mrs.
M. Thornley)

Tayside
Glendoick Gardens, Perth (Mr. & Mrs.
P. A. Cox)

WALES
Clwyd
Bodnant Gardens, Tal-y-Cafn (National
Trust)

Gwynedd
Plas Newydd, Isle of Anglesey (National
Trust)

West Glamorgan
Margam Park, Port Talbot (Neath and
Port Talbot Borough Council)

IRELAND
County Cork
Fota Island, Carringtuohill (Fota Trust
Company)

County Down
Rowallane Gardens, Saintfield (National
Trust)

County Dublin
National Botanic Garden, Glasnevin
(Office of Public Works)

County Kerry
Muckross Gardens and Arboretum, Killarney (Office of Public Works)

County Offaly
Birr Castle (Earl of Rosse)

County Waterford
Mount Congreve, Waterford (Ambrose
Congreve)

County Wexford
Dunloe Castle Hotel (Killarney Hotels)

County Wicklow
Mount Usher, Ashford (Madelaine Jay)
Kilmacurragh, Rathdrum (Department
of Fisheries and Forestry)

CANADA
University of British Columbia Botanical
Garden, Vancouver, British Columbia
V6T 1Z4
Van Dusen Botanical Garden, Vancouver,
British Columbia V6M 4H1

CHINA
Beijing Botanical Garden (Academia
Sinica)
Guilin Botanical Garden (Guangxi Acad-
emy of Sciences)
Hangzhou Botanical Garden (Municipal)
Kunming Botanical Garden (Academia
Sinica), Yunnan
Lu Shan Botanic Garden, Jiangxi
Nanjing Botanical Garden Mem. Sun Yat-
Sen
Nanyue Arboretum (The Forestry Bureau
of Hunnan)
The South China Institute of Botany,
Guangzhou, Guandong

DENMARK
Royal Vet and Agricultural University Arboretum, DK-2970 Horsholm
University Botanic Garden, O Farimags-
gade, 2B, DK-1353 Copenhagen

FRANCE
Arboretum de Balaine, F-03460, Vil-
leneuve-sur-Allier
Ferme des Tourelles, Ingrannes, 45450
Fay-aux-Loges (Count Bernard de la
Rochefoucauld)

Jardin Botanique de la Ville, Nantes (Municipal), 44094 Nantes Cedex 1

Pépinières de Kerisnel, St. Pol-de-Leon (Société d'Initiatives et de Cooperation Agricoles Sica)

Le Vasterival, F76119 Varengeville-sur-Mer (Princess G. Sturdza)

GEORGIA, REPUBLIC OF
Batumi Botanical Garden (Georgian Academy of Sciences)

GERMANY
Palmengarten, Frankfurt

ITALY
Isola Madre, Lake Maggiore

Villa Taranto, Pallanza, Lake Maggiore

JAPAN
Japan Association for Shidekobushi Conservation, S. Yamaguchi, Ashimata, Okute-cho, Mizunami City 509-64

Koshigaya, Aritaki Arboretum (T. Aritaki)

KOREA, SOUTH
Chollipo Arboretum, T'aean-gun, Chungchong Namdo 357-930 (Ferris Miller)

NETHERLANDS
Arboretum Von Gimborn, Doorn (University of Utrecht)

Trompenburg Arboretum, Rotterdam (J. R. P. van Hoey Smith)

NEW ZEALAND
North Island
Auckland Botanic Garden (Auckland Regional Council)

Eastwoodhill Arboretum, Ngatapa (Bill Williams)

Hackfalls Arboretum, Gisborne (Bob and Lady Anne Berry)

Pukeiti, New Plymouth (Pukeiti Rhododendron Trust)

Tikorangi, Waitara (Mark and Abbie Jury)

South Island
Christchurch Botanic Garden (Christchurch City Council)

Dunedin Botanic Garden (Dunedin City Council)

POLAND
Kornick, Polish Academy of Sciences (Governmental)

SWEDEN
Botaniska Tradgarden, S41319 Göteborg

Norrauramov, S26700 Bjuv (K. E. Flinck)

SWITZERLAND
San Nazzaro CH 6575 Ticino (Otto Eisenhut)

Vico Morcote, Lugano CH 6921 (Sir Peter Smithers)

Vira Gambarogno CH 6574 (Piet van Veen)

UNITED STATES OF AMERICA
Alabama
Magnolia Nursery and Display Gardens, Chunchula 36521

California
Huntington Botanical Gardens, San Marino 91108

Los Angeles County Arboretum, Arcadia 91007

Strybing Arboretum and Botanical Gardens, San Francisco 94122

Delaware
Henry Francis du Pont Garden, Winterthur 19735

District of Columbia
Dumbarton Oaks, Washington 20007
U.S. National Arboretum, Washington 20002

Georgia
Callaway Gardens, Pine Mountains 31822

Illinois
Chicago Horticultural Society Botanic Garden, Glencoe 60022
University of Illinois, Urbana 61801

Massachusetts
Arnold Arboretum of Harvard University, Jamaica Plain 02130
Polly Hill Arboretum, West Tisbury 02575

Michigan
Phil J. Savage Jr., 2150 Woodward Avenue, Bloomfield Hills 48013

Mississippi
Gloster Arboretum, Gloster 39638

Missouri
Missouri Botanical Garden, St. Louis 36110

New Jersey
The Arboretum of Rutgers University, Gladstone 07935

New York
Brooklyn Botanic Garden, Brooklyn 11225

The Cary Arboretum, Millbrook 12545
New York Botanical Garden, Bronx 10458

North Carolina
North Carolina State University, Raleigh 27695

Pennsylvania
Gardens of the Henry Foundation, Gladwyne 19035
Longwood Gardens, Kennett Square 19348
Morris Arboretum, Philadelphia 19118
Scott Arboretum, Swarthmore College, Swarthmore 19081

Ohio
The Holden Arboretum, Kirtland 44094

Oregon
Gossler Farms Nursery and Gardens, Springfield 97478
John W. S. Platt, Portland 97221

South Carolina
Magnolia Plantation and Gardens, Charleston 29407
Middleton Place, Charleston 29407
Wayside Gardens, Hodges 29695

Tennessee
Great Smoky Mountains National Park, Gatlinburg 37738

Washington
Washington Park Arboretum, Seattle 98112

Where to Buy Magnolias

Most garden centres in the British Isles will stock some magnolias, but those listed here carry a particularly wide range. It is always worthwhile looking through the RHS Plant Finder for an up to date list. A list of international sales centres is also included, however the Magnolia Society periodically carries a list and needs to be consulted.

AUSTRALIA

East Coast Perennials (Jan Carson), P.O. Box 323, Wauchope 2446, N.S.W.

W. J. Simpson, Wayside, 602 Nepean Highway, Frankston, Victoria 3199

Woodbank Nursery (Ken Gillanders), 2040 Huon Road, Longley, Tasmania 7150

Yamina Rare Plants (Don Tesse), 25 Moores Road, Monbulk, Victoria 3993

BELGIUM

C.E.C.E., Avenue Leopold III n. 12, 7130 Bray (Binche)

BRITISH ISLES
ENGLAND
Cheshire

Bridgemere Garden World, Nantwich CW5 7QB

Cornwall

Burncoose and Southdown Nurseries, Gwennap, Redruth TR16 6BJ
http://www.eclipse.co.uk/burncoose

Duchy of Cornwall Nursery, Cott Road, Lostwithiel PL22 0BW

The Lanhydrock Gardens, Bodmin PL30 5AD

Trewithen Nurseries, Grampound Road, Truro TR2 4DD

Devon

Knightshayes Garden Trust, Tiverton EX16 7RG

RHS Garden, Rosemoor, Great Torrington EX38 8PH

Dorset

J. Trehane & Sons, Stapehill Road, Hampreston, Wimborne BH21 7NE

Hampshire

Hillier Nurseries (Winchester), Ampfield House, Ampfield, Romsey SO51 9PA

Spinners Garden, Boldre, Lymington SO41 5QE

Somerset

Mallet Court Nursery, Curry Mallet, Taunton TA3 6SY

Suffolk

BE & JL Humphrey, Ramblers, Benhall Low Street, Nr. Farnham, Saxmundham IP17 1JE

Suffolk, continued

Notcutts Nurseries, Woodbridge IP12 4AF
Email: sales@notcutts.demon.co.uk

Surrey

RHS Plant Centre, RHS Garden, Wisley,
Woking GU23 6QB

Savill Garden Plant Centre, Wick Lane,
Englefield Green, Egham TW20 0UU

WALES

Bodnant Garden Nursery, Tal-y-Cafn,
Colwyn Bay, Clwyd LL28 5RE
Email: ianshutes@enterprise.net

CANADA

Ocean Park Nurseries, 2124 Stevenson
Road, White Rock, British Columbia
V4A 3V6

DENMARK

Plantekassen, Jaegersborg Alle 172, 2820
Gentofte

FRANCE

Pepiniere de L'Arboretum de Balaine,
Chateau de Balaine, F-03460, Vil-
leneuve-sur-Allier

JAPAN

Yamaguchi Plantsman's Nursery, 509-
6471, 22-45 Okute-cho, Mizunami City

NETHERLANDS

Bulkhard Nurseries, Rijnveld 115, Boskoop (Rein and Mark Bulk)

Firma C. Esveld, Rijnveld 72, 2771 X.S.
Boskoop

Wim. A. M. Rutten, Zevenhuisen 1, NL
5595XE Leende
Email: wruttene@iaehv.nl

Zwijnenburg, Pieter Jr., Halve Raak 18,
2771 AD Boskoop

NEW ZEALAND

Caves Tree Nursery, Pukeroro R.D. 3
Hamilton, North Island

Duncan and Davies Nurseries, P.O. Box
5203, New Plymouth, Taranaki, North
Island

Jury, Mark and Abbie, Tikorangi, 591
Otaraoa Road, R.D. 43 Waitara, North
Taranaki, North Island

Oswald Blumhardt, No. 9 R.D.
Whangarei, North Island

SWEDEN

Zetas Nursery, Gä Södertäljevägen 194,
141 70 Huddinge

SWITZERLAND

Otto Eisenhut Nurseries, Ch6575, San
Nazzaro/Ticino

UNITED STATES OF AMERICA
Alabama

Tom Dodd Nurseries, U.S. Highway 98,
P.O. Drawer 45, Semmes 36575

Dodd & Dodd Nursery, 9585 Wulff Road,
P.O. Drawer 439, Semmes 36575

Magnolia Nursery, 12615 Roberts Road,
Chunchula 36521

Southern Plants, P.O. Box 232, Semmes
36575

Georgia

Homeplace Garden, Harden Bridge
Road, P.O. Box 300, Commerce 30529

Sweetbay Farm, 4260 Enon Road,
Coolidge 31738

Illinois

Klehm Nursery, 4210 North Duncan
Road, Champaign 61821
Email: klehm@duracef.shout.net

Louisiana

Louisiana Nursery, Route 7, Box 43,
Opelousas 70570

Missouri

Arborville Farm Nursery, 15604 County
Road CC, P.O. Box 227, Holt 64068

New Jersey

Fairweather Gardens, P.O. Box 330,
Greenwich 08323

New York

Roslyn Nursery, 211 Burrs Lane, Dix Hills
11746

North Carolina

Camellia Forest Nursery, 125 Carolina
Forest Road, Chapel Hill 27516

Oregon

Forestfarm, 990 Tetherow Road, Williams
97544
Gossler Farms Nursery, 1200 Weaver
Road, Springfield 97479
Greer Gardens, 1280 Goodpasture Island
Road, Eugene 97401

Whitman Farms, 3995 Gibson Road NW,
Salem 97304
Stanley and Sons Nursery, 11740 SE Ori-
ent Drive, Boring 97009

South Carolina

Wayside Gardens, 1 Garden Lane,
Hodges 29695
Woodlanders, 1128 Colleton Avenue,
Aiken 29801

Tennessee

Beaver Creek Nursery, 7526 Pelleaux
Road, Knoxville 37938
Owen Farms, 2951 Curve-Nankipoo
Road, Ripley 38063
Toole's Bend Nursery, 3530 Toole's Bend
Road, Knoxville 37922

Texas

Yucca Do Nursery, P.O. Box 655, Waller
77484

Washington

Wells Medina Nursery, 8300 NE 24th St.,
Bellevue 98004
Molbak's, 13625 NE 175 St., Woodinville
98072

Societies

The Magnolia Society

Secretary: Roberta Hagen, 6616 81st Street, Cabin John, MD 20818, U.S.A

International Cultivar Registrar: Dorothy Callaway, c/o The Magnolia Society, 6616 81st Street, Cabin John, MD 20818, U.S.A. Email: RHagen6902@aol.com

Founded in 1963 for the purpose of promoting education and exchange of information on these beautiful plants. Benefits include *Magnolia* twice yearly journal, newsletter, seed exchange, round robin, slide library, research grants, and cultivar registration.

The Royal Horticultural Society

P. O. Box 313

London SW1P 2PE

http://www.rhs.org.uk

Benefits include *The Garden* monthly journal, access to 27 gardens in the United Kingdom and Europe, access to flower shows such as Chelsea, Hampton Court, and Vincent Square, free gardening advice, admission to talks and demonstrations, free seed from Wisley, access to the Lindley Library.

Incorporating Rhododendrons with Camellias and Magnolias

Royal Horticultural Society

80 Vincent Square

London SW1P 2PE

The International Dendrology Society

James Greenfield

Hergest Estate Office

Kington

Herefordshire HR5 3EG

Benefits include publications, outings, conservation, and research.

The National Council for the Conservation of Plants and Gardens

The RHS Garden Wisley

Woking

Surrey GU23 6QB

To encourage the conservation of plants and gardens through national plant collections, lectures, publications, and outings.

The Tree Register of the British Isles

Secretary: Mrs. P. A. Stevenson, 77a Hall End, Wootton, Bedford MK43 9HP

Email: trobi@aol.com

Bibliography

Bean, W. J. 1973. *Trees and Shrubs Hardy in the British Isles.* Vol. 2, 8th edition.

Bond, John. 1992. "The National Magnolia Collection." *RHS Rhododendrons.*

Bond, John. 1994. "The National Magnolia Collection (Part 2)." *RHS Rhododendrons.*

Borlase, Peter. 1988, 1989. "Magnolias at Lanhydrock." *RHS Rhododendrons.*

Borlase, Peter. 1998. "The 3 'Star Magnolias' of Lanhydrock." *RHS Rhododendrons.*

Briggs, Roy W. 1993. *"Chinese" Wilson—A Life of Ernest H. Wilson 1876–1930.*

Callaway, Dorothy J. 1994. *The World of Magnolias.*

Chen, B. L., and H. P. Nooteboom. 1993. "Notes on Magnoliaceae III. The Magnoliaceae of China." *Annals of the Missouri Botanical Garden.*

Coats, Alice. 1969. *The Quest for Plants.*

Cowdray, Lady Anne. 1995. "Magnolias at Broadleas." *RHS Rhododendrons.*

Cox, E. H. M. 1926. *Farrer's Last Journey.*

Cox, E. H. M., editor. 1928–1940. *The New Flora and Silva.*

Cox, E. H. M. 1945. *Plant Hunting in China.*

Dandy, J. E. 1950. "The Highdown Magnolia." *Journal of the Royal Horticultural Society.*

Dirr, Michael A. 1990. *Manual of Woody Landscape Plants.* 4th edition.

Elias, T. D. 1980. *Trees of North America.*

Facciola, Stephen. 1990. *Cornucopia. A Source Book of Edible Plants.*

Figlar, Richard B. 1993. "Stone Magnolias." *Arnoldia.*

Figlar, Richard B. 1994. "Magnolias in Stone: Exploring an Ancient *Magnolia* Forest in Northern Idaho. *Magnolia.*

Fletcher, Harold R. 1975. *A Quest of Flowers.*

Flinck, Karl. 1991. "A Magnolia Breeder with Flair." *RHS Rhododendrons.*

Foley, Daniel J. 1969. *The Flowering World of "Chinese" Wilson.*

Forrest, George. 1927. "Magnolias of Yunnan." In *Magnolias,* by J. G. Millais.

Forrest, Todd. 1995. "Two Thousand Years of Eating Bark." *Arnoldia.*

Forster, W. Arnold. 1948. *Trees and Shrubs for the Milder Counties.*

Foster, Maurice. 1991. "The Brooklyn 'Yellows'." *RHS Rhododendrons.*

Foster, Maurice. 1996a. "The Best Yellow Magnolia." *RHS Rhododendrons.*

Foster, Maurice. 1996b. "*Magnolia campbellii* var. *alba* in Bhutan." *RHS Rhododendrons.*

Gardiner, J. M. 1989. "Magnificent Magnolias." *Plants and Gardens*.

Gardiner, J. M. 1994. "*Magnolia* 'Gold Star' and Other Yellow-Flowered Magnolias." *The New Plantsman*.

Gardiner, J. M. 1997a. "*Magnolia ×soulangeana*." *The Garden*.

Gardiner, J. M. 1997b. *Propagation from Cuttings*.

Gardiner, J. M. 1997c. *Propagation from Seed*.

Gardiner, J. M. 1998. "Magnificent Magnolias." Part 4. *The Garden*.

Gresham, Todd. 1964. "Deciduous Magnolias of California Origin." *Journal of the Royal Horticultural Society*.

Hartmann, Hudson T., and Dale E. Kester. 1968. *Plant Propagation, Principles and Practices*. 2d edition.

Heywood, V. H. 1978. *Flowering Plants of the World*.

Hillier Nurseries. 1991. *The Hillier Manual of Trees and Shrubs*. 6th edition.

Holman, Nigel. 1973. "Asiatic Magnolias in a Cornish Garden." *RHS Rhododendrons*.

Holman, Nigel. 1988, 1989. "Naming Seedlings of *Magnolia campbellii* subsp. *mollicomata*." *RHS Rhododendrons*.

Hunt, David, ed. 1998. *Magnolias and Their Allies*.

Jacobson, Arthur Lee. 1996. *North American Landscape Trees*.

Johnstone, George H. 1950. "Chinese Magnolias in Cultivation." *Camellias and Magnolias*. RHS Conference Report.

Johnstone, George H. 1955. *Asiatic Magnolias in Cultivation*.

Jury, Abbie. 1994. "Felix Jury's Magnolias." *RHS Rhododendrons*.

Kingdon Ward, Frank. 1930. *Plant Hunting on the Edge of the World*.

Kingdon Ward, Frank. 1960. *Pilgrimage for Plants*.

Krüssmann, Gerd. 1984. *Manual of Cultivated Broad-leaved Trees and Shrubs*. Vol. 2.

Lancaster, Roy. 1981. *Plant Hunting in Nepal*.

Lancaster, Roy. 1987. *Garden Plants for Connoisseurs*.

Lancaster, Roy. 1989. *Travels in China—A Plantsman's Paradise*.

Lancaster, Roy. 1994. "*Magnolia cylindrica*." *The Garden*.

Loudon, J. C. 1844. *Arboretum et Fruticetum Britannicum*. 2d edition.

Magnolia Society. 1965–1998. *Magnolia* (journal) and *Newsletter*.

Magnolia Society. 1994. *Checklist of Cultivated Magnolia*.

McClintock, Elizabeth. 1985. *Magnolias and Their Relatives in Strybing Arboretum, Golden Gate Park*.

McMillan Browse, Philip. 1979. *Plant Propagation*.

Meyer, F. G., and E. McClintock. 1987. "Rejection of the Names *Magnolia heptapeta* and *M. quinquepeta* (Magnoliaceae)." *Taxon*.

Millais, J. G. 1927. *Magnolias*.

Miller, P. 1731. *The Gardeners' Dictionary*. 1st edition.

Mitchell, Alan F., Victoria E. Schilling, and John E. J. White. 1994. *Champion Trees in the British Isles*. 4th edition.

The New Royal Horticultural Society. 1992. *Dictionary of Gardening*.

Nooteboom, H. P. 1985. "Notes on Magnoliaceae." *Blumea* 31.

Ohba, Hideaki. 1994. "A Brief Overview of the Woody Vegetation of Japan and Its Conservation Status." *I.D.S. Symposium on Temperate Trees Under Threat*.

Ohwi, J. 1965. *Flora of Japan*.

Quest-Ritson, Charles, and Christopher Blair. 1998. *RHS Gardeners' Year Book*.

Rehder, Alfred. 1958. *Manual of Cultivated Trees and Shrubs Hardy in North America*.

The Royal Horticultural Society. 1950. *Camellias and Magnolias*. RHS Conference Report.

The Royal Horticultural Society. 1997, 1998. *The Plant Finder*.

Schilling, V. (née Hallett). 1991. "Champion Magnolias." *RHS Rhododendrons*.

Sheat, Wilfrid G. 1948. *Propagation of Trees, Shrubs and Conifers*.

Smithers, Sir Peter. 1985, 1986. "An Experiment with Magnolias: Updated." *RHS Rhododendrons*.

Smithers, Sir Peter. 1993. "Which Magnolia?" *RHS Rhododendrons*.

Smithers, Sir Peter. 1995. *Adventures of a Gardener*.

Spongberg, Stephen A. 1976. "Magnoliaceae Hardy in Temperate North America." *Journal of the Arnold Arboretum*.

Spongberg, Stephen A. 1990. *A Reunion of Trees*.

Spongberg, Stephen A. 1998. "Magnoliaceae Hardy in Cooler Temperate Regions." In *Magnolias and Their Allies*, ed. David Hunt.

Spongberg, Stephen A., and Peter Del Tredici. 1992. "The 'Hope of Spring' *Magnolia* Finally Flowers in Boston." *Arnoldia*.

Stern, F. C. 1960. *A Chalk Garden*.

Stiff, Ruth L. A. 1988. *Flowers from the Royal Gardens of Kew*.

Sunset. 1990. *Western Garden Book*.

Sutton, S. B. 1971. *The Arnold Arboretum, the First Century*.

Taylor, Jane. 1988. *Collecting Garden Plants*.

Treseder, Neil G. *Magnolias*. 1978.

Treseder, Neil G., and Marjorie Blamey. 1981. *The Book of Magnolias*.

Ueda, K. 1980. "Taxonomic Study of *Magnolia sieboldii* C. Koch." *Acta Phytotaxonomica et Geobotanica*.

Weibang, Sun, and Zhao Tianbang. 1998. *Investigations of Henan Xinyi and Some New Taxa of Magnoliaceae from Henan and Jiangxi of China*.

Wharton, A. Peter. 1987, 1988, "The Purple Lanarth Magnolia in the Wild." *RHS Rhododendrons*.

Wilson, Ernest H. 1906. "Magnolias." *Gardeners Chronicle*.

Wilson, Ernest H. 1913. *A Naturalist in Western China*.

Yamaguchi Plantsman's Nursery. 1992. *Wildstand Shidekobushi in Japan*.

Index of *Magnolia* Names

Bold-faced page numbers indicate main descriptions.

General Index

Bold-faced page numbers indicate main descriptions.